AN ESSAY ON THE
PRINCIPLE OF POPULATION

A NORTON CRITICAL EDITION

Norton Critical Editions in the History of Ideas

A NORTON CRITICAL EDITION

THOMAS ROBERT MALTHUS

AN ESSAY ON THE PRINCIPLE OF POPULATION

TEXT

SOURCES AND BACKGROUND

CRITICISM

Edited by

PHILIP APPLEMAN

INDIANA UNIVERSITY

W · W · NORTON & COMPANY

New York · London

"Outlines of a Critique of Political Economy" by Friedrich Engels, from *Marx and Engels on Malthus*. Copyright © 1954, International Publishers Co., Inc.
"The Structure of Malthus' Population Theory" by Antony Flew, from *Australasian Journal of Philosophy*, Vol. XXXV (1957). Copyright © 1957 by Antony Flew. Reprinted with permission of the author and the *Australasian Journal of Philosophy*.
"Was Malthus Right?" by Joseph J. Spengler. Copyright © 1947; 1948; 1966. Reprinted from the *Southern Economic Journal* (1972), Chapel Hill, North Carolina.
"The Closing Circle" from *The Closing Circle* by Barry Commoner. Copyright © 1971 by Barry Commoner. Reprinted by permission of Alfred A. Knopf, Inc. Portions of this book originally appeared in *The New Yorker*.
"The New Breed of Malthusians" by Goran Ohlin. Copyright © 1974 by Goran Ohlin. Reprinted with permission from *Family Planning Perspectives*, Vol. 6, No. 3, 1974.
"Population: A Problem for Democracy" from *Population: A Problem for Democracy* by Gunnar Myrdal (Harvard University Press). Copyright © by the President and Fellows of Harvard College; 1968 by Gunnar Myrdal.
"The Economics of the Coming Spaceship Earth" by Kenneth E. Boulding, from *Environmental Quality in a Growing Economy* edited by Henry Jarrett. Copyright © 1966, the Johns Hopkins Press.
"Population, GNP, and the Environment" by Alan R. Sweezy, from *Are Our Descendants Doomed?* edited by Harrison Brown and Edward Hutchings. Copyright © 1970, 1972 by California Institute of Technology. Reprinted with permission of The Viking Press, Inc.
"An Inquiry into the Human Prospect" from *An Inquiry into the Human Prospect* by Robert L. Heilbroner. By permission of W. W. Norton & Company, Inc. Copyright © 1974 by W. W. Norton & Company, Inc.
"My Fight for Birth Control" from *My Fight for Birth Control* by Margaret Sanger. Copyright © 1931; 1959 by Margaret Sanger. Reprinted by permission of Grant Sanger, M.D.
"Unmet Needs in Family Planning: A World Survey" by John Robbins. Copyright © 1973 by John Robbins. Reprinted with permission from *Family Planning Perspectives*, Vol. 5, No. 4, 1973.
"Population Policy: Will Current Programs Succeed?" by Kingsley Davis, *Science*, Vol. 158 (10 November 1967), pp. 730–39. Copyright © 1967 by the American Association for the Advancement of Science.
"Demographic Chic at the UN" by J. Mayone Stycos. Copyright © 1974 by J. Mayone Stycos. Reprinted with permission from *Family Planning Perspectives*, Vol. 6, No. 3, 1974.
"Proposal for the Use of American Food: 'Triage'" by William and Paul Paddock, from *Famine 1975! America's Decision: Who Will Survive?* by William and Paul Paddock, Copyright © 1967 by William and Paul Paddock. By permission of Little, Brown and Co.
"The Tragedy of the Commons" by Garrett Hardin, from *Exploring New Ethics for Survival* by Garrett Hardin. Copyright © 1968, 1972 by Garrett Hardin. Reprinted by permission of The Viking Press, Inc.
"Population, Resources, Environment" from *Population, Resources, Environment: Issues in Human Ecology* by Paul R. and Anne H. Ehrlich. W. H. Freeman and Company. Copyright © 1970.
"In the Human Interest" from *In the Human Interest* by Lester R. Brown. By permission of W. W. Norton & Company, Inc. Copyright © 1974 by W. W. Norton and Company, Inc.

Library of Congress Cataloging in Publication Data
Malthus, Thomas Robert, 1766–1834.
    An essay on the principle of population.
    (A Norton critical edition)
    The text of the 1798 ed. together with commentaries from the 19th and 20th centuries.
    Includes bibliographical references and index.
    1. Population.   I. Appleman, Philip, 1926–
II. Title.
HB861.E7   1976   301.32   75–26853

ISBN 0-393-04419-X
ISBN 0-393-09202-X pbk.

5 6 7 8 9

Contents

Some "Neo-Malthusian" Proposals

Preface

An anthology is always a compromise between the richness of the outside world and the meager insides of a book. This one is no exception: the literature of Malthusianism is vast and various, and to try to represent it in a single volume is a frustrating task. I hope that this collection will at least outline some of the more important influences which Malthus' thinking has had, both on his own world and on ours.

Malthus' *Essay on the Principle of Population* is represented here by the 1798 text, but without the antique *s*'s and *c*'s of the first edition. I have also taken the editorial liberty of deleting a multitude of commas, colons, and semicolons, and inserting a few of my own.

I wish to thank the following persons, who have offered various kinds of advice and assistance in the planning of this book; none of them, of course, bears any responsibility for any faults remaining in the volume: Lester R. Brown, Lynton K. Caldwell, Phillips Cutright, H. Scott Gordon, William D. Grampp, Donald J. Gray, Kenneth Gros Louis, Patricia James, Karl Kroeber, Richard A.. Levine, Richard Lincoln, Helene Moglen, Joseph J. Spengler, George Stade, George J. Stolnitz, and John Woodcock.

Special thanks are due to my editor, James L. Mairs, for his understanding, counsel, and friendship during the making of this volume and of the Norton Critical Edition of *Darwin*, as well.

And I am happy to record once again my gratitude to my wife, Margie, for her acute and creative criticism.

PHILIP APPLEMAN

Introduction

At the end of each day, the world now has over two hundred thousand more mouths to feed than it had the day before; at the end of every week, one and one-half million more; at the close of each year, an additional eighty million. Aware of these alarming statistics, many national governments, influential institutions, and private enterprises are trying to encourage increased production of all the necessities of life, particularly food, in the hope of preventing mass starvation, privation, and social disorder. Fortunately there has been enough success in recent years to forestall, at least temporarily, a major disaster; but some serious regional famines have already occurred, and in the world's poorest countries, where population growth is most rapid, the lives of hundreds of millions of people are constantly plagued by hunger and by diseases aggravated by malnutrition. Humankind, now doubling its numbers every thirty-five years, has fallen into an ambush of its own making; economists call it the "Malthusian trap," after the man who most forcefully stated our biological predicament: population growth tends to outstrip the supply of food.

Thomas Robert Malthus was born in 1766, in a country house near the town of Dorking, in England, the son of a gentleman who prided himself on his advanced ideas and was an admirer and friend of both Hume and Rousseau. Young Robert (he was never called Thomas) was at first privately educated; then, in 1784, he went up to Jesus College, Cambridge, where he graduated creditably as Ninth Wrangler (an honors degree in mathematics) in 1788. In that same year he took holy orders, and later was appointed to a rectory. In livelihood, however, he was less a "parson" (as his detractors have often chosen to call him), than a college professor; for in 1805 he became the first professor of political economy in the English-speaking world, at the new East India College, in Hertfordshire, a post he held until his death in 1834.

According to the testimony of his friends, Robert Malthus was amiable, gentle, and good-natured—"one of the most serene and cheerful" of men, the writer Harriet Martineau called him. He was a devoted family man: he married Harriet Eckersall, one of his "pretty cousins," in 1804, and they had three children, two of whom survived to maturity. He was a faithful friend: his correspondence with the economist David Ricardo covered the last dozen years of Ricardo's life in amicable and generous disagreement ("I should not like you more than I do," Ricardo wrote him, "if you agreed in opinion with me"). He was a dutiful teacher: one of his students' class notes survive, and they refer to Malthus as "Pop." And he was a prophet of what might be called long-range benevolence: "My ultimate object," he wrote, "is to diminish vice and misery." When he died, he was remembered fondly by his friends, one of whom wrote for his epitaph at Bath Abbey:

> The spotless integrity of his principles,
> The equity and candour of his nature,
> His sweetness of temper, urbanity of manners,
> And tenderness of heart,
> His benevolence and piety,
> Are the still dearer recollections of his family and friends.

Yet this was the man whose social views were immediately and persistently assailed by humanitarians and social reformers all over Europe: "that black and terrible demon that is always ready to stifle the hopes of humanity" (Godwin); "this abominable tenet" (Coleridge); "the dismal science" (Carlyle); "this vile and infamous doctrine, this repulsive blasphemy against man and nature" (Engels). "Unless Mr. Malthus can contrive to starve someone," Hazlitt fumed, "he thinks he does nothing." "He was the 'best-abused man of the age,' " James Bonar wrote in *Malthus and His Work*; "For thirty years it rained refutations."[1] And the chorus of dissent has continued into our own time: Malthusianism is "a warning against all attempts to ameliorate the condition of society," wrote a tendentious scholar in 1953; it is a "gospel of despair," added another in 1955.[2]

It is not difficult to understand this bitter and sustained hostility toward the genial Malthus and his work, for the basic idea he enunciated—that population tends to increase at a faster rate than its food supplies—is indeed an ominous one, and few people are fond of prophets of doom. How did Malthus arrive at such a bleak view of the human condition?

It helps to recall that Malthus grew up during the Enlightenment, was ten years old when the American Revolution began, and came to maturity at the time of the French Revolution. Hume and Rousseau had visited at his father's house when Robert Malthus was a baby, and the dates of his life also overlap those of Voltaire, Diderot, and d'Alembert, as well as Washington, Jefferson, and Franklin. The late eighteenth century was for European nations

1. James Bonar, *Malthus and His Work* (London, 1885), pp. 1–2.
2. Ronald L. Meek, ed., *Marx and Engels on the Population Bomb* (Berkeley, Calif., 1971), p. 10; Harold A. Boner, *Hungry Generations* (New York, 1955), p. 195.

what the late twentieth century is for much of the Third World: on the one hand, a time of economic hardship and social despair; on the other hand, a time of intellectual ferment, of movements for social and political reform, a time of energetic speculation about the possible improvement of societies and of people. Enthusiasm for science ran high; and hopes that science, applied to society, would transform the world, were reinforced by the recent discoveries of "paradises"—supposedly "perfect" societies—in the South Seas. "Our hopes for the future condition of the human race," wrote Condorcet, "can be subsumed under three important heads: the abolition of inequality between nations, the progress of equality within each nation, and the true perfection of mankind." To these ideals, European intellectuals were giving their sympathetic attention, and often their loyalty. It may have been the worst of times for some people, but it was the best of times for visionaries.

Then in 1789 came the French Revolution, and in its wake regicide, the Reign of Terror, and the savaging of half of Europe by that imperialistic Jacobin, Bonaparte; the Directory then governing France was rumored to be planning an invasion of England. British suspicion of French institutions and French intentions, never at that time far below the surface, boiled up in widespread alarm and hostility. In England it was no longer the best of times for social reformers; and yet the infection of "French philosophy" was still there, and determined social critics like William Godwin went on with their work. Godwin's influential *Enquiry concerning Political Justice* appeared in 1793, and in 1797 he issued a collection of essays called *The Enquirer*, in one of which, "Of Avarice and Profusion," he continued his examinations of the "first principles of morality," "justice between man and man," and "the extensive diffusion of liberty and happiness." Robert Malthus and his father read that essay, with far-reaching results.

As it happened, the two men differed on precisely the question of whether "the extensive diffusion of liberty and happiness" was possible in human affairs. The elder Malthus, true to his advanced ideas, held that it was. Robert disagreed; the reasons for his pessimism were fundamental. He had been reading Hume and Robert Wallace on the question of whether human populations had grown or declined since ancient times (Hume believed they had grown; Wallace, the reverse) and Adam Smith on how the numbers of laborers affect wages ("The demand for men, like that for any other commodity, necessarily regulates the production of men"); and Robert had arrived at a theory of population which, if "certainly not new" (as he said), had just as certainly never been presented as forcefully as he was now to present it. "I mean to place it in a point of view," he wrote, "in some degree different from any that I have hitherto seen" (p. 18)[3]—a remarkable under-statement, as it turned out. In his systematic way, he immediately wrote down his thoughts in a manuscript which he entitled *An Essay on the Principle of Population, as It Affects the Future Improvement of Society.* It was published anonymously in London in 1798.

The discrete parts of what Malthus had to say on his subject were, indeed, "not new." He had been anticipated by the book of Ecclesiastes by some twenty-five hundred years: "When goods increase, they are increased who eat them"; and by thinkers as reverend and diverse as Confucius and Plato, who had explored similar notions. More to the point, contemporary social theorists like Hume, Smith, and Benjamin Franklin had shown an aware-ness of the tendency of populations to increase very rapidly unless somehow "checked." Eighteenth-century thinkers, however, viewed population growth as a mark of social well-being, not as a threat to the "improvement of society." An increase in people was generally taken to imply an increase in wealth: "Every wise, just and mild government," Hume wrote, "by rendering the condition of its sub-jects easy and secure will always abound most in people, as well as in commodities and riches" (p. 3).

Malthus saw it differently. He began with the awesome redun-dancy of nature: "Through the animal and vegetable kingdoms," he wrote, "nature has scattered the seeds of life abroad with the most profuse and liberal hand. . . . The germs of life contained in this spot of earth, with ample food and ample room to expand in, would fill millions of worlds in the course of a few thousand years" (p. 20). That observation may not have been "new" with Malthus; but it always *seems* new, simply because it is always, upon contem-plation, staggering. And it always gives rise to the inevitable next question: if all organisms have this potential for rapid multiplica-tion, if any single species could, in a comparatively brief time, overrun the earth—why does it not happen?

In *The Wealth of Nations* (1776), Adam Smith had already implied the question and given the answer: "Every species of ani-mals naturally multiplies in proportion to the means of their sub-sistence, and no species can ever multiply beyond it." Nature, Malthus asserted, "has been comparatively sparing in the room and the nourishment necessary to rear them" (p. 20). "Room," then, is one of Malthus' two ineluctable limitational factors; but his emphasis in the *Essay* falls upon the second one: "nourish-ment." Malthus could not reasonably anticipate (or, as he put it, "The most enthusiastic speculator cannot suppose") an increase in food supply that was greater than arithmetical, each generation.

3. Parenthetical page references are to passages in this volume.

It follows that the tendency of population to multiply, if unchecked by other means, will be checked by "vice and misery"; it will simply (and of course only temporarily) outrun the supply of food. This is the most brutal and final of "positive" checks to population growth.

For Malthus' contemporaries, the immediate force of his argument derived from the quasi-scientific way he chose to illustrate his premises. The former mathematics student could not resist a mathematical illustration; population can increase geometrically, he said, whereas agricultural production can only increase arithmetically:

> Taking the population of the world at any number, a thousand millions, for instance, the human species would increase in the ratio of —1, 2, 4, 8, 16, 32, 64, 128, 256, 512, &c. and subsistence as—1, 2, 3, 4, 5, 6, 7, 8, 9, 10, &c. In two centuries and a quarter, the population would be to the means of subsistence as 512 to 10, in three centuries as 4096 to 13, and in two thousand years the difference would be almost incalculable [p. 23].

It was a persuasive illustration, partly because of its stark simplicity and partly because the first half of it—the geometric power of population increase—is true on its face: the reproductive potential of any plant or animal species verifies it. (Charles Darwin and Alfred Russel Wallace, impressed with Malthus' argument, found in it the key to their theory of natural selection.[4]) The other half—the arithmetic maximum for agricultural production—was a conjecture rather than an observation, and its history is more complicated. It certainly seemed a safe conjecture when Malthus wrote his essay: to imagine agricultural production increasing even by arithmetic progression each generation, given the farming methods of the eighteenth century, seemed generous. Malthus tried always to be empirical, which is why he steadily took issue with the Utopians of his time; the *Essay* persistently appeals to experience:

> —We shall be assisted in our review by what we daily see around us, by actual experience, by facts that come within the scope of every man's observation [p. 31].

> —Such establishments and calculations may appear very promising upon paper, but when applied to real life they will be found to be absolutely nugatory [p. 58].

> —How little Mr. Godwin has turned the attention of his penetrating mind to the real state of man on earth will sufficiently appear . . . [p. 67].

4. See Peter Vorzimmer, "Darwin, Malthus, and the Theory of Natural Selection," *Journal of the History of Ideas*, 30 (1969), 527–42; and Howard E. Gruber and Paul H. Barrett, *Darwin on Man* (New York, 1974), chapter 8.

And so on, throughout the *Essay*.

Ironically, when he came to the crux of his own argument, Malthus himself had to speculate. No better than others at foreseeing the future, he extrapolated from the best evidence he had, which was the agricultural practice of the late eighteenth century. The steam engine had been invented in that eventful year 1776, but it was not yet apparent in 1798 that the emerging shift from muscle power to machine power would revolutionize agriculture, making possible unprecedented increases in food supplies. (The application of modern biochemistry and genetics to agriculture was of course still further in the future and even less conceivable in Malthus' time.) When this began to happen, in the course of the nineteenth century, Malthus' celebrated ratios seemed to be discredited; and by the early twentieth century (as people of the industrialized countries increasingly chose to have smaller families), when someone spoke of the "population problem," he was as likely to mean the threat of underpopulation ("race suicide," it was often called) as of overpopulation. Malthus' fears then seemed distant and groundless. But after World War II, when death rates in many of the less developed countries were abruptly reduced to the levels of the industrialized countries, population growth rates shot up, and Malthus' handwriting once again appeared, clear and portentous, on the wall.[5]

Today, even in the face of a Malthusian crisis of vast proportions, we in the West tend to remain the philosophical heirs of the eighteenth- and nineteenth-century prophets of Progress. We are inclined to be problem-solvers; we pattern our mental futures on the success of the recent past. And yet, the rapidly increasing food production of the last two centuries may be as misleading a guide as was the relatively static situation in Malthus' time. Many people are now becoming uneasy about our reliance on agricultural and industrial technologies which often have hidden, sometimes frightening, costs. We have been in the habit of taking accelerated agricultural productivity as the norm for a modern society; but we now recognize that it may be a splendid but temporary luxury, a historical aberration. For it is increasingly clear that the necessity

5. Although he did not foresee the great increases in food production of the nineteenth and twentieth centuries, Malthus believed that his theory allowed for such a possibility without loss of force. See, e.g., his letter to Nassau Senior, dated March 23, 1829: "The meaning which I intended to convey . . . was, that population was always ready, and inclined, to increase faster than food, if the checks which repressed it were removed; and that though these checks might be such as to prevent population from advancing upon subsistence, or even to keep it at a greater distance behind; yet, that whether population were *actually* increasing faster than food, or food faster than population, it was true that, except in new colonies, favourably circumstanced, population was always pressing against food, and was always ready to start off at a faster rate than that at which the food was actually increasing." (See Nassau W. Senior, *Selected Writings on Economics* [New York, 1966], p. 61.)

of supplying food to very large and rapidly growing populations has pollution and resource-depletion effects that are more imminent and more destructive than they would be in a less densely populated world. The large amounts of pesticides and herbicides that are required to protect high crop yields in Sri Lanka or Indonesia, so that larger and larger populations can be supported there, are inevitably being carried down to the sea, with toxic effects, often widespread and persistent, upon the living resources of the ocean; so the short-range gain in rice will be paid for by a long-range loss of much of the world's supply of protein-rich sea food.

Depletion of natural resources is also aggravated by overpopulation: "When a 10,000 ton freighter loaded . . . with Food for Peace wheat sails out of New York," write the Paddock brothers, "a specific component of American wealth is shipped out, wealth in the form of 200 tons of nitrogen, 41 tons of phosphorus and 50 tons of potassium. Multiply these figures by the approximately 14,600 freighter loads shipped out from 1954 to July 1965 and one sees that the portion of our soil's fertility thus lost forever is a significant part of our national resources . . ." (p. 232). Furthermore, the spectacular productiveness of American agriculture is based upon methods that demand such massive investments of fossil fuels and machinery that the energy required to produce some foods has now become greater than the energy obtained from them.[6]

Thus, even with the "green revolution" fresh in our memories (see pp. 246–49) Malthus' speculation about agriculture seems rather less mistaken these days, than it once did. The validity of Malthus' argument depends, after all, not on the mathematical accuracy of his two ratios, but on their long-range relation to each other. And if Malthus was right—if population growth does, in the long run, have a tendency to outstrip food supplies—what, then, could he have hoped for by way of "the future improvement of society"? The answer is that as of 1798 he saw no real hope for permanent improvement, because he thought of the ratios as representing a law of nature as immutable as Newton's; and he saw no effective way of averting the grim consequences of that law. In Malthus' time, after all, there were only the crudest and most barbarous kinds of population control: undependable methods of contraception, abortion by shockingly dangerous self-induced means, and infanticide. To Malthus all of these were unacceptable, on moral grounds, and they therefore played no part in his first

6. See Eric Hirst, "Food-Related Energy Requirements," *Science*, 184 (1974), 134–38.

Essay[7]—which means that he was left without any practicable options, any effective way of preventing that excessive growth of population that is decreed by the redundancy of nature. So, he wrote, "This argument appears to be conclusive . . . against any marked and striking change for the better . . . any great and decided amelioration of the lower classes of mankind" (p. 95).

That is almost how he left it at the end of his first *Essay* in 1798—but not quite. Despite the relentless logic that drove him to this gloomy judgment, he apparently could not feel comfortable in a conclusion that seemed to recommend only an inhumane and fatalistic acquiescence in human misery. Malthus therefore recommended policies which would help to alleviate human suffering: land reform (p. 115), the transfer of laborers from luxury manufactures to farming (p. 111), and a shift of national emphasis from foreign trade to agriculture (p. 112).

Still, his conclusion was undeniably "melancholy," as he himself called it, and in his preface he apologizes for that, pleading "that he has drawn these dark tints from a conviction that they are really in the picture, and not from a jaundiced eye." He would have been pleased, he says, to believe the optimistic visions of a Godwin or a Condorcet, but (in an ironic thrust) he "has not acquired that command over his understanding which would enable him to believe what he wishes, without evidence . . ." (p. 15).

That is where the matter rested with Malthus in 1798. Then, for five years, he pondered the matter further and collected new evidence, and in 1803 brought out a revised edition of the *Essay* which was greatly enlarged (from 50,000 to 250,000 words) and less pessimistic than before. In those five years of reconsideration, Malthus had thought of the possibility of "another check to population which does not come under the head of either vice or misery" (p. 130). He called this check "moral restraint"; by which he meant simply delayed marriage. "It is clearly the duty of each individual," Malthus wrote, "not to marry till he has a prospect of supporting his children" (p. 132).

The importance of recognizing this third potential check to population growth was that it admitted into Malthus' equation for the first time a conscious and potentially benevolent human element, a possibility that undesirable population growth could conceivably be brought under human control. This tended, as Malthus said, to "soften some of the harshest conclusions of the first

7. When in 1822 Francis Place suggested contraception as a remedy for overpopulation, he felt obliged to put it in the most circumspect and defensive terms (see pp. 209–10); and for more than a century thereafter, those who publicly advocated birth control risked imprisonment (see pp. 213–16). Ironically, although Malthus himself disapproved of birth control, contraceptives were often called "Malthusian appliances" later in the century; see Peter Fryer, *The Birth Controllers* (London, 1965).

Essay" (p. 130); and it prompted Malthus' new way of viewing his grim subject—no longer simply as a sort of biological juggernaut, but rather in terms of a moral imperative: "If moral restraint be the only virtuous mode of avoiding the evils arising from this principle [of population], our obligation to practise it will evidently rest exactly upon the same foundation as our obligation to practise any of the other virtues" (p. 132).[8]

Malthus' first *Essay*, by not accounting for the possibility of effective human intervention, described a real biological tendency without showing all of the possible alternatives. The second *Essay*, by allowing for conscious human intervention, showed the same consequences as before, plus one more possibility, and a far preferable one; but the biological problem represented in the first *Essay* remained the same in the second *Essay* and remains a problem to this day. Whether or not people will in fact interpose prudential checks to catastrophic population growth seems to have been answered in the affirmative for the industrialized countries; but it has by no means been answered yet for the 600 million people of India, currently doubling their numbers in twenty-eight years, or for Mexico, currently doubling its numbers in twenty-one years, or for Egypt, currently doubling its numbers in thirty-three years; or for Ghana, or Colombia, or Turkey, or Brazil, or for most of the other less developed countries, doubling at similarly alarming rates. There is a vast difference between the abstract possibility of problem-solving, and the actual achievement of solutions.

For Malthus the human obligations were clear:

> We are not, however, to relax our efforts in increasing the quantity of provisions, but to combine another effort with it; that of keeping the population, when once it has been overtaken, at such a distance behind as to effect the relative proportion which we desire; and thus unite the two grand *desiderata*, a great actual population and a state of society in which abject poverty and dependence are comparatively but little known; two objects which are far from being incompatible [p. 133].

That reasoning, and even that kind of optimism, cautious and qualified, have never been improved upon.

After nearly two centuries of disparaging the so-called Malthu-

8. Walter Bagehot later commented acidly, "He does not seem to see that he has cut away the ground of his whole argument . . . In its first form the *Essay on Population* was conclusive as an argument, only it was based on untrue facts; in its second form it was based on true facts, but it was inconclusive as an argument" (*Economic Studies* [London, 1880], p. 179). Bagehot's analysis of Malthus' position, however, is itself de-fective. It is not the "facts" that are changed in Malthus' second edition; they remain exactly as before, and are as true, or untrue, as they had previously been. What Malthus changed was the range of possible alternatives in the face of these facts, now for the first time admitting the possibility of human intervention into a situation he previously considered unalterable.

sian gloom, it may seem odd to hear Malthus called optimistic; but the conventional labels have been misleading. It is often the cheery voices of the self-proclaimed "optimists" of the far right (theologians, businessmen, and technologists who argue that bigger is better, and that unlimited population growth and material growth are not only possible, but desirable) which encourage the neglect of pressing social problems, thereby condemning multitudes of unfortunate people to continuing misery; whereas the "doomsayers," the so-called pessimists, are often the ones to raise an alarm, thus sometimes producing effective social action. (Rachel Carson, passionately opposed to the indiscriminate use of DDT, was no doubt a more genuine benefactor of humanity, and therefore a truer optimist, than some of her smooth-spoken antagonists in the pesticide industry.) Similarly, the "optimists" of the far left, by obdurately refusing to recognize rapid population growth as a threat to social improvement, have compromised their own—and others'—attempts to deal with poverty, crime, racial injustice, and other problems. It is ironic that in the continuing attacks on "Malthusianism," the far left of Marxists and other radicals have joined hands with the far right of conservative economists and the conservative hierarchy of the Roman Catholic Church (which is still categorically opposed to "artificial" birth control; see below, pp. 183–85).

What Malthus did was to oppose an effective and tough-minded empiricism to the often woolly-headed Utopianism so popular during his youth. Only after he had done this could Malthus propose a different sort of optimism, a qualified and wary optimism, about a future for humankind that recognizes and accounts for the dangers implicit in our biological nature. "Though our future prospects may not be so bright as we could wish," Malthus concluded his revised *Essay*, "yet they . . . by no means preclude that gradual and progressive improvement in human society which, before the late wild speculations on this subject, was the object of rational expectation" (p. 138).

To call this attitude, this message, a "warning against all attempts to ameliorate the condition of society" or a "gospel of despair" (see above, p. xii) is obviously a misreading.[9] John Maynard

9. About the "willful misrepresentations" of Malthus' ideas that are frequently assigned to the adjective "Malthusian," William Peterson writes: "Is this word ever used to designate, say, the first significant economist to recognize the importance of effective demand and thus the only nineteenth-century figure in the main line of classical economic thought to suggest the serious lacks in laissez-faire policies; or, in social thought, a pioneer advocate of universal education, the initiator of political science as a university discipline; or, specifically with respect to population, the theorist who analyzed both the relation between humans and resources and the effect of social man's rising aspirations on his fertility? Very little of the full and well rounded thought of Professor Thomas Robert Malthus is recalled in the commentary even of professionals" ("The Malthus-Godwin Debate, Then and Now," *Demography*, 8 [1971], 25).

Keynes' tribute to Malthus is far more accurate. Commenting in 1933 on the *Essay on Population*, he wrote:

> The book can claim a place amongst those which have had great influence on the progress of thought. It is profoundly in the English tradition of humane science—in that tradition of Scotch and English thought, in which there has been, I think, an extraordinary continuity of *feeling*, if I may so express it, from the eighteenth century to the present time—the tradition which is suggested by the names of Locke, Hume, Adam Smith, Paley, Bentham, Darwin, and Mill, a tradition marked by a love of truth and a most noble lucidity, by a prosaic sanity free from sentiment or metaphysic, and by an immense disinterestedness and public spirit. There is a continuity in these writings, not only of feeling, but of actual matter. It is in this company that Malthus belongs.[1]

Malthus' theory of population originated, as we have seen, in an argument with his father about "the future improvement of society"; significantly, nearly all of the subsequent controversies, still animated after more than 175 years, ultimately turn on that question. Discussions of "Malthusianism" have always been, and still are, compounded less of economics, narrowly defined, than of social philosophy, less of demography than of moral exhortation. The early followers of Malthus included classical economists like David Ricardo, Nassau Senior, and James and John Stuart Mill. The long correspondence between Ricardo and Malthus, in fact, bears little on the question of population, simply because Ricardo agreed so thoroughly with Malthus on that subject, differing only in certain emphases. Similarly, Senior wrote that Malthus' theory places him "as a benefactor to mankind on a level with Adam Smith" (p. 148); though Senior was more optimistic than Malthus about the effectiveness of "preventive" checks to population growth.

John Stuart Mill published his *Principles of Political Economy* in 1848; by that time he was heir not only to Malthus' original generalizations but also to the subsequent discovery, made almost simultaneously by Malthus, Ricardo, and two other British economists, of the Law of Diminishing Returns in agriculture. In his 1814 essay on the Corn Laws, and again in 1815, in a discussion of rent, Malthus had described the operation of Diminishing Returns. In fact, as early as the second edition of the *Essay on Population* (1803), Malthus had casually anticipated his own later discovery:

> It must be evident to those who have the slightest acquaintance with agricultural subjects, that in proportion as cultivation ex-

1. John Maynard Keynes, *Essays in Biography* (New York, 1933), p. 120.

tended, the additions that could yearly be made to the former average produce, must be gradually and regularly diminishing.[2]

However, he made only passing reference to Diminishing Returns in the *Essay on Population*, thinking perhaps that the *Essay* rested on other generalizations that were already sufficiently convincing. When John Stuart Mill published his *Principles of Political Economy*, however, he regarded Diminishing Returns as fundamental to agricultural production:

> It is vain to say, that all mouths which the increase of mankind calls into existence, bring with them hands. The new mouths require as much food as the old ones, and the hands do not produce as much [p. 151].

Mill's work was so influential that he may be said to have shifted permanently the post-Malthusian emphasis, away from Malthus' ratios and onto the Law of Diminishing Returns; in doing so, he gave new force to the Malthusian principle.

Meanwhile, the anti-Malthusians, who were largely well-intentioned social reformers of various persuasions, were rallying against the hated notion that population growth is an inevitable and insuperable "natural" obstacle to human betterment. Malthus, having argued for the retention of the protectionist Corn Laws (and thus for higher food prices) and for the abolition of poor relief, was soon characterized as a "hard-hearted" public enemy of poor people, despite his sincere insistence that these short-range severities were in their long-range best interest. Malthus may have been a "serene and cheerful" man, as Harriet Martineau said; but some of his social nostrums were undeniably hard-hearted in the short run:

> —I should propose a regulation to be made, declaring that no child born from any marriage . . . should ever be entitled to parish assistance.

> —With regard to illegitimate children . . . they should not be allowed to have any claim to parish assistance . . .

> —The infant is, comparatively speaking, of little value to the society, as others will immediately supply its place [pp. 135–36].

Stripped of their context of "long-range benevolence," these notions have the odor of barbarity about them. With the advantage of hindsight and knowledge of subsequent agricultural successes, we now realize—as Malthus did not—that such severity was not necessary. It may be instructive to Americans in the 1970s, faced with proposals of food-triage (see pp. 230–32), to remember that

2. Malthus, *An Essay on Population*, Everyman's Library ed., Vol. I, p. 11.

where Malthus was least humane, he was most wrong. In view of present population growth rates, it is clear that it will require unprecedented good will and social discipline to avert an imminent human tragedy of vast proportions; and despite the best that contemporary societies can do (or are willing to do), we may yet live to see mass starvation in our lifetime. But cold-bloodedly to cut off food aid to the most needy countries, even on the grounds of using the food more effectively elsewhere, would be an act of national arrogance which Americans might well come to repent as intensely as Germans repent Nazi genocide.

At any rate, nineteenth-century humanitarians refused to accept the inevitability of Malthus' grim "law" of population and his draconian remedies, stressing instead the need to reform society itself in order to rescue humanity from poverty and misery. Godwin (Malthus' original target) responded:

> Man is to a considerable degree the artificer of his own fortune. We can apply our reflections and our ingenuity to whatever we regret [p. 143].

Moralists like William Cobbett repeatedly voiced their distaste for Malthus:

> Talk as long as Parson Malthus likes about "moral *restraint*"; and report as long as the Committees of Parliament please about preventing "*premature* and *improvident* marriages" amongst the labouring classes, the passion that they would *restrain*, while it is necessary to the existence of mankind, is the greatest of all the compensations for the inevitable cares, troubles, hardships, and sorrows of life; and, as to the *marriages*, if they could once be rendered universally *provident*, every generous sentiment would quickly be banished from the world.[3]

And as the century wore on, some well-known economists joined the assault on "Parson Malthus." Walter Bagehot's ill-considered criticism, in his *Economic Studies* (1880), has already been noted (see above, p. xix, note 8). In the same year, the American Henry George was writing, in *Progress and Poverty*:

> I assert that in any given state of civilization a greater number of people can collectively be better provided for than a smaller. I assert that the injustice of society, not the niggardliness of nature, is the cause of want and misery which the current theory attributes to over-population. . . . I assert that, other things being equal, the greater the population, the greater the comfort . . .[4]

3. William Cobbett, *Advice to Young Men* (London, 1829), p. 85.

4. Henry George, *Progress and Poverty* (New York, 1942), pp. 141–42.

It is revealing that many literary people in the nineteenth century were also anti-Malthusians—revealing, because it demonstrates how deeply Malthus' message offended humanitarian values. "The voice of objective reason," Keynes said of Malthus' theory, "had been raised against a deep instinct which the evolutionary struggle had been implanting from the commencement of life . . ." That same voice spoke against the religious command to "increase and multiply"; and, despite Malthus' protestations from 1803 on, his doctrine was also held, by socialists and other radical reformers, to be an immovable obstacle to any human action for social betterment. It was no wonder, then, that nineteenth-century writers, characteristically thinking of themselves as humanitarians, resisted the Malthusian propositions. Shelley (Godwin's son-in-law), Coleridge, Wordsworth, and Hazlitt all spoke out; Carlyle's sarcasm is well known; Dickens' Scrooge, in his most misanthropic moods, speaks as a pseudo-Malthusian ("If they would rather die . . . they had better do it, and decrease the surplus population"); and others of Dickens' villains are Malthusian caricatures:

> "A man may live to be as old as Methuselah," said Mr. Filer, "and may labour all his life for the benefit of such people as those; and may heap up facts on figures, facts on figures, facts on figures, mountains high and dry; and he can no more hope to persuade 'em that they have no right or business to be married, than he can hope to persuade 'em that they have no earthly right or business to be born. And *that* we know they haven't. We reduced it to a mathematical certainty long ago!"[5]

The most persistent of Malthus' critics have been Marxists. By stressing the pessimism of Malthus' first *Essay*, and ignoring the qualified optimism of the later editions, Marxists have characteristically painted Malthus as (in Marx's own words) "the great destroyer of all hankerings after human development," and as a capitalist hireling, a defender of class privilege. Until the 1960s, Marxists were virtually unanimous in holding that overpopulation is a problem only of capitalist societies, not of socialist societies. The Marxian labor theory of value does not admit the Law of Diminishing Returns (under socialism, every pair of hands "can" produce sufficient food for every stomach, without limit); so socialist societies should be capable of supporting any foreseeable population.[6] Recently, however, solid Marxist agreement on this subject has broken down, and, while "Malthusianism" is still ritualistically

5. Charles Dickens, *The Chimes*, in *Works* (New York, 1911), Vol. 16, p. 97.
6. Compare, however, the dissenting view of Michael Harrington, in his *Socialism* (New York, 1970, page 149): "One cannot foresee a socialism capable of meeting the needs of a world which increases its numbers by the billions in the course of a single generation."

denounced, Chinese and Russian demographers and economists now openly debate the advisability of population control.[7]

One reason for the changing Marxist attitudes toward population may be the difficulties that both the Soviet Union and the People's Republic of China have had in producing enough food to sustain their own burgeoning populations. The Soviet Union is now increasing by about two and a half million people per year; China, according to United Nations estimates, by over thirteen million per year. And Russia, a former grain exporter, has in recent years had to import massive supplies of food grains from the capitalist West;[8] while China, which was once the major exporter of soybeans on the world market, has now become a soybean importer as well as a large wheat importer. Another reason may be that some Marxist demographers have stared into the gaunt face of overpopulation in the less developed countries and seen it for the ominous thing it actually is, not disguised by the rosy vision of what socialism might one day make of it.

In any case, both the Soviet Union and China now consider population growth to be a matter of national interest and state planning, thus implicitly conceding Malthus' fundamental proposition. Population growth in the Soviet Union has been reduced (by individual family decisions, not by state planning) in ten years' time from a relatively high 1.7 percent to a more moderate 1.0 percent; while in China a vigorous national policy of population control—perhaps "the most comprehensive, ambitious effort to reduce births of any major country in the world," according to Lester Brown[9]—has brought its population growth rate down from 2.0 percent to 1.7 percent. So whatever the Marxists' official views on "Malthusianism" may be, the actual practice of the two largest communist nations confirms their tacit agreement with Malthus' proposition: that in the face of unchecked population growth, *"no possible form of society* could prevent the almost constant action of misery upon a great part of mankind, if in a state of inequality, *and upon all, if all were equal"* (p. 26; emphasis added).

When Mathus died in 1834, the total population of the world was about one billion. If he were to return today, he would find a world population that is over four billion, and is now doubling

7. See, e.g., James W. Brackett, "The Evolution of Marxist Theories of Population: Marxism Recognizes the Population Problem," *Demography*, 5 (1968), 158–73; and Michael F. Brewer, ed., "The Soviet Peoples: Population Growth and Policy," *Population Bulletin*, 28 (1972), passim.
8. The huge Russian grain imports are partly due to a Kremlin policy decision to increase supplies of meat and animal products in the Soviet Union; but Russia also has fifty million more mouths to feed now than at the end of World War II.
9. Lester Brown, *In the Human Interest* (New York, 1974), p. 130.

itself within thirty-five years. Malthus would no doubt be surprised
to learn that in only 140 years the world food supply had increased
sufficiently to keep so many people alive; but he would be far less
surprised to hear that of those four billion people, nearly half of
them—almost twice as many people as existed in his own time—
are suffering from malnutrition and are threatened by starvation.[1]
Despite a century and a half of progress in agricultural technology,
there is little in today's world situation to suggest that Malthus
would now change his mind: in many of the less developed countries, there is simply not enough domestic food to nourish the
population adequately; widespread bad weather conditions in the
mid-1970s have reduced world crop yields; food from foreign
sources is increasingly expensive due to higher costs of oil and
fertilizer; and meanwhile the world population keeps growing by
eighty million mouths per year. World food reserves, which as
recently as 1961 were at nearly a hundred days' supply, were down
to a mere twenty-seven-day supply in 1974—a reminder that Malthus once wrote:

> Where a country is so populous in proportion to the means of
> subsistence that the average produce of it is but barely sufficient
> to support the inhabitants, any deficiency from the badness of
> seasons must be fatal [p. 53].

Complicating and worsening the situation is the fact that the
large numbers of babies born in the less developed countries after
World War II have for some years now been coming to adulthood
(and parenthood). They have flooded the labor markets, and,
because so large a percentage of them are unable to find employment, they constitute a huge and growing reservoir of human
misery. Other social problems, of varying degrees of urgency, have
also been aggravated by rapid increases in population: shortages
of housing and hospitals, of schools and teachers; inadequate clean
water supplies, sanitation, and health care. Some of these may
seem less alarming than shortages of food; but they compound
human misery and are therefore part of the total cost of overpopulation.

That is why most Western humanitarians in the post–World War
II period (unlike some of their counterparts in the nineteenth century) see population control as an urgent necessity for "the future
improvement of society," and consider Malthus an important social
prophet. Suspicious of "colonialist" and "imperialist" ideas, many
scholars and political leaders in the socialist and Third World
countries do not agree (see below, pp. 181 ff. and 193 ff.). They

1. See, e.g., "Nutrition, Development, and Population Growth," *Population Bulletin*,
29 (1973), 6.

are persuaded that population limitation is less important for their social welfare than are economic redistribution and reform. They cling to the hope that a demographic transition toward lower growth rates will occur in their societies in the same way it did in the West: as a consequence, not a precondition, of economic development. Western economists and demographers, on the other hand, point out that the currently industrialized countries had a much more favorable starting position with regard to development, including smaller populations, more available natural resources, the possibility of large-scale emigration, and a century or more for the demographic transition to take place before low modern death rates were achieved; the less developed countries, lacking all of these conditions, can hardly depend upon repeating the Western experience.

Still, this is rather a difference of emphasis than a direct confrontation of strategies, because most contemporary Western social critics have abandoned the "either-or" approach of earlier ones. It has now become compellingly obvious that since the world already *has* population growth rates which threaten millions with starvation, therefore it *must* attempt to bring these growth rates down— eventually to zero, but in the meantime as much as possible. And since the world also already *has* food shortages and at the same time the ability to raise more food, therefore it *must* do everything possible to increase food supplies. There is nothing mutually exclusive about these two social necessities; on the contrary, they can be mutually reinforcing (see below, pp. 250–52). In part because of rapid population growth, the world faces a future full of uncertainty and prodigious challenge; it is easy to be pessimistic, even fatalistic, in the face of such forbidding conditions. But the same man who anticipated the present condition also prescribed the only tenable response to it: "Sufficient remains to be done for mankind," Malthus wrote, "to animate us to the most unremitted exertion" (p. 116).

PART I

Influences on Malthus

DAVID HUME

Of the Populousness of Antient Nations (1752) †

In general, we may observe, that the question with regard to the comparative populousness of ages or kingdoms implies very important consequences * * *. For as there is in all men, both male and female, a desire and power of generation more active than is ever universally exerted, the restraints, which it lyes under, must proceed from some difficulties in men's situation, which it belongs to a wise legislature carefully to observe and remove. Almost every man, who thinks he can maintain a family, will have one; and the human species, at this rate of propagation, wou'd more than double every generation, were every one coupled as soon as he comes to the age of puberty. How fast do mankind multiply in every colony or new settlement; where it is an easy matter to provide for a family; and where men are no way straitned or confin'd, as in long establish'd governments? History tells us frequently of plagues, that have swept away the third or fourth part of a people: Yet in a generation or two, the destruction was not perceiv'd; and the society had again acquir'd their former number. The lands, that were cultivated, the houses built, the commodities rais'd, the riches acquir'd, enabled the people, who escap'd, immediately to marry, and to rear families, which supply'd the place of those who had perish'd. And for a like reason, every wise, just, and mild government, by rendering the condition of its subjects easy and secure, will always abound most in people, as well as in commodities and riches. A country, indeed, whose climate and soil are fitted for vines, will naturally be more populous than one, which produces only corn, and that more populous than one, which is only fitted for pasturage. But if every thing else be equal, it seems natural to expect, that wherever there are most happiness and virtue and the wisest institutions, there also be most people.

* * *

† David Hume (1711–1776), Scottish philosopher and historian. The present text is from Discourse X of his *Political Discourses*.

ROBERT WALLACE

A Dissertation on the Numbers of Mankind in Antient and Modern Times (1753) †

It will be proper to lay down some general maxims taken from nature and constant observation, which may be useful to guide us in a more particular comparison.

1. A rude and barbarous people, living by hunting, fishing, or pasturage, or on the spontaneous product of the earth, without agriculture, commerce and arts, can never be so numerous as a people inhabiting the same tracts of land, who are well skilled in agriculture and civilized by commerce: since uncultivated can never maintain so many inhabitants, as cultivated lands. In every country, there shall always be found a greater number of inhabitants, *cæteris paribus*, in proportion to the plenty of provisions it affords, as plenty will always encourage the generality of the people to marry.

* * *

2. As the earth could not be well peopled in rude and barbarous ages, neither are all countries, climates and soils, equally favourable to propagation.

* * *

3. Besides the nature of the climate or soil, the number of people in every country depends greatly on its political maxims and institutions concerning the division of lands.

* * *

Hence we may conclude, that when any antient nation divided its lands into small shares, and when even eminent citizens had but a few acres to maintain their families; tho' such a nation had but little commerce, and had learned only a few simple and more necessary arts, it must have abounded greatly in people. This was in a particular manner the case in *Rome* for several ages, as we shall see afterwards.

* * *

4. As the number of people in every nation depends most immediately on the number and fruitfulness of marriages, and the encouragement that is given to marry; where-ever the greatest care is taken in this respect, the number of people, *cæteris paribus*,

† Robert Wallace (1697–1771), Scottish clergyman and amateur economist.

shall be greatest; and a bad policy in this article must give a considerable check to propagation.

Hence, in a debauched nation, addicted to sensuality and irregular amours, and where luxury and a high taste of delicate living prevails, the number of the people must be proportionally small, as their debauchery will hinder many from marrying, and their luxury and delicacy will render them less able to maintain families.

For the same reason, a nation shall be more populous in proportion as good morals and a simplicity of taste and manners prevail, or as the people are more frugal and virtuous.

5. As mankind can only be supported by the fruits of the earth and animal food, and it is only by agriculture, fishing and hunting, that food can be provided, to render the earth as populous as possible, these arts must be duly cherished, especially agriculture and fishing.

Hence, the more persons employ themselves in agriculture and fishing, and the arts which are necessary for managing them to greatest advantage, the world in general will be more populous; and as fewer hands are employed in this manner, there will be fewer people. * * *

Philosophers have been advising, and Divines calling upon mankind to cultivate frugality, temperance, simplicity, contentment with a little, and patience of labour, demonstrating, that these humble virtues are the only means by which they can expect to secure solid, lasting, and independent felicity. * * *

But the cultivation of these virtues not only makes individuals happy; but, from what has been maintained in the preceding *Dissertation*, appears further to be the surest way of rendering the earth populous, and making society flourish. 'Twas simplicity of taste, frugality, patience of labour, and contentment with a little, which made the world so populous in antient times. * * *

In this manner the most humble virtues are found to be not only consistent with, but greatly conducive to the populousness and grandeur of society.

ADAM SMITH

An Inquiry into the Nature and Causes of the Wealth of Nations (1776) †

Though the wealth of a country should be very great, yet if it has been long stationary, we must not expect to find the wages of labour very high in it. The funds destined for the payment of

† Adam Smith (1723–1790), British economist and moral philosopher.

wages, the revenue and stock of its inhabitants, may be of the greatest extent; but if they have continued for several centuries of the same, or very nearly of the same extent, the number of labourers employed every year could easily supply, and even more than supply, the number wanted the following year. There could seldom be any scarcity of hands, nor could the masters be obliged to bid against one another in order to get them. The hands, on the contrary, would, in this case, naturally multiply beyond their employment. * * *

Poverty, though it no doubt discourages, does not always prevent marriage. It seems even to be favourable to generation. A half-starved Highland woman frequently bears more than twenty children, while a pampered fine lady is often incapable of bearing any, and is generally exhausted by two or three. Barrenness, so frequent among women of fashion, is very rare among those of inferior station. Luxury in the fair sex, while it inflames perhaps the passion for enjoyment, seems always to weaken, and frequently to destroy altogether, the powers of generation.

But poverty, though it does not prevent the generation, is extremely unfavorable to the rearing of children. The tender plant is produced, but in so cold a soil and so severe a climate, soon withers and dies. It is not uncommon, I have been frequently told, in the Highlands of Scotland for a mother who has borne twenty children not to have two alive. * * * In some places one half the children born die before they are four years of age; in many places before they are seven; and in almost all places before they are nine or ten. This great mortality, however, will everywhere be found chiefly among the children of the common people, who cannot afford to tend them with the same care as those of better station. Though their marriages are generally more fruitful than those of people of fashion, a smaller proportion of their children arrive at maturity. In foundling hospitals, and among the children brought up by parish charities, the mortality is still greater than among those of the common people.

Every species of animals naturally multiplies in proportion to the means of their subsistence, and no species can ever multiply beyond it. But in civilised society it is only among the inferior ranks of people that the scantiness of subsistence can set limits to the further multiplication of the human species; and it can do so in no other way than by destroying a great part of the children which their fruitful marriages produce.

The liberal reward of labour, by enabling them to provide better for their children, and consequently to bring up a greater number, naturally tends to widen and extend those limits. It deserves to be remarked, too, that it necessarily does this as nearly as possible in the proportion which the demand for labour requires. If this demand is continually increasing, the reward of labour must necessarily encourage in such a manner the marriage and multiplication of labourers, as may enable them to supply that continually increasing demand by a continually increasing population. If the reward should at any time be less than what was requisite for this purpose, the deficiency of hands would soon raise it; and if it should at any time be more, their excessive multiplication would soon lower it to this necessary rate. The market would be so much under-stocked with labour in the one case, and so much over-stocked in the other, as would soon force back its price to that proper rate which the circumstances of the society required. It is in this manner that the demand for men, like that for any other commodity, necessarily regulates the production of men; quickens it when it goes on too slowly, and stops it when it advances too fast. * * *

CONDORCET

The Future Progress of the Human Mind (1795) †

If man can, with almost complete assurance, predict phenomena when he knows their laws, and if, even when he does not, he can still, with great expectation of success, forecast the future on the basis of his experience of the past, why, then, should it be regarded as a fantastic undertaking to sketch, with some pretence to truth, the future destiny of man on the basis of his history? The sole foundation for belief in the natural sciences is this idea, that the general laws directing the phenomena of the universe, known or unknown, are necessary and constant. Why should this principle be any less true for the development of the intellectual and moral faculties of man than for the other operations of nature? * * *

If we glance at the state of the world today we see first of all that in Europe the principles of the French constitution are already those of all enlightened men. We see them too widely propagated, too seriously professed, for priests and despots to prevent their gradual penetration even into the hovels of their slaves; there they will soon awaken in these slaves the remnants of their common sense and inspire them with that smouldering indignation which

† Marie Jean Antoine Nicolas Caritat, Marquis de Condorcet (1743–1794), French mathematician and philosopher. The present text is from the last chapter of his *Sketch for a Historical Picture of the Progress of the Human Mind*.

not even constant humiliation and fear can smother in the soul of the oppressed.

* * *

Let us turn to the enlightened nations of Europe, and observe the size of their present populations in relation to the size of their territories. Let us consider, in agriculture and industry the proportion that holds between labour and the means of subsistence, * * * new instruments, machines and looms can add to man's strength and can improve at once the quality and the accuracy of his productions, and can diminish the time and labour that has to be expended on them. The obstacles still in the way of this progress will disappear, accidents will be foreseen and prevented, the insanitary conditions that are due either to the work itself or to the climate will be eliminated.

A very small amount of ground will be able to produce a great quantity of supplies of greater utility or higher quality; more goods will be obtained for a smaller outlay; the manufacture of articles will be achieved with less wastage in raw materials and will make better use of them. Every type of soil will produce those things which satisfy the greatest number of needs; of several alternative ways of satisfying needs of the same order, that will be chosen which satisfies the greatest number of people and which requires least labour and least expenditure. So, without the need for sacrifice, methods of preservation and economy in expenditure will improve in the wake of progress in the arts of producing and preparing supplies and making articles from them.

So not only will the same amount of ground support more people, but everyone will have less work to do, will produce more, and satisfy his wants more fully.

With all this progress in industry and welfare which establishes a happier proportion between men's talents and their needs, each successive generation will have larger possessions, either as a result of this progress or through the preservation of the products of industry; and so, as a consequence of the physical constitution of the human race, the number of people will increase. Might there not then come a moment when these necessary laws begin to work in a contrary direction; when, the number of people in the world finally exceeding the means of subsistence, there will in consequence ensue a continual diminution of happiness and population, a true retrogression, or at best an oscillation between good and bad? In societies that have reached this stage will not this oscillation be a perennial source of more or less periodic disaster? Will it not show that a point has been attained beyond which all further improvement is impossible, that the perfectibility of the human race has after long years arrived at a term beyond which it may never go?

There is doubtless no-one who does not think that such a time is still very far from us; but will it ever arrive? It is impossible to pronounce about the likelihood of an event that will occur only when the human species will have necessarily acquired a degree of knowledge of which we can have no inkling. And who would take it upon himself to predict the condition to which the art of converting the elements to the use of man may in time be brought?

But even if we agree that the limit will one day arrive, nothing follows from it that is in the least alarming as far as either the happiness of the human race or its indefinite perfectibility is concerned; if we consider that, before all this comes to pass, the progress of reason will have kept pace with that of the sciences, and that the absurd prejudices of superstition will have ceased to corrupt and degrade the moral code by its harsh doctrines instead of purifying and elevating it, we can assume that by then men will know that, if they have a duty towards those who are not yet born, that duty is not to give them existence but to give them happiness; their aim should be to promote the general welfare of the human race or of the society in which they live or of the family to which they belong, rather than foolishly to encumber the world with useless and wretched beings. It is, then, possible that there should be a limit to the amount of food that can be produced, and, consequently, to the size of the population of the world, without this involving that untimely destruction of some of those creatures who have been given life, which is so contrary to nature and to social prosperity.

WILLIAM GODWIN

Of Avarice and Profusion (1797) †

Riches and poverty are in some degree necessarily incidental to the social existence of man. There is no alternative, but that men must either have their portion of labour assigned them by the society at large, and the produce collected into a common stock; or that each man must be left to exert the portion of industry, and cultivate the habits of economy, to which his mind shall prompt him.

* * *

† William Godwin (1756–1836), British social philosopher. The present text is from Essay II of his *The Enquirer: Reflections on Education, Manners and Literature*.

Inequality * * * being to a certain extent unavoidable, it is the province of justice and virtue to counteract the practical evils which inequality has a tendency to produce. It is certain that men will differ from each other in their degrees of industry and economy. But it is not less certain, that the wants of one man are similar to the wants of another, and that the same things will conduce to the improvement and happiness of each, except so far as either is corrupted by the oppressive and tyrannical condition of the society in which he is born. * * *

How far does the conduct of the rich man who lives up to his fortune on the one hand, and of the avaricious man on the other, contribute to the placing of human beings in the condition in which they ought to be placed?

* * * It is a gross and ridiculous error to suppose that the rich pay for any thing. There is no wealth in the world except this, the labour of man.[1] What is misnamed wealth, is merely a power vested in certain individuals by the institutions of society, to compel others to labour for their benefit. So much labour is requisite to produce the necessaries of life; so much more to produce those superfluities which at present exist in any country. Every new luxury is a new weight thrown into the scale. The poor are scarcely ever benefited by this. It adds a certain portion to the mass of their labour; but it adds nothing to their conveniences.[2] Their wages are not changed. They are paid no more now for the work of ten hours, than before for the work of eight. They support the burthen; but they come in for no share of the fruit. * * *

* * * Let us see what is the tendency of the conduct of the avaricious man in this respect.

He recognises, in his proceedings at least, if not as an article of his creed, that great principle of austere and immutable justice, that the claims of the rich man are no more extensive than those of the poor, to the sumptuousness and pamperings of human existence. He watches over his expenditure with unintermitted scrupulosity; and, though enabled to indulge himself in luxuries, he has the courage to practise an entire self-denial.

It may be alleged indeed that, if he do not consume his wealth upon himself, neither does he impart it to another; he carefully locks it up, and pertinaciously withholds it from general use. But this point does not seem to have been rightly understood. The true development and definition of the nature of wealth have not been applied to illustrate it. Wealth consists in this only, the commodities raised and fostered by human labour. But he locks up neither corn, nor oxen, nor clothes, nor houses. These things are used and

1. *Political Justice*, Book VIII, Chap. II, octavo edition.
2. Ibid.

consumed by his contemporaries, as truly and to as great an extent, as if he were a beggar. * * *

His conduct is much less pernicious to mankind, and much more nearly conformable to the unalterable principles of justice, than that of the man who disburses his income in what has been termed, a liberal and spirited style. * * *

Such appears to be the genuine result of the comparison between the votary of avarice and the man of profusion. It by no means follows from the preference we feel compelled to cede to the former, that he is not fairly chargeable with enormous mistakes. Money, though in itself destitute of any real value, is an engine enabling us to vest the actual commodities of life in such persons and objects, as our understandings may point out to us. This engine, which might be applied to most admirable purposes, the miser constantly refuses to employ. The use of wealth is no doubt a science attended with uncommon difficulties. But it is not less evident that, by a master in the science, it might be applied, to chear the miserable, to relieve the oppressed, to assist the manly adventurer, to advance science, and to encourage art. A rich man, guided by the genuine principles of virtue, would be munificent, though not with that spurious munificence that has so often usurped the name. It may however almost be doubted whether the conduct of the miser, who wholly abstains from the use of riches, be not more advantageous to mankind, than the conduct of the man who, with honourable intentions, is continually misapplying his wealth to what he calls public benefits and charitable uses.

* * *

This speculation upon the comparative merits of avarice and profusion, may perhaps be found to be of greater importance than at first sight might be imagined. It includes in it the first principles of morality, and of justice between man and man. It strikes at the root of a deception that has long been continued, and long proved a curse to all the civilised nations of the earth. It tends to familiarise the mind to those strict and severe principles of judging, without which our energy, as well as our usefulness, will lie in a very narrow compass. It contains the germs of a code of political science, and may perhaps be found intimately connected with the extensive diffusion of liberty and happiness.

PART II

Selections from Malthus' Work

An Essay on the Principle of Population†

Preface

The following Essay owes its origin to a conversation with a friend, on the subject of Mr. Godwin's Essay on avarice and profusion, in his Enquirer. The discussion started the general question of the future improvement of society; and the Author at first sat down with an intention of merely stating his thoughts to his friend, upon paper, in a clearer manner than he thought he could do in conversation. But as the subject opened upon him, some ideas occurred which he did not recollect to have met with before; and as he conceived that every the least light, on a topic so generally interesting, might be received with candour, he determined to put his thoughts in a form for publication.

The Essay might undoubtedly have been rendered much more complete by a collection of a greater number of facts in elucidation of the general argument. But a long and almost total interruption from very particular business, joined to a desire (perhaps imprudent) of not delaying the publication much beyond the time that he originally proposed, prevented the Author from giving to the subject an undivided attention. He presumes, however, that the facts which he has adduced will be found to form no inconsiderable evidence for the truth of his opinion respecting the future improvement of mankind. As the Author contemplates this opinion at present, little more appears to him to be necessary than a plain statement, in addition to the most cursory view of society, to establish it.

It is an obvious truth, which has been taken notice of by many writers, that population must always be kept down to the level of the means of subsistence; but no writer that the Author recollects has inquired particularly into the means by which this level is effected: and it is a view of these means which forms, to his mind, the strongest obstacle in the way to any very great future improvement of society. He hopes it will appear that, in the discussion of this interesting subject, he is actuated solely by a love of truth, and not by any prejudices against any particular set of men, or of opinions. He professes to have read some of the speculations on the future improvement of society in a temper very different from a wish to find them visionary, but he has not acquired that command over his understanding which would enable him to

† This text of the *Essay on the Principle of Population* is Malthus' first essay of 1798; the typography and punctuation (and, in a few instances, spelling) have been modernized.

believe what he wishes, without evidence, or to refuse his assent to what might be unpleasing, when accompanied with evidence.

The view which he has given of human life has a melancholy hue, but he feels conscious that he has drawn these dark tints from a conviction that they are really in the picture, and not from a jaundiced eye or an inherent spleen of disposition. The theory of mind which he has sketched in the two last chapters accounts to his own understanding in a satisfactory manner for the existence of most of the evils of life, but whether it will have the same effect upon others must be left to the judgment of his readers.

If he should succeed in drawing the attention of more able men to what he conceives to be the principal difficulty in the way to the improvement of society and should, in consequence, see this difficulty removed, even in theory, he will gladly retract his present opinions and rejoice in a conviction of his error.

June 7, 1798

CHAPTER I

Question stated—Little prospect of a determination of it, from the enmity of the opposing parties—The principal argument against the perfectibility of man and of society has never been fairly answered—Nature of the difficulty arising from population—Outline of the principal argument of the essay.

The great and unlooked for discoveries that have taken place of late years in natural philosophy, the increasing diffusion of general knowledge from the extension of the art of printing, the ardent and unshackled spirit of inquiry that prevails throughout the lettered and even unlettered world, the new and extraordinary lights that have been thrown on political subjects which dazzle and astonish the understanding, and particularly that tremendous phenomenon in the political horizon, the French revolution, which, like a blazing comet, seems destined either to inspire with fresh life and vigour, or to scorch up and destroy the shrinking inhabitants of the earth, have all concurred to lead many able men into the opinion that we were touching on a period big with the most important changes, changes that would in some measure be decisive of the future fate of mankind.

It has been said that the great question is now at issue, whether man shall henceforth start forwards with accelerated velocity towards illimitable, and hitherto unconceived improvement, or be condemned to a perpetual oscillation between happiness and misery, and after every effort remain still at an immeasurable distance from the wished-for goal.

Yet, anxiously as every friend of mankind must look forwards to the termination of this painful suspense, and eagerly as the inquiring mind would hail every ray of light that might assist its view into futurity, it is much to be lamented that the writers on each side of this momentous question still keep far aloof from each other. Their mutual arguments do not meet with a candid examination. The question is not brought to rest on fewer points, and even in theory scarcely seems to be approaching to a decision.

The advocate for the present order of things is apt to treat the sect of speculative philosophers either as a set of artful and designing knaves who preach up ardent benevolence and draw captivating pictures of a happier state of society only the better to enable them to destroy the present establishments and to forward their own deep-laid schemes of ambition, or as wild and madheaded enthusiasts whose silly speculations and absurd paradoxes are not worthy the attention of any reasonable man.

The advocate for the perfectibility of man and of society retorts on the defender of establishments a more than equal contempt. He brands him as the slave of the most miserable and narrow prejudices; or as the defender of the abuses of civil society only because he profits by them. He paints him either as a character who prostitutes his understanding to his interest, or as one whose powers of mind are not of a size to grasp any thing great and noble, who cannot see above five yards before him, and who must therefore be utterly unable to take in the views of the enlightened benefactor of mankind.

In this unamicable contest the cause of truth cannot but suffer. The really good arguments on each side of the question are not allowed to have their proper weight. Each pursues his own theory, little solicitous to correct or improve it by an attention to what is advanced by his opponents.

The friend of the present order of things condemns all political speculations in the gross. He will not even condescend to examine the grounds from which the perfectibility of society is inferred. Much less will he give himself the trouble in a fair and candid manner to attempt an exposition of their fallacy.

The speculative philosopher equally offends against the cause of truth. With eyes fixed on a happier state of society, the blessings of which he paints in the most captivating colours, he allows himself to indulge in the most bitter invectives against every present establishment, without applying his talents to consider the best and safest means of removing abuses and without seeming to be aware of the tremendous obstacles that threaten, even in theory, to oppose the progress of man towards perfection.

It is an acknowledged truth in philosophy that a just theory will always be confirmed by experiment. Yet so much friction and so many minute circumstances occur in practice, which it is next to impossible for the most enlarged and penetrating mind to foresee, that on few subjects can any theory be pronounced just, that has not stood the test of experience. But an untried theory cannot fairly be advanced as probable, much less as just, till all the arguments against it have been maturely weighed and clearly and consistently refuted.

I have read some of the speculations on the perfectibility of man and of society with great pleasure. I have been warmed and delighted with the enchanting picture which they hold forth. I ardently wish for such happy improvements. But I see great, and, to my understanding, unconquerable difficulties in the way to them. These difficulties it is my present purpose to state, declaring, at the same time, that so far from exulting in them, as a cause of triumph over the friends of innovation, nothing would give me greater pleasure than to see them completely removed.

The most important argument that I shall adduce is certainly not new. The principles on which it depends have been explained in part by Hume, and more at large by Dr. Adam Smith. It has been advanced and applied to the present subject, though not with its proper weight, or in the most forcible point of view, by Mr. Wallace, and it may probably have been stated by many writers that I have never met with. I should certainly therefore not think of advancing it again, though I mean to place it in a point of view in some degree different from any that I have hitherto seen, if it had ever been fairly and satisfactorily answered.

The cause of this neglect on the part of the advocates for the perfectibility of mankind is not easily accounted for. I cannot doubt the talents of such men as Godwin and Condorcet. I am unwilling to doubt their candour. To my understanding, and probably to that of most others, the difficulty appears insurmountable. Yet these men of acknowledged ability and penetration scarcely deign to notice it, and hold on their course in such speculations, with unabated ardour and undiminished confidence. I have certainly no right to say that they purposely shut their eyes to such arguments. I ought rather to doubt the validity of them, when neglected by such men, however forcibly their truth may strike my own mind. Yet in this respect it must be acknowledged that we are all of us too prone to err. If I saw a glass of wine repeatedly presented to a man, and he took no notice of it, I should be apt to think that he was blind or uncivil. A juster philosophy might teach me rather to think that my eyes deceived me and that the offer was not really what I conceived it to be.

In entering upon the argument I must premise that I put out of the question, at present, all mere conjectures, that is, all suppositions, the probable realization of which cannot be inferred upon any just philosophical grounds. A writer may tell me that he thinks man will ultimately become an ostrich. I cannot properly contradict him. But before he can expect to bring any reasonable person over to his opinion, he ought to shew that the necks of mankind have been gradually elongating, that the lips have grown harder and more prominent, that the legs and feet are daily altering their shape, and that the hair is beginning to change into stubs of feathers. And till the probability of so wonderful a conversion can be shewn, it is surely lost time and lost eloquence to expatiate on the happiness of man in such a state; to describe his powers, both of running and flying, to paint him in a condition where all narrow luxuries would be contemned, where he would be employed only in collecting the necessaries of life, and where, consequently, each man's share of labour would be light, and his portion of leisure ample.

I think I may fairly make two postulata.

First, That food is necessary to the existence of man.

Secondly, That the passion between the sexes is necessary and will remain nearly in its present state.

These two laws, ever since we have had any knowledge of mankind, appear to have been fixed laws of our nature, and, as we have not hitherto seen any alteration in them, we have no right to conclude that they will ever cease to be what they now are, without an immediate act of power in that Being who first arranged the system of the universe, and for the advantage of his creatures, still executes, according to fixed laws, all its various operations.

I do not know that any writer has supposed that on this earth man will ultimately be able to live without food. But Mr. Godwin has conjectured that the passion between the sexes may in time be extinguished. As, however, he calls this part of his work a deviation into the land of conjecture, I will not dwell longer upon it at present than to say that the best arguments for the perfectibility of man are drawn from a contemplation of the great progress that he has already made from the savage state and the difficulty of saying where he is to stop. But towards the extinction of the passion between the sexes, no progress whatever has hitherto been made. It appears to exist in as much force at present as it did two thousand or four thousand years ago. There are individual exceptions now as there always have been. But, as these exceptions do not appear to increase in number, it would surely be a very

unphilosophical mode of arguing, to infer merely from the existence of an exception, that the exception would, in time, become the
rule, and the rule the exception.

Assuming then, my postulata as granted, I say that the power of
population is indefinitely greater than the power in the earth to
produce subsistence for man.

Population, when unchecked, increases in a geometrical ratio.
Subsistence increases only in an arithmetical ratio. A slight
acquaintance with numbers will shew the immensity of the first
power in comparison of the second.

By that law of our nature which makes food necessary to the life
of man, the effects of these two unequal powers must be kept
equal.

This implies a strong and constantly operating check on population from the difficulty of subsistence. This difficulty must fall some
where and must necessarily be severely felt by a large portion of
mankind.

Through the animal and vegetable kingdoms, nature has scattered
the seeds of life abroad with the most profuse and liberal hand.
She has been comparatively sparing in the room and the nourishment necessary to rear them. The germs of existence contained in
this spot of earth, with ample food and ample room to expand in,
would fill millions of worlds in the course of a few thousand
years. Necessity, that imperious all pervading law of nature,
restrains them within the prescribed bounds. The race of plants
and the race of animals shrink under this great restrictive law.
And the race of man cannot, by any efforts of reason, escape from
it. Among plants and animals its effects are waste of seed, sickness,
and premature death. Among mankind, misery and vice. The
former, misery, is an absolutely necessary consequence of it. Vice
is a highly probable consequence, and we therefore see it abundantly prevail, but it ought not, perhaps, to be called an absolutely
necessary consequence. The ordeal of virtue is to resist all temptation to evil.

This natural inequality of the two powers of population and of
production in the earth and that great law of our nature which
must constantly keep their effects equal form the great difficulty
that to me appears insurmountable in the way to the perfectibility
of society. All other arguments are of slight and subordinate consideration in comparison of this. I see no way by which man can
escape from the weight of this law which pervades all animated
nature. No fancied equality, no agrarian regulations in their utmost
extent, could remove the pressure of it even for a single century.
And it appears, therefore, to be decisive against the possible existence of a society, all the members of which should live in ease,

happiness, and comparative leisure, and feel no anxiety about providing the means of subsistence for themselves and families.

Consequently, if the premises are just, the argument is conclusive against the perfectibility of the mass of mankind.

I have thus sketched the general outline of the argument, but I will examine it more particularly, and I think it will be found that experience, the true source and foundation of all knowledge, invariably confirms its truth.

CHAPTER II

The different ratios in which population and food increase—The necessary effects of these different ratios of increase—Oscillation produced by them in the condition of the lower classes of society—Reasons why this oscillation has not been so much observed as might be expected—Three propositions on which the general argument of the essay depends—The different states in which mankind have been known to exist proposed to be examined with reference to these three propositions.

I said that population, when unchecked, increased in a geometrical ratio, and subsistence for man in an arithmetical ratio.

Let us examine whether this position be just.

I think it will be allowed that no state has hitherto existed (at least that we have any account of) where the manners were so pure and simple, and the means of subsistence so abundant, that no check whatever has existed to early marriages, among the lower classes, from a fear of not providing well for their families, or among the higher classes, from a fear of lowering their condition in life. Consequently in no state that we have yet known has the power of population been left to exert itself with perfect freedom.

Whether the law of marriage be instituted or not, the dictate of nature and virtue seems to be an early attachment to one woman. Supposing a liberty of changing in the case of an unfortunate choice, this liberty would not affect population till it arose to a height greatly vicious; and we are now supposing the existence of a society where vice is scarcely known.

In a state therefore of great equality and virtue, where pure and simple manners prevailed, and where the means of subsistence were so abundant that no part of the society could have any fears about providing amply for a family, the power of population being left to exert itself unchecked, the increase of the human species would evidently be much greater than any increase that has been hitherto known.

In the United States of America, where the means of subsistence have been more ample, the manners of the people more pure, and consequently the checks to early marriages fewer than in any of the modern states of Europe, the population has been found to double itself in twenty-five years.

This ratio of increase, though short of the utmost power of population, yet as the result of actual experience, we will take as our rule, and say, that population, when unchecked, goes on doubling itself every twenty-five years or increases in a geometrical ratio.

Let us now take any spot of earth, this Island for instance, and see in what ratio the subsistence it affords can be supposed to increase. We will begin with it under its present state of cultivation.

If I allow that by the best possible policy, by breaking up more land and by great encouragements to agriculture, the produce of this Island may be doubled in the first twenty-five years, I think it will be allowing as much as any person can well demand.

In the next twenty-five years, it is impossible to suppose that the produce could be quadrupled. It would be contrary to all our knowledge of the qualities of land. The very utmost that we can conceive is that the increase in the second twenty-five years might equal the present produce. Let us then take this for our rule, though certainly far beyond the truth, and allow that by great exertion, the whole produce of the Island might be increased every twenty-five years, by a quantity of subsistence equal to what it at present produces. The most enthusiastic speculator cannot suppose a greater increase than this. In a few centuries it would make every acre of land in the Island like a garden.

Yet this ratio of increase is evidently arithmetical.

It may be fairly said, therefore, that the means of subsistence increase in an arithmetical ratio. Let us now bring the effects of these two ratios together.

The population of the Island is computed to be about seven millions, and we will suppose the present produce equal to the support of such a number. In the first twenty-five years the population would be fourteen millions, and the food being also doubled, the means of subsistence would be equal to this increase. In the next twenty-five years the population would be twenty-eight millions, and the means of subsistence only equal to the support of twenty-one millions. In the next period the population would be fifty-six millions, and the means of subsistence just sufficient for half that number. And at the conclusion of the first century the population would be one hundred and twelve millions and the means of subsistence only equal to the support of thirty-five millions, which would leave a population of seventy-seven millions totally unprovided for.

A great emigration necessarily implies unhappiness of some kind or other in the country that is deserted. For few persons will leave their families, connections, friends, and native land, to seek a settlement in untried foreign climes, without some strong subsisting causes of uneasiness where they are, or the hope of some great advantages in the place to which they are going.

But to make the argument more general and less interrupted by the partial views of emigration, let us take the whole earth, instead of one spot, and suppose that the restraints to population were universally removed. If the subsistence for man that the earth affords was to be increased every twenty-five years by a quantity equal to what the whole world at present produces, this would allow the power of production in the earth to be absolutely unlimited and its ratio to increase much greater than we can conceive that any possible exertions of mankind could make it.

Taking the population of the world at any number, a thousand millions, for instance, the human species would increase in the ratio of—1, 2, 4, 8, 16, 32, 64, 128, 256, 512, &c. and subsistence as—1, 2, 3, 4, 5, 6, 7, 8, 9, 10, &c. In two centuries and a quarter, the population would be to the means of subsistence as 512 to 10, in three centuries as 4096 to 13, and in two thousand years the difference would be almost incalculable, though the produce in that time would have increased to an immense extent.

No limits whatever are placed to the productions of the earth; they may increase for ever and be greater than any assignable quantity; yet still the power of population being a power of a superior order, the increase of the human species can only be kept commensurate to the increase of the means of subsistence by the constant operation of the strong law of necessity acting as a check upon the greater power.

The effects of this check remain now to be considered.

Among plants and animals the view of the subject is simple. They are all impelled by a powerful instinct to the increase of their species, and this instinct is interrupted by no reasoning or doubts about providing for their offspring. Wherever therefore there is liberty, the power of increase is exerted, and the super-abundant effects are repressed afterwards by want of room and nourishment, which is common to animals and plants, and among animals, by becoming the prey of others.

The effects of this check on man are more complicated. Impelled to the increase of his species by an equally powerful instinct, reason interrupts his career and asks him whether he may not bring beings into the world, for whom he cannot provide the means of subsistence. In a state of equality, this would be the simple question. In the present state of society, other considerations occur. Will he not lower his rank in life? Will he not subject himself to greater difficulties than he at present feels? Will he not be obliged to labour harder? and if he has a large family, will his utmost exertions enable him to support them? May he not see his offspring in rags and misery, and clamouring for bread that he cannot give them? And may he not be reduced to the grating necessity of forfeiting his independence and of being obliged to the sparing hand of charity for support?

These considerations are calculated to prevent, and certainly do prevent, a very great number in all civilized nations from pursuing the dictate of nature in an early attachment to one woman. And this restraint almost necessarily, though not absolutely so, produces vice. Yet in all societies, even those that are most vicious, the tendency to a virtuous attachment is so strong that there is a constant effort towards an increase of population. This constant effort as constantly tends to subject the lower classes of the society to distress and to prevent any great permanent amelioration of their condition.

The way in which these effects are produced seems to be this.

We will suppose the means of subsistence in any country just equal to the easy support of its inhabitants. The constant effort towards population, which is found to act even in the most vicious societies, increases the number of people before the means of subsistence are increased. The food therefore which before supported seven millions must now be divided among seven millions and a half or eight millions. The poor consequently must live much worse, and many of them be reduced to severe distress. The number of labourers also being above the proportion of the work in the market, the price of labour must tend toward a decrease, while the price of provisions would at the same time tend to rise. The labourer therefore must work harder to earn the same as he did before. During this season of distress, the discouragements to marriage and the difficulty of rearing a family are so great that population is at a stand. In the mean time the cheapness of labour, the plenty of labourers, and the necessity of an increased industry amongst them, encourage cultivators to employ more labour upon their land, to turn up fresh soil, and to manure and improve more completely what is already in tillage, till ultimately the means of subsistence become in the same proportion to the population as at the period from which we set out. The situation of the labourer being then again tolerably comfortable, the restraints to population are in some degree loosened, and the same retrograde and progressive movements with respect to happiness are repeated.

This sort of oscillation will not be remarked by superficial observers, and it may be difficult even for the most penetrating mind to calculate its periods. Yet that in all old states some such vibration does exist, though from various transverse causes, in a much less marked, and in a much more irregular manner than I have described it, no reflecting man who considers the subject deeply can well doubt.

Many reasons occur why this oscillation has been less obvious, and less decidedly confirmed by experience, than might naturally be expected.

One principal reason is that the histories of mankind that we possess are histories only of the higher classes. We have but few accounts that can be depended upon of the manners and customs of that part of mankind, where these retrograde and progressive movements chiefly take place. A satisfactory history of this kind, of one people, and of one period, would require the constant and minute attention of an observing mind during a long life. Some of the objects of enquiry would be, in what proportion to the number of adults was the number of marriages, to what extent vicious customs prevailed in consequence of the restraints upon matrimony, what was the comparative mortality among the children of the most distressed part of the community and those who lived rather more at their ease, what were the variations in the real price of labour, and what were the observable differences in the state of the lower classes of society with respect to ease and happiness, at different times during a certain period.

Such a history would tend greatly to elucidate the manner in which the constant check upon population acts and would probably prove the existence of the retrograde and progressive movements that have been mentioned, though the times of their vibration must necessarily be rendered irregular, from the operation of many interrupting causes, such as the introduction or failure of certain manufactures, a greater or less prevalent spirit of agriculture enterprize, years of plenty, or years of scarcity, wars and pestilence, poor laws, the invention of processes for shortening labour without the proportional extension of the market for the commodity, and, particularly, the difference between the nominal and real price of labour, a circumstance which has perhaps more than any other contributed to conceal this oscillation from common view.

It very rarely happens that the nominal price of labour universally falls, but we well know that it frequently remains the same, while the nominal price of provisions has been gradually increasing. This is, in effect, a real fall in the price of labour, and during this period the condition of the lower orders of the community must gradually grow worse and worse. But the farmers and capitalists are growing rich from the real cheapness of labour. Their increased capitals enable them to employ a greater number of men. Work therefore may be plentiful, and the price of labour would consequently rise. But the want of freedom in the market of labour, which occurs more or less in all communities, either from parish laws, or the more general cause of the facility of combination among the rich, and its difficulty among the poor, operates to prevent the price of labour from rising at the natural period, and keeps it down some time longer; perhaps, till a year of scarcity, when the clamour is too loud, and the necessity too apparent to be resisted.

The true cause of the advance in the price of labour is thus concealed, and the rich affect to grant it as an act of compassion and favour to the poor, in consideration of a year of scarcity, and, when plenty returns, indulge themselves in the most unreasonable of all complaints, that the price does not again fall, when a little reflection would shew them that it must have risen long before but from an unjust conspiracy of their own.

But though the rich by unfair combinations contribute frequently to prolong a season of distress among the poor, yet no possible form of society could prevent the almost constant action of misery upon a great part of mankind, if in a state of inequality, and upon all, if all were equal.

The theory on which the truth of this position depends appears to me so extremely clear that I feel at a loss to conjecture what part of it can be denied.

That population cannot increase without the means of subsistence is a proposition so evident that it needs no illustration.

That population does invariably increase where there are the means of subsistence, the history of every people that have ever existed will abundantly prove.

And that the superior power of population cannot be checked without producing misery or vice, the ample portion of these too bitter ingredients in the cup of human life and the continuance of the physical causes that seem to have produced them bear too convincing a testimony.

But in order more fully to ascertain the validity of these three propositions, let us examine the different states in which mankind have been known to exist. Even a cursory review will, I think, be sufficient to convince us that these propositions are incontrovertible truths.

CHAPTER III

*The savage or hunter state shortly reviewed—The shep-
herd state, or the tribes of barbarians that overran the
Roman Empire—The superiority of the power of population to the means of subsistence—The cause of the great
tide of Northern Emigration.*

In the rudest state of mankind, in which hunting is the principal
occupation and the only mode of acquiring food, the means of subsistence being scattered over a large extent of territory, the comparative population must necessarily be thin. It is said that the
passion between the sexes is less ardent among the North American Indians than among any other race of men. Yet notwithstanding this apathy, the effort towards population, even in this people,
seems to be always greater than the means to support it. This
appears from the comparatively rapid population that takes place
whenever any of the tribes happen to settle in some fertile spot
and to draw nourishment from more fruitful sources than that of
hunting, and it has been frequently remarked that when an Indian
family has taken up its abode near any European settlement and
adopted a more easy and civilized mode of life, that one woman
has reared five or six, or more children, though in the savage state
it rarely happens, that above one or two in a family grow up to
maturity. The same observation has been made with regard to the
Hottentots near the Cape. These facts prove the superior power of
population to the means of subsistence in nations of hunters, and
that this power always shews itself the moment it is left to act
with freedom.

It remains to inquire whether this power can be checked, and its
effects kept equal to the means of subsistence, without vice or
misery.

The North American Indians, considered as a people, cannot justly
be called free and equal. In all the accounts we have of them, and,
indeed, of most other savage nations, the women are represented
as much more completely in a state of slavery to the men than
the poor are to the rich in civilized countries. One half the nation
appears to act as Helots to the other half, and the misery that
checks population falls chiefly, as it always must do, upon that
part whose condition is lowest in the scale of society. The infancy
of man in the simplest state requires considerable attention, but
this necessary attention the women cannot give, condemned as they
are to the inconveniences and hardships of frequent change of

place and to the constant and unremitting drudgery of preparing every thing for the reception of their tyrannic lords. These exertions, sometimes during pregnancy or with children at their backs, must occasion frequent miscarriages, and prevent any but the most robust infants from growing to maturity. Add to these hardships of the women, the constant war that prevails among savages, and the necessity which they frequently labour under of exposing their aged and helpless parents, and of thus violating the first feelings of nature, and the picture will not appear very free from the blot of misery. In estimating the happiness of a savage nation, we must not fix our eyes only on the warrior in the prime of life: he is one of a hundred: he is the gentleman, the man of fortune, the chances have been in his favour; and many efforts have failed ere this fortunate being was produced, whose guardian genius should preserve him through the numberless dangers with which he would be surrounded from infancy to manhood. The true points of comparison between two nations, seem to be, the ranks in each which appear nearest to answer to each other. And in this view, I should compare the warriors in the prime of life with the gentlemen, and the women, children, and aged, with the lower classes of the community in civilized states.

May we not then fairly infer from this short review, or rather, from the accounts that may be referred to of nations of hunters, that their population is thin from the scarcity of food, that it would immediately increase if food was in greater plenty, and that, putting vice out of the question among savages, misery is the check that represses the superior power of population and keeps its effects equal to the means of subsistence. Actual observation and experience tell us that this check, with a few local and temporary exceptions, is constantly acting now upon all savage nations, and the theory indicates, that it probably acted with nearly equal strength a thousand years ago, and it may not be much greater a thousand years hence.

Of the manners and habits that prevail among nations of shepherds, the next state of mankind, we are even more ignorant than of the savage state. But that these nations could not escape the general lot of misery arising from the want of subsistence, Europe, and all the fairest countries in the world, bear ample testimony. Want was the goad that drove the Scythian shepherds from their native haunts, like so many famished wolves in search of prey. Set in motion by this all powerful cause, clouds of Barbarians seemed to collect from all points of the northern hemisphere. Gathering fresh darkness and terror as they rolled on, the congregated bodies at length obscured the sun of Italy and sunk the whole world in universal night. These tremendous effects, so long and so deeply felt throughout the fairest portions of the earth, may be traced to the simple cause of the superior power of population, to the means of subsistence.

It is well known that a country in pasture cannot support so many inhabitants as a country in tillage, but what renders nations of shepherds so formidable is the power which they possess of moving all together and the necessity they frequently feel of exerting this power in search of fresh pasture for their herds. A tribe that was rich in cattle had an immediate plenty of food. Even the parent stock might be devoured in a case of absolute necessity. The women lived in greater ease than among nations of hunters. The men bold in their united strength and confiding in their power of procuring pasture for their cattle by change of place, felt, probably, but few fears about providing for a family. These combined causes soon produced their natural and invariable effect on extended population. A more frequent and rapid change of place became then necessary. A wider and more extensive territory was successively occupied. A broader desolation extended all around them. Want pinched the less fortunate members of the society, and, at length, the impossibility of supporting such a number together became too evident to be resisted. Young scions were then pushed out from the parent-stock and instructed to explore fresh regions and to gain happier seats for themselves by their swords. "The world was all before them where to chuse." Restless from present distress, flushed with the hope of fairer prospects, and animated with the spirit of hardy enterprize, these daring adventurers were likely to become formidable adversaries to all who opposed them. The peaceful inhabitants of the countries on which they rushed could not long withstand the energy of men acting under such powerful motives of exertion. And when they fell in with any tribes like their own, the contest was a struggle for existence, and they fought with a desperate courage, inspired by the reflection that death was the punishment of defeat and life the prize of victory.

In these savage contests many tribes must have been utterly exterminated. Some probably perished by hardship and famine. Others, whose leading star had given them a happier direction, became great and powerful tribes, and, in their turns, sent off fresh adventurers in search of still more fertile seats. The prodigious waste of human life occasioned by this perpetual struggle for room and food was more than supplied by the mighty power of population, acting, in some degree, unshackled from the constant habit of emigration. The tribes that migrated towards the South, though they won these more fruitful regions by continual battles, rapidly increased in number and power, from the increased means of subsistence. Till at length the whole territory, from the confines of China to the shores of the Baltic, was peopled by a various race of Barbarians, brave, robust, and enterprising, inured to hardship, and delighting in war. Some tribes maintained their independence. Others ranged themselves under the standard of some barbaric chieftain who led them to victory after victory, and what was of more importance, to regions abounding in corn, wine, and oil, the long wished for consummation and great reward of their labours. An Alaric, an Attila, or a Zingis Khan, and the chiefs around them, might fight for glory, for the fame of extensive conquests; but the true cause that set in motion the great tide of northern emigration, and that continued to propel it till it rolled at different periods, against China, Persia, Italy, and even Egypt, was a scarcity of food, a population extended beyond the means of supporting it.

The absolute population at any one period, in proportion to the extent of territory, could never be great, on account of the unproductive nature of some of the regions occupied; but there appears to have been a most rapid succession of human beings, and as fast as some were mowed down by the scythe of war or of famine, others rose in increased numbers to supply their place. Among these bold and improvident Barbarians, population was probably but little checked, as in modern states, from a fear of future difficulties. A prevailing hope of bettering their condition by change of place, a constant expectation of plunder, a power even, if distressed, of selling their children as slaves, added to the natural carelessness of the barbaric character, all conspired to raise a population which remained to be repressed afterwards by famine or war.

Where there is any inequality of conditions, and among nations of shepherds this soon takes place, the distress arising from a scarcity of provisions, must fall hardest upon the least fortunate members of the society. This distress also must frequently have been felt by the women, exposed to casual plunder in the absence of their husbands, and subject to continual disappointments in their expected return.

But without knowing enough of the minute and intimate history of these people, to point out precisely on what part the distress for want of food chiefly fell, and to what extent it was generally felt, I think we may fairly say, from all the accounts that we have of nations of shepherds, that population invariably increased among them whenever, by emigration or any other cause, the means of subsistence were increased, and that a further population was checked, and the actual population kept equal to the means of subsistence, by misery and vice.

For independently of any vicious customs that might have prevailed amongst them with regard to women, which always operate as checks to population, it must be acknowledged I think, that the commission of war is vice, and the effect of it misery, and none can doubt the misery of want of food.

CHAPTER IV

State of civilized nations—Probability that Europe is much more populous now than in the time of Julius Caesar—Best criterion of population—Probable error of Hume in one of the criterions that he proposes as assisting in an estimate of population—Slow increase of population at present in most of the states of Europe—The two principal checks to population—The first, or preventive check examined with regard to England.

In examining the next state of mankind with relation to the question before us, the state of mixed pasture and tillage, in which with some variation in the proportions the most civilized nations must always remain, we shall be assisted in our review by what we daily see around us, by actual experience, by facts that come within the scope of every man's observation.

Notwithstanding the exaggerations of some old historians, there can remain no doubt in the mind of any thinking man that the population of the principal countries of Europe, France, England, Germany, Russia, Poland, Sweden, and Denmark is much greater than ever it was in former times. The obvious reason of these exaggerations is the formidable aspect that even a thinly peopled nation must have, when collected together and moving all at once in search of fresh seats. If to this tremendous appearance be added a succession at certain intervals of similar emigrations, we shall not be much surprised that the fears of the timid nations of the South represented the North as a region absolutely swarming with human beings. A nearer and juster view of the subject at present enables us to see that the inference was as absurd as if a man in this country, who was continually meeting on the road droves of cattle from Wales and the North, was immediately to conclude that these countries were the most productive of all the parts of the kingdom.

The reason that the greater part of Europe is more populous now than it was in former times is that the industry of the inhabitants has made these countries produce a greater quantity of human subsistence. For I conceive that it may be laid down as a position not to be controverted, that taking a sufficient extent of territory to include within it exportation and importation, and allowing some variation for the prevalence of luxury or of frugal habits, that population constantly bears a regular proportion to the food that the earth is made to produce. In the controversy concerning the populousness of ancient and modern nations, could it be clearly ascertained that the average produce of the countries in question, taken altogether, is greater now than it was in the times of Julius Caesar, the dispute would be at once determined.

When we are assured that China is the most fertile country in the world, that almost all the land is in tillage, and that a great part of it bears two crops every year, and further, that the people live very frugally, we may infer with certainty that the population must be immense, without busying ourselves in inquiries into the manners and habits of the lower classes and the encouragements to early marriages. But these inquiries are of the utmost importance, and a minute history of the customs of the lower Chinese would be of the greatest use in ascertaining in what manner the checks to a further population operate; what are the vices, and what are the distresses that prevent an increase of numbers beyond the ability of the country to support.

Hume, in his essay on the populousness of ancient and modern nations, when he intermingles, as he says, an inquiry concerning causes with that concerning facts, does not seem to see with his usual penetration how very little some of the causes he alludes to could enable him to form any judgment of the actual population of ancient nations. If any inference can be drawn from them, perhaps it should be directly the reverse of what Hume draws, though I certainly ought to speak with great diffidence in dissenting from a man, who of all others on such subjects was the least likely to be deceived by first appearances. If I find that at a certain period in ancient history, the encouragements to have a family were great, that early marriages were consequently very prevalent, and that few persons remained single, I should infer with certainty that population was rapidly increasing, but by no means that it was then actually very great, rather, indeed, the contrary, that it was then thin and that there was room and food for a much greater number. On the other hand, if I find that at this period the difficulties attending a family were very great, that consequently few early marriages took place, and that a great number of both sexes remained single, I infer with certainty that population was at a stand, and probably because the actual population was very great in proportion to the fertility of the land and that there was scarcely room and food for more. The number of footmen, housemaids, and other persons remaining unmarried in modern states Hume allows to be rather an argument against their population. I should rather draw a contrary inference and consider it an argument of their fullness, though this inference is not certain, because there are many thinly inhabited states that are yet stationary in their population. To speak, therefore, correctly, perhaps it may be said that the number of unmarried persons in proportion to the whole number existing at different periods, in the same or different states will enable us to judge whether population at these periods was increasing, stationary, or decreasing, but will form no criterion by which we can determine the actual population.

There is, however, a circumstance taken notice of in most of the accounts we have of China that it seems difficult to reconcile with this reasoning. It is said that early marriages very generally prevail through all the ranks of the Chinese. Yet Dr. Adam Smith supposes that population in China is stationary. These two circumstances appear to be irreconcileable. It certainly seems very little probable that the population of China is fast increasing. Every acre of land has been so long in cultivation that we can hardly conceive there is any great yearly addition to the average produce. The fact, perhaps, of the universality of early marriages may not be sufficiently ascertained. If it be supposed true, the only way of accounting for the difficulty, with our present knowledge of the subject, appears to be that the redundant population, necessarily occasioned by the prevalence of early marriages, must be repressed by occasional famines, and by the custom of exposing children, which, in times of distress, is probably more frequent than is ever acknowledged to Europeans. Relative to this barbarous practice, it is difficult to avoid remarking that there cannot be a stronger proof of the distresses that have been felt by mankind for want of food, than the existence of a custom that thus violates the most natural principle of the human heart. It appears to have been very general among ancient nations, and certainly tended rather to increase population.

In examining the principal states of modern Europe, we shall find that though they have increased very considerably in population since they were nations of shepherds, yet that at present, their progress is but slow, and instead of doubling their numbers every twenty-five years they require three or four hundred years or more for that purpose. Some, indeed, may be absolutely stationary, and others even retrograde. The cause of this slow progress in population cannot be traced to a decay of the passion between the sexes. We have sufficient reason to think that this natural propensity exists still in undiminished vigour. Why then do not its effects appear in a rapid increase of the human species? An intimate view of the state of society in any one country in Europe, which may serve equally for all, will enable us to answer this question, and to say that a foresight of the difficulties attending the rearing of a family acts as a preventive check, and the actual distresses of some of the lower classes, by which they are disabled from giving the proper food and attention to their children, acts as a positive check to the natural increase of population.

England, as one of the most flourishing states of Europe, may be fairly taken for an example, and the observations made will apply with but little variation to any other country where the population increases slowly.

The preventive check appears to operate in some degree through all the ranks of society in England. There are some men, even in the highest rank, who are prevented from marrying by the idea of the expenses that they must retrench, and the fancied pleasures that they must deprive themselves of, on the supposition of having a family. These considerations are certainly trivial, but a preventive foresight of this kind has objects of much greater weight for its contemplation as we go lower.

A man of liberal education, but with an income only just suffi-cient to enable him to associate in the rank of gentlemen, must feel absolutely certain that if he marries and has a family he shall be obliged, if he mixes at all in society, to rank himself with moderate farmers and the lower class of tradesmen. The woman that a man of education would naturally make the object of his choice would be one brought up in the same tastes and sentiments with himself and used to the familiar intercourse of a society totally different from that to which she must be reduced by marriage. Can a man consent to place the object of his affection in a situation so dis-cordant, probably, to her tastes and inclinations? Two or three steps of descent in society, particularly at this round of the ladder, where education ends and ignorance begins, will not be consid-ered by the generality of people as a fancied and chimerical, but a real and essential evil. If society be held desireable, it surely must be free, equal, and reciprocal society, where benefits are conferred as well as received, and not such as the dependent finds with his patron or the poor with the rich.

These considerations undoubtedly prevent a great number in this rank of life from following the bent of their inclinations in an early attachment. Others, guided either by a stronger passion, or a weaker judgment, break through these restraints, and it would be hard indeed, if the gratification of so delightful a passion as virtu-ous love did not sometimes more than counterbalance all its attendant evils. But I fear it must be owned, that the more general consequences of such marriages, are rather calculated to justify than to repress the forebodings of the prudent.

The sons of tradesmen and farmers are exhorted not to marry, and generally find it necessary to pursue this advice till they are settled in some business or farm that may enable them to support a family. These events may not, perhaps, occur till they are far advanced in life. The scarcity of farms is a very general complaint in England. And the competition in every kind of business is so great that it is not possible that all should be successful.

The labourer who earns eighteen pence a day and lives with some degree of comfort as a single man, will hesitate a little before he divides that pittance among four or five, which seems to be but just sufficient for one. Harder fare and harder labour he would submit to for the sake of living with the woman that he loves, but he must feel conscious, if he thinks at all, that should he have a large family, and any ill luck whatever, no degree of frugality, no possible exertion of his manual strength could preserve him from the heart rending sensation of seeing his children starve, or of forfeiting his independence, and being obliged to the parish for their support. The love of independence is a sentiment that surely none would wish to be erased from the breast of man, though the parish law of England, it must be confessed, is a system of all others the most calculated gradually to weaken this sentiment, and in the end may eradicate it completely.

The servants who live in gentlemen's families have restraints that are yet stronger to break through in venturing upon marriage. They possess the necessaries, and even the comforts of life, almost in as great plenty as their masters. Their work is easy and their food luxurious compared with the class of labourers. And their sense of dependence is weakened by the conscious power of changing their masters, if they feel themselves offended. Thus comfortably situated at present, what are their prospects in marrying? Without knowledge or capital, either for business or farming, and unused, and therefore unable, to earn a subsistence by daily labour, their only refuge seems to be a miserable alehouse, which certainly offers no very enchanting prospect of a happy evening to their lives. By much the greater part, therefore, deterred by this uninviting view of their future situation, content themselves with remaining single where they are.

If this sketch of the state of society in England be near the truth, and I do not conceive that it is exaggerated, it will be allowed that the preventive check to population in this country operates, though with varied force, through all the classes of the community. The same observation will hold true with regard to all old states. The effects, indeed, of these restraints upon marriage are but too conspicuous in the consequent vices that are produced in almost every part of the world, vices that are continually involving both sexes in inextricable unhappiness.

CHAPTER V

The positive check to population, by which I mean the check that represses an increase which is already begun, is confined chiefly, though not perhaps solely, to the lowest orders of society. This check is not so obvious to common view as the other I have mentioned, and to prove distinctly the force and extent of its operation would require, perhaps, more data than we are in possession of. But I believe it has been very generally remarked by those who have attended to bills of mortality that of the number of children who die annually, much too great a proportion belongs to those who may be supposed unable to give their offspring proper food and attention, exposed as they are occasionally to severe distress and confined, perhaps, to unwholesome habitations and hard labour. This mortality among the children of the poor has been constantly taken notice of in all towns. It certainly does not prevail in an equal degree in the country, but the subject has not hitherto received sufficient attention to enable any one to say that there are not more deaths in proportion among the children of the poor, even in the country, than among those of the middling and higher classes. Indeed, it seems difficult to suppose that a labourer's wife who has six children, and who is sometimes in absolute want of bread, should be able always to give them the food and attention necessary to support life. The sons and daughters of peasants will not be found such rosy cherubs in real life as they are described to be in romances. It cannot fail to be remarked by those who live much in the country that the sons of labourers are very apt to be stunted in their growth, and are a long while arriving at maturity. Boys that you would guess to be fourteen or fifteen, are upon inquiry, frequently found to be eighteen or nineteen. And the lads who drive plough, which must certainly be a healthy exercise, are very rarely seen with any appearance of calves to their legs; a circumstance which can only be attributed to a want either of proper or of sufficient nourishment.

To remedy the frequent distresses of the common people, the poor laws of England have been instituted; but it is to be feared that though they may have alleviated a little the intensity of individual misfortune, they have spread the general evil over a much larger surface. It is a subject often started in conversation and mentioned always as a matter of great surprise that notwithstanding the immense sum that is annually collected for the poor in England, there is still so much distress among them. Some think that the money must be embezzled, others that the churchwardens and overseers consume the greater part of it in dinners. All agree that some how or other it must be very ill-managed. In short the fact that nearly three millions are collected annually for the poor and yet that their distresses are not removed is the subject of continual astonishment. But a man who sees a little below the surface of things would be very much more astonished if the fact were otherwise than it is observed to be, or even if a collection universally of eighteen shillings in the pound instead of four, were materially to alter it. I will state a case which I hope will elucidate my meaning.

Suppose, that by a subscription of the rich, the eighteen pence a day which men earn now was made up five shillings, it might be imagined, perhaps, that they would then be able to live comfortably and have a piece of meat every day for their dinners. But this would be a very false conclusion. The transfer of three shillings and sixpence a day to every labourer would not increase the quantity of meat in the country. There is not at present enough for all to have a decent share. What would then be the consequence? The competition among the buyers in the market of meat would rapidly raise the price from six pence or seven pence, to two or three shillings in the pound, and the commodity would not be divided among many more than it is at present. When an article is scarce, and cannot be distributed to all, he that can shew the most valid patent, that is, he that offers most money becomes the possessor. If we can suppose the competition among the buyers of meat to continue long enough for a greater number of cattle to be reared annually, this could only be done at the expense of the corn, which would be a very disadvantageous exchange, for it is well known that the country could not then support the same population, and when subsistence is scarce in proportion to the number of people, it is of little consequence whether the lowest members of the society possess eighteen pence or five shillings. They must at all events be reduced to live upon the hardest fare and in the smallest quantity.

It will be said, perhaps, that the increased number of purchasers in every article would give a spur to productive industry and that the whole produce of the island would be increased. This might in some degree be the case. But the spur that these fancied riches would give to population would more than counterbalance it, and the increased produce would be to be divided among a more than proportionately increased number of people. All this time I am supposing that the same quantity of work would be done as before. But this would not really take place. The receipt of five shillings a day, instead of eighteen pence, would make every man fancy himself comparatively rich and able to indulge himself in many hours or days of leisure. This would give a strong and immediate check to productive industry, and in a short time not only the nation would be poorer, but the lower classes themselves would be much more distressed than when they received only eighteen pence a day.

A collection from the rich of eighteen shillings in the pound, even if distributed in the most judicious manner, would have a little the same effect as that resulting from the supposition I have just made, and no possible contributions of sacrifices of the rich, particularly in money, could for any time prevent the recurrence of distress among the lower members of society whoever they were. Great changes might, indeed, be made. The rich might become poor, and some of the poor rich, but a part of the society must necessarily feel a difficulty of living, and this difficulty will naturally fall on the least fortunate members.

It may at first appear strange, but I believe it is true, that I cannot by means of money raise a poor man and enable him to live much better than he did before, without proportionably depressing others in the same class. If I retrench the quantity of food consumed in my house, and give him what I have cut off, I then benefit him, without depressing any but myself and family, who, perhaps, may be well able to bear it. If I turn up a piece of uncultivated land, and give him the produce, I then benefit both him and all the members of the society, because what he before consumed is thrown into the common stock, and probably some of the new produce with it. But if I only give him money, supposing the produce of the country to remain the same, I give him a title to a larger share of that produce than formerly, which share he cannot receive without diminishing the shares of others. It is evident that this effect, in individual instances, must be so small as to be totally imperceptible; but still it must exist, as many other effects do, which like some of the insects that people the air, elude our grosser perceptions.

Supposing the quantity of food in any country to remain the

same for many years together, it is evident that this food must be divided according to the value of each man's patent,[1] or the sum of money that he can afford to spend in this commodity so universally in request. It is a demonstrative truth, therefore, that the patents of one set of men could not be increased in value without diminishing the value of the patents of some other set of men. If the rich were to subscribe and give five shillings a day to five hundred thousand men without retrenching their own tables, no doubt can exist that as these men would naturally live more at their ease and consume a greater quantity of provisions, there would be less food remaining to divide among the rest, and consequently each man's patent would be diminished in value or the same number of pieces of silver would purchase a smaller quantity of subsistence.

An increase of population without a proportional increase of food will evidently have the same effect in lowering the value of each man's patent. The food must necessarily be distributed in smaller quantities, and consequently a day's labour will purchase a smaller quantity of provisions. An increase in the price of provisions would arise either from an increase of population faster than the means of subsistence, or from a different distribution of the money of the society. The food of a country that has been long occupied, if it be increasing, increases slowly and regularly and cannot be made to answer any sudden demands, but variations in the distribution of the money of a society are not unfrequently occurring, and are undoubtedly among the causes that occasion the continual variations which we observe in the price of provisions.

The poor-laws of England tend to depress the general condition of the poor in these two ways. Their first obvious tendency is to increase population without increasing the food for its support. A poor man may marry with little or no prospect of being able to support a family in independence. They may be said therefore in some measure to create the poor which they maintain, and as the provisions of the country must, in consequence of the increased population, be distributed to every man in smaller proportions, it is evident that the labour of those who are not supported by parish assistance will purchase a smaller quantity of provisions than before and consequently more of them must be driven to ask for support.

Secondly, the quantity of provisions consumed in workhouses upon a part of the society that cannot in general be considered as the most valuable part diminishes the shares that would otherwise

---

1. Mr. Godwin calls the wealth that a man receives from his ancestors a mouldy patent. It may, I think, very properly be termed a patent, but I hardly see the propriety of calling it a mouldy one, as it is an article in such constant use.

belong to more industrious and more worthy members, and thus in the same manner forces more to become dependent. If the poor in the workhouses were to live better than they now do, this new distribution of the money of the society would tend more conspicuously to depress the condition of those out of the workhouses by occasioning a rise in the price of provisions.

Fortunately for England, a spirit of independence still remains among the peasantry. The poor-laws are strongly calculated to eradicate this spirit. They have succeeded in part, but had they succeeded as completely as might have been expected, their pernicious tendency would not have been so long concealed.

Hard as it may appear in individual instances, dependent poverty ought to be held disgraceful. Such a stimulus seems to be absolutely necessary to promote the happiness of the great mass of mankind, and every general attempt to weaken this stimulus, however benevolent its apparent intention, will always defeat its own purpose. If men are induced to marry from a prospect of parish provision, with little or no chance of maintaining their families in independence, they are not only unjustly tempted to bring unhappiness and dependence upon themselves and children, but they are tempted, without knowing it, to injure all in the same class with themselves. A labourer who marries without being able to support a family may in some respects be considered as an enemy to all his fellow-labourers.

I feel no doubt whatever that the parish laws of England have contributed to raise the price of provisions and to lower the real price of labour. They have therefore contributed to impoverish that class of people whose only possession is their labour. It is also difficult to suppose that they have not powerfully contributed to generate that carelessness and want of frugality observable among the poor, so contrary to the disposition frequently to be remarked among petty tradesmen and small farmers. The labouring poor, to use a vulgar expression, seem always to live from hand to mouth. Their present wants employ their whole attention, and they seldom think of the future. Even when they have an opportunity of saving they seldom exercise it, but all that is beyond their present necessities goes, generally speaking, to the ale-house. The poor-laws of England may therefore be said to diminish both the power and the will to save among the common people, and thus to weaken one of the strongest incentives to sobriety and industry, and consequently to happiness.

It is a general complaint among master manufacturers that high wages ruin all their workmen, but it is difficult to conceive that these men would not save a part of their high wages for the future support of their families, instead of spending it in drunkenness and dissipation, if they did not rely on parish assistance for support in case of accidents. And that the poor employed in manufactures consider this assistance as a reason why they may spend all the wages they earn and enjoy themselves while they can appears to be evident from the number of families that, upon the failure of any great manufactory, immediately fall upon the parish, when perhaps the wages earned in this manufactory while it flourished were sufficiently above the price of common country labour to have allowed them to save enough for their support till they could find some other channel for their industry.

A man who might not be deterred from going to the ale-house from the consideration that on his death, or sickness, he should leave his wife and family upon the parish might yet hesitate in thus dissipating his earnings if he were assured that, in either of these cases, his family must starve or be left to the support of casual bounty. In China, where the real as well as nominal price of labour is very low, sons are yet obliged by law to support their aged and helpless parents. Whether such a law would be adviseable in this country I will not pretend to determine. But it seems at any rate highly improper, by positive institutions, which render dependent poverty so general, to weaken that disgrace, which for the best and most humane reasons ought to attach to it.

The mass of happiness among the common people cannot but be diminished, when one of the strongest checks to idleness and dissipation is thus removed, and when men are thus allured to marry with little or no prospect of being able to maintain a family in independence. Every obstacle in the way of marriage must undoubtedly be considered as a species of unhappiness. But as from the laws of our nature some check to population must exist, it is better that it should be checked from a foresight of the difficulties attending a family and the fear of dependent poverty than that it should be encouraged, only to be repressed afterwards by want and sickness.

It should be remembered always that there is an essential difference between food and those wrought commodities, the raw materials of which are in great plenty. A demand for these last will not fail to create them in as great a quantity as they are wanted. The demand for food has by no means the same creative power. In a country where all the fertile spots have been seized, high offers are necessary to encourage the farmer to lay his dressing on land from which he cannot expect a profitable return for some years. And before the prospect of advantage is sufficiently great to encourage this sort of agricultural enterprize, and while the new produce is rising, great distresses may be suffered from the want of it. The demand for an increased quantity of subsistence is, with few exceptions, constant every where, yet we see how slowly it is answered in all those countries that have been long occupied.

The poor-laws of England were undoubtedly instituted for the most benevolent purpose, but there is great reason to think that they have not succeeded in their intention. They certainly mitigate some cases of very severe distress which might otherwise occur, yet the state of the poor who are supported by parishes, considered in all its circumstances, is very far from being free from misery. But one of the principal objections to them is that for this assistance which some of the poor receive, in itself almost a doubtful blessing, the whole class of the common people of England is subjected to a set of grating, inconvenient, and tyrannical laws, totally inconsistent with the genuine spirit of the constitution. The whole business of settlements, even in its present amended state, is utterly contradictory to all ideas of freedom. The parish persecution of men whose families are likely to become chargeable, and of poor women who are near lying-in, is a most disgraceful and disgusting tyranny. And the obstructions continually occasioned in the market of labour by these laws, have a constant tendency to add to the difficulties of those who are struggling to support themselves without assistance.

These evils attendant on the poor-laws are in some degree irremediable. If assistance be to be distributed to a certain class of people, a power must be given somewhere of discriminating the proper objects and of managing the concerns of the institutions that are necessary, but any great interference with the affairs of other people, is a species of tyranny, and in the common course of things the exercise of this power may be expected to become grating to those who are driven to ask for support. The tyranny of Justices, Churchwardens, and Overseers, is a common complaint among the poor, but the fault does not lie so much in these persons, who probably before they were in power were not worse than other people, but in the nature of all such institutions.

The evil is perhaps gone too far to be remedied, but I feel little doubt in my own mind that if the poor-laws had never existed, though there might have been a few more instances of very severe distress, yet that the aggregate mass of happiness among the common people would have been much greater than it is at present.

Mr. Pitt's Poor-bill has the appearance of being framed with benevolent intentions, and the clamour raised against it was in many respects ill directed and unreasonable. But it must be confessed that it possesses in a high degree the great and radical defect of all systems of the kind, that of tending to increase population without increasing the means for its support, and thus to depress the condition of those that are not supported by parishes, and, consequently, to create more poor.

To remove the wants of the lower classes of society is indeed an arduous task. The truth is that the pressure of distress on this part of a community is an evil so deeply seated that no human ingenuity can reach it. Were I to propose a palliative, and palliatives are all that the nature of the case will admit, it should be, in the first place, the total abolition of all the present parish-laws. This would at any rate give liberty and freedom of action to the peasantry of England, which they can hardly be said to possess at present. They would then be able to settle without interruption, wherever there was a prospect of a greater plenty of work and a higher price for labour. The market of labour would then be free, and those obstacles removed, which as things are now, often for a considerable time prevent the price from rising according to the demand.

Secondly, Premiums might be given for turning up fresh land, and all possible encouragements held out to agriculture above manufactures, and to tillage above grazing. Every endeavour should be used to weaken and destroy all those institutions relating to corporations, apprenticeships, &c, which cause the labours of agriculture to be worse paid than the labours of trade and manufactures. For a country can never produce its proper quantity of food while these distinctions remain in favour of artizans. Such encouragements to agriculture would tend to furnish the market with an increasing quantity of healthy work, and at the same time, by augmenting the produce of the country, would raise the comparative price of labour and ameliorate the condition of the labourer. Being now in better circumstances, and seeing no prospect of parish assistance, he would be more able, as well as more inclined, to enter into associations for providing against the sickness of himself or family.

Lastly, for cases of extreme distress, county workhouses might be established, supported by rates upon the whole kingdom and free for persons of all counties, and indeed of all nations. The fare should be hard, and those that were able obliged to work. It would be desireable that they should not be considered as comfortable asylums in all difficulties, but merely as places where severe distress might find some alleviation. A part of these houses might be separated, or others built for a most beneficial purpose, which has not been unfrequently taken notice of, that of providing a place where any person, whether native or foreigner, might do a day's work at all times and receive the market price for it. Many cases would undoubtedly be left for the exertion of individual benevolence.

A plan of this kind, the preliminary of which should be an abolition of all the present parish laws, seems to be the best calculated to increase the mass of happiness among the common people in England. To prevent the recurrence of misery is, alas! beyond the power of man. In the vain endeavour to attain what in the nature of things is impossible, we now sacrifice not only possible but certain benefits. We tell the common people that if they will submit to a code of tyrannical regulations, they shall never be in want. They do submit to these regulations. They perform their part of the contract, but we do not, nay cannot, perform ours, and thus the poor sacrifice the valuable blessing of liberty and receive nothing that can be called an equivalent in return.

Notwithstanding then, the institution of the poor-laws in England, I think it will be allowed that considering the state of the lower classes altogether, both in the towns and in the country, the distresses which they suffer from the want of proper and sufficient food, from hard labour and unwholesome habitations, must operate as a constant check to incipient population.

To these two great checks to population, in all long occupied countries, which I have called the preventive and the positive checks, may be added vicious customs with respect to women, great cities, unwholesome manufactures, luxury, pestilence, and war.

All these checks may be fairly resolved into misery and vice. And that these are the true causes of the slow increase of population in all the states of modern Europe, will appear sufficiently evident from the comparatively rapid increase that has invariably taken place whenever these causes have been in any considerable degree removed.

CHAPTER VI

New colonies—Reasons of their rapid increase—North American Colonies—Extraordinary instance of increase in the back settlements—Rapidity with which even old states recover the ravages of war, pestilence, famine, or the convulsions of nature.

It has been universally remarked that all new colonies settled in healthy countries where there was plenty of room and food have constantly increased with astonishing rapidity in their population. Some of the colonies from ancient Greece, in no very long period, more than equalled their parent states in numbers and strength. And not to dwell on remote instances, the European settlements in the new world bear ample testimony to the truth of a remark which, indeed, has never, that I know of, been doubted. A plenty of rich land, to be had for little or nothing, is so powerful a cause of population as to overcome all other obstacles. No settlements could well have been worse managed than those of Spain in Mexico, Peru, and Quito. The tyranny, superstition, and vices of the mother-country were introduced in ample quantities among her children. Exorbitant taxes were exacted by the Crown. The most arbitrary restrictions were imposed on their trade. And the governors were not behind hand in rapacity and extortion for themselves as well as their master. Yet, under all these difficulties, the colonies made a quick progress in population. The city of Lima, founded since the conquest, is represented by Ulloa as containing fifty thousand inhabitants near fifty years ago. Quito, which had been but a hamlet of Indians, is represented by the same author as in his time equally populous. Mexico is said to contain a hundred thousand inhabitants, which, notwithstanding the exaggerations of the Spanish writers, is supposed to be five times greater than what it contained in the time of Montezuma.

In the Portuguese colony of Brazil, governed with almost equal tyranny, there were supposed to be, thirty years since, six hundred thousand inhabitants of European extraction.

The Dutch and French colonies, though under the government of exclusive companies of merchants, which, as Dr. Adam Smith says very justly, is the worst of all possible governments, still persisted in thriving under every disadvantage.

But the English North American colonies, now the powerful People of the United States of America, made by far the most rapid progress. To the plenty of good land which they possessed in common with the Spanish and Portuguese settlements, they added a greater degree of liberty and equality. Though not without some restrictions on their foreign commerce, they were allowed a perfect liberty of managing their own internal affairs. The political institutions that prevailed were favourable to the alienation and division of property. Lands that were not cultivated by the proprietor within a limited time were declared grantable to any other person. In Pennsylvania there was no right of primogeniture, and in the provinces of New England the eldest had only a double share. There were no tythes in any of the States, and scarcely any taxes. And on account of the extreme cheapness of good land a capital could not be more advantageously employed than in agriculture which at the same time that it supplies the greatest quantity of healthy work affords much the most valuable produce to the society.

The consequence of these favourable circumstances united was a

rapidity of increase, probably without parallel in history. Throughout all the northern colonies, the population was found to double
itself in 25 years. The original number of persons who had settled
in the four provinces of new England in 1643, was 21,200.[2] Afterwards, it is supposed that more left them than went to them. In
the year 1760, they were increased to half a million. They had
therefore all along doubled their own number in 25 years. In New
Jersey the period of doubling appeared to be 22 years; and in
Rhode Island still less. In the back settlements, where the inhabitants applied themselves solely to agriculture, and luxury was not
known, they were found to double their own number in 15 years, a
most extraordinary instance of increase.[3] Along the sea coast,
which would naturally be first inhabited, the period of doubling
was about 35 years; and in some of the maritime towns, the population was absolutely at a stand.

These facts seem to shew that population increases exactly in the
proportion that the two great checks to it, misery and vice, are
removed and that there is not a truer criterion of the happiness
and innocence of a people than the rapidity of their increase. The
unwholesomeness of towns, to which some persons are necessarily
driven from the nature of their trades, must be considered as a
species of misery; and every the slightest check to marriage, from
a prospect of the difficulty of maintaining a family, may be fairly
classed under the same head. In short it is difficult to conceive any
check to population which does not come under the description of
some species of misery or vice.

The population of the thirteen American States before the war,
was reckoned at about three millions. Nobody imagines that Great
Britain is less populous at present for the emigration of the small
parent stock that produced these numbers. On the contrary, a certain degree of emigration is known to be favourable to the popula-

---

2. I take these facts from Dr. Price's two
volumes of Observations [Richard Price,
Observations on Reversionary Payments
(1771), 2 vols. (*Editor*)], not having Dr.
Styles's pamphlet, from which he quotes,
by me.

3. In instances of this kind the powers of
the earth appear to be fully equal to
answer all the demands for food that
can be made upon it by man. But we
should be led into an error if we were
thence to suppose that population and
food ever really increase in the same
ratio. The one is still a geometrical and
the other an arithmetical ratio, that is,
one increases by multiplication, and the
other by addition. Where there are few
people, and a great quantity of fertile
land, the power of the earth to afford a
yearly increase of food may be compared to a great reservoir of water, supplied by a moderate stream. The faster
population increases, the more help will
be got to draw off the water, and consequently an increasing quantity will be
taken every year. But the sooner, undoubtedly, will the reservoir be exhausted, and the streams only remain.
When acre has been added to acre, till
all the fertile land is occupied, the
yearly increase of food will depend upon
the amelioration of the land already in
possession; and even this moderate
stream will be gradually diminishing.
But population, could it be supplied
with food, would go on with unex-
hausted vigour, and the increase of one
period would furnish the power of a
greater increase the next, and this without any limit.

tion of the mother country. It has been particularly remarked that the two Spanish provinces from which the greatest number of people emigrated to America became in consequence more populous. Whatever was the original number of British Emigrants that increased so fast in the North American Colonies, let us ask, why does not an equal number produce an equal increase in the same time in Great Britain? The great and obvious cause to be assigned is the want of room and food, or, in other words, misery, and that this is a much more powerful cause even than vice appears sufficiently evident from the rapidity with which even old States recover the desolations of war, pestilence, or the accidents of nature. They are then for a short time placed a little in the situation of new states, and the effect is always answerable to what might be expected. If the industry of the inhabitants be not destroyed by fear or tyranny, subsistence will soon increase beyond the wants of the reduced numbers, and the invariable consequence will be, that population which before, perhaps, was nearly stationary, will begin immediately to increase.

The fertile province of Flanders, which has been so often the seat of the most destructive wars, after a respite of a few years, has appeared always as fruitful and as populous as ever. Even the Palatinate lifted up its head again after the execrable ravages of Louis the Fourteenth. The effects of the dreadful plague in London in 1666 were not perceptible 15 or 20 years afterwards. The traces of the most destructive famines in China and Indostan are by all accounts very soon obliterated. It may even be doubted whether Turkey and Egypt are upon an average much less populous for the plagues that periodically lay them waste. If the number of people which they contain be less now than formerly, it is, probably, rather to be attributed to the tyranny and oppression of the government under which they groan, and the consequent discouragements to agriculture, than to the loss which they sustain by the plague. The most tremendous convulsions of nature, such as volcanic eruptions and earthquakes, if they do not happen so frequently as to drive away the inhabitants or to destroy their spirit of industry, have but a trifling effect on the average population of any state. Naples, and the country under Vesuvius, are still very populous, notwithstanding the repeated eruptions of that mountain. And Lisbon and Lima are now, probably, nearly in the same state with regard to population, as they were before the last earthquakes.

CHAPTER VII

A probable cause of epidemics—Extracts from Mr. Sus-milch's tables—Periodical returns of sickly seasons to be expected in certain cases—Proportion of births to burials for short periods in any country an inadequate criterion of the real average increase of population—Best criterion of a permanent increase of population—Great frugality of living one of the causes of the famines of China and Indostan—Evil tendency of one of the clauses in Mr. Pitt's Poor Bill—Only one proper way of encouraging population—Causes of the happiness of nations—Famine, the last and most dreadful mode by which nature represses a redundant population—The three propositions considered as established.

By great attention to cleanliness, the plague seems at length to be completely expelled from London. But it is not improbable that among the secondary causes that produce even sickly seasons and epidemics ought to be ranked a crowded population and unwholesome and insufficient food. I have been led to this remark, by looking over some of the tables of Mr. Susmilch, which Dr. Price has extracted in one of his notes to the postscript on the controversy respecting the population of England and Wales. They are considered as very correct, and if such tables were general, they would throw great light on the different ways by which population is repressed and prevented from increasing beyond the means of subsistence in any country. I will extract a part in the tables, with Dr. Price's remarks.

IN THE KINGOM OF PRUSSIA, AND DUKEDOM OF LITHUANIA

Annual Average	Births	Burials	Marriages	Proportion of Births to Marriages	Proportion of Births to Burials
10 Yrs. to 1702	21963	14718	5928	37 to 10	150 to 100
5 Yrs. to 1716	21602	11984	4968	37 to 10	180 to 100
5 Yrs. to 1756	28392	19154	5599	50 to 10	148 to 100

"N. B. In 1709 and 1710, pestilence carried off 247,733 of the inhabitants of this country, and in 1736 and 1737, epidemics prevailed, which again checked its increase."

It may be remarked, that the greatest proportion of births to burials, was in the five years after the great pestilence.

DUTCHY OF POMERANIA

Annual Average	Births	Burials	Marriages	Proportion of Births to Marriages	Proportion of Births to Burials
6 Yrs. to 1702	6540	4647	1810	36 to 10	140 to 100
6 Yrs. to 1708	7455	4208	1875	39 to 10	177 to 100
6 Yrs. to 1726	8432	5627	2131	39 to 10	150 to 100
4 Yrs. to 1756	12767	9281	2957	43 to 10	137 to 100

"In this instance the inhabitants appear to have been almost doubled in 56 years, no very bad epidemics having once interrupted the increase, but the three years immediately following the last period (to 1759) were years so sickly that the births were sunk to 10,229, and the burials raised to 15,068."

Is it not probable that in this case the number of inhabitants had increased faster than the food and the accommodations necessary to preserve them in health? The mass of the people would, upon this supposition, be obliged to live harder, and a greater number would be crowded together in one house, and it is not surely improbable that these were among the natural causes that produced the three sickly years. These causes may produce such an effect, though the country, absolutely considered, may not be extremely crowded and populous. In a country even thinly inhabited, if an increase of population take place before more foods is raised and more houses are built, the inhabitants must be distressed in some degree for room and subsistence. Were the marriages in England, for the next eight or ten years, to be more prolifick than usual, or even were a greater number of marriages than usual to take place, supposing the number of houses to remain the same, instead of five or six to a cottage, there must be seven or eight, and this, added to the necessity of harder living, would probably have a very unfavourable effect on the health of the common people.

NEUMARK OF BRANDENBURGH

Annual Average	Births	Burials	Marriages	Proportion of Births to Marriages	Proportion of Births to Burials
5 Yrs. to 1701	5433	3483	1436	37 to 10	155 to 100
5 Yrs. to 1726	7012	4254	1713	40 to 10	164 to 100
5 Yrs. to 1756	7978	5567	1891	42 to 10	143 to 100

"Epidemics prevailed for six years, from 1736, to 1741, which checked the increase."

DUKEDOM OF MAGDEBURGH

Annual Average	Births	Burials	Marriages	Proportion of Births to Marriages	Proportion of Births to Burials
5 Yrs. to 1702	6431	4103	1681	38 to 10	156 to 100
5 Yrs. to 1717	7590	5335	2076	36 to 10	142 to 100
5 Yrs. to 1756	8850	8069	2193	40 to 10	109 to 100

"The years 1738, 1740, 1750, and 1751, were particularly sickly."

For further information on this subject, I refer the reader to Mr. Susmilch's tables. The extracts that I have made are sufficient to shew the periodical though irregular returns of sickly seasons, and it seems highly probable that a scantiness of room and food was one of the principal causes that occasioned them.

It appears from the tables that these countries were increasing rather fast for old states, notwithstanding the occasional sickly seasons that prevailed. Cultivation must have been improving, and marriages, consequently, encouraged. For the checks to population appear to have been rather of the positive than of the preventive kind. When from a prospect of increasing plenty in any country, the weight that represses population is in some degree removed, it is highly probable that the motion will be continued beyond the operation of the cause that first impelled it. Or, to be more particular, when the increasing produce of a country, and the increasing demand for labour, so far ameliorate the condition of the labourer as greatly to encourage marriage, it is probable that the custom of early marriages will continue till the population of the country has gone beyond the increased produce, and sickly seasons appear to be the natural and necessary consequence. I should expect, therefore, that those countries where subsistence was increasing sufficiently at times to encourage population but not to answer all its demands, would be more subject to periodical epidemics than those where the population could more completely accommodate itself to the average produce.

An observation the converse of this will probably also be found true. In those countries that are subject to periodical sicknesses, the increase of population, or the excess of births above the burials, will be greater in the intervals of these periods than is usual, caeteris paribus, in the countries not so much subject to such disorders. If Turkey and Egypt have been nearly stationary in their average population for the last century, in the intervals of their periodical plagues, the births must have exceeded the burials in a greater proportion than in such countries as France and England.

The average proportion of births to burials in any country for a period of five or ten years will hence appear to be a very inadequate criterion by which to judge of its real progress in population. This proportion certainly shews the rate of increase during those five or ten years; but we can by no means thence infer what had been the increase for the twenty years before, or what would be the increase for the twenty years after. Dr. Price observes that Sweden, Norway, Russia, and the kingdom of Naples are increasing fast; but the extracts from registers that he has given are not for periods of sufficient extent to establish the fact. It is highly probable, however, that Sweden, Norway, and Russia are really increasing in their population, though not at the rate that the proportion of births to burials for the short periods that Dr. Price takes would seem to shew.[4] For five years, ending in 1777, the proportion of births to burials in the kingdom of Naples was 144 to 100, but there is reason to suppose that this proportion would indicate an increase much greater than would be really found to have taken place in that kingdom during a period of a hundred years.

Dr. Short compared the registers of many villages and market towns in England for two periods; the first from Queen Elizabeth to the middle of the last century, and the second from different years at the end of the last century to the middle of the present. And from a comparison of these extracts, it appears that in the former period the births exceeded the burials in the proportion of 124 to 100 but in the latter, only in the proportion of 111 to 100. Dr. Price thinks that the registers in the former period are not to be depended upon, but probably in this instance they do not give incorrect proportions. At least there are many reasons for expecting to find a greater excess of births above the burials in the former period than in the latter. In the natural progress of the population of any country, more good land will, caeteris paribus,[5] be taken into cultivation in the earlier stages of it than in the later. And a greater proportional yearly increase of produce will almost invariably be followed by a greater proportional increase of population. But besides this great cause, which would naturally give the excess of births above the burials greater at the end of Queen Elizabeth's reign than in the middle of the present century, I cannot help thinking that the occasional ravages of the plague in the former period must have had some tendency to increase this proportion. If an average of ten years had been taken in the intervals of the returns of this dreadful disorder, or if the years of plague had been rejected as accidental, the registers would certainly give the pro-

4. See Dr. Price's Observation, 2 Vol. Postscript to the controversy on the population of England and Wales.

5. I say caeteris paribus, because the increase of the produce of any country will always very greatly depend on the spirit of industry that prevails and the way in which it is directed. The knowledge and habits of the people, and other temporary causes, particularly the degree of civil liberty and equality existing at the time, must always have great influence in exciting and directing this spirit.

portion of births to burials too high for the real average increase of the population. For some few years after the great plague in 1666, it is probable that there was a more than usual excess of births above burials, particularly if Dr. Price's opinion be founded, that England was more populous at the revolution (which happened only 22 years afterwards) than it is at present.

Mr. King, in 1693, stated the proportion of the births to the burials throughout the Kingdom, exclusive of London, as 115 to 100. Dr. Short makes it, in the middle of the present century, 111 to 100, including London. The proportion in France for five years, ending in 1774, was 117 to 100. If these statements are near the truth, and if there are no very great variations at particular periods in the proportions, it would appear that the population of France and England has accommodated itself very nearly to the average produce of each country. The discouragements to marriage, the consequent vicious habits, war, luxury, the silent though certain depopulation of large towns, and the close habitations and insufficient food of many of the poor, prevent population from increasing beyond the means of subsistence; and, if I may use an expression which certainly at first appears strange, supersede the necessity of great and ravaging epidemics to repress what is redundant. Were a wasting plague to sweep off two millions in England and six millions in France, there can be no doubt whatever that after the inhabitants had recovered from the dreadful shock, the proportion of births to burials would be much above what it is in either country at present.

In New Jersey, the proportion of births to deaths on an average of seven years, ending in 1743, was as 300 to 100. In France and England, taking the highest proportion, it is as 117 to 100. Great and astonishing as this difference is, we ought not to be so wonderstruck at it as to attribute it to the miraculous interposition of heaven. The causes of it are not remote, latent and mysterious; but near us, round about us, and open to the investigation of every inquiring mind. It accords with the most liberal spirit of philosophy to suppose that not a stone can fall, or a plant rise, without the immediate agency of divine power. But we know from experience that these operations of what we call nature have been conducted almost invariably according to fixed laws. And since the world began, the causes of population and depopulation have probably been as constant as any of the laws of nature with which we are acquainted.

The passion between the sexes has appeared in every age to be so nearly the same that it may always be considered, in algebraic language, as a given quantity. The great law of necessity which prevents population from increasing in any country beyond the food which it can either produce or acquire, is a law so open to our view, so obvious and evident to our understandings, and so completely confirmed by the experience of every age, that we cannot for a moment doubt it. The different modes which nature takes to prevent or repress a redundant population do not appear, indeed, to us so certain and regular, but though we cannot always predict the mode we may with certainty predict the fact. If the proportion of births to deaths for a few years, indicate an increase of numbers much beyond the proportional increased or acquired produce of the country, we may be perfectly certain that unless an emigration takes place, the deaths will shortly exceed the births, and that the increase that had taken place for a few years cannot be the real average increase of the population of the country. Were there no other depopulating causes, every country would, without doubt, be subject to periodical pestilences or famines.

The only true criterion of a real and permanent increase in the population of any country is the increase of the means of subsistence. But even this criterion is subject to some slight variations which are, however, completely open to our view and observations. In some countries population appears to have been forced, that is, the people have been habituated by degrees to live almost upon the smallest possible quantity of food. There must have been periods in such countries when population increased permanently, without an increase in the means of subsistence. China seems to answer to this description. If the accounts we have of it are to be trusted, the lower classes of people are in the habit of living almost upon the smallest possible quantity of food and are glad to get any putrid offals that European labourers would rather starve than eat. The law in China which permits parents to expose their children has tended principally thus to force the population. A nation in this state must necessarily be subject to famines. Where a country is so populous in proportion to the means of subsistence that the average produce of it is but barely sufficient to support the lives of the inhabitants, any deficiency from the badness of seasons must be fatal. It is probable that the very frugal manner in which the Gentoos are in the habit of living contributes in some degree to the famines of Indostan.

In America, where the reward of labour is at present so liberal, the lower classes might retrench very considerably in a year of scarcity without materially distressing themselves. A famine therefore seems to be almost impossible. It may be expected that in the progress of the population of America, the labourers will in time be much less liberally rewarded. The numbers will in this case permanently increase without a proportional increase in the means of subsistence.

In the different States of Europe there must be some variations in the proportion between the number of inhabitants and the quantity of food consumed, arising from the different habits of living that prevail in each State. The labourers of the South of England are so accustomed to eat fine wheaten bread that they will suffer themselves to be half starved before they will submit to live like the Scotch peasants. They might perhaps in time, by the constant operation of the hard law of necessity, be reduced to live even like the lower Chinese, and the country would then, with the same quantity of food, support a greater population. But to effect this must always be a most difficult, and every friend to humanity will hope, an abortive attempt. Nothing is so common as to hear of encouragements that ought to be given to population. If the tendency of mankind to increase be so great as I have represented it to be, it may appear strange that this increase does not come when it is thus repeatedly called for. The true reason is that the demand for a greater population is made without preparing the funds necessary to support it. Increase the demand for agricultural labour by promoting cultivation, and with it consequently increase the produce of the country, and ameliorate the condition of the labourer, and no apprehensions whatever need be entertained of the proportional increase of population. An attempt to effect this purpose in any other way is vicious, cruel, and tyrannical, and in any state of tolerable freedom cannot therefore succeed. It may appear to be the interest of the rulers, and the rich of a State, to force population and thereby lower the price of labour, and consequently the expense of fleets and armies and the cost of manufactures for foreign sale, but every attempt of the kind should be carefully watched and strenuously resisted by the friends of the poor, particularly when it comes under the deceitful garb of benevolence and is likely, on that account, to be cheerfully and cordially received by the common people.

I entirely acquit Mr. Pitt of any sinister intention in that clause of his poor bill which allows a shilling a week to every labourer for each child he has above three. I confess that before the bill was brought into Parliament, and for some time after, I thought that such a regulation would be highly beneficial; but further reflection on the subject has convinced me that if its object be to better the condition of the poor, it is calculated to defeat the very purpose which it has in view. It has no tendency that I can discover to increase the produce of the country, and if it tend to increase the population without increasing the produce, the necessary and inevitable consequence appears to be that the same produce must be divided among a greater number, and consequently that a day's labour will purchase a smaller quantity of provisions, and the poor therefore in general must be more distressed.

I have mentioned some cases where population may permanently increase without a proportional increase in the means of subsistence. But it is evident that the variation in different States, between the food and the numbers supported by it, is restricted to a limit beyond which it cannot pass. In every country, the population of which is not absolutely decreasing, the food must be necessarily sufficient to support, and to continue, the race of labourers.

Other circumstances being the same, it may be affirmed that countries are populous according to the quantity of human food which they produce, and happy according to the liberality with which that food is divided, or the quantity which a day's labour will purchase. Corn countries are more populous than pasture countries, and rice countries more populous that corn countries. The lands in England are not suited to rice, but they would all bear potatoes; and Dr. Adam Smith observes that if potatoes were to become the favourite vegetable food of the common people, and if the same quantity of land was employed in their culture as is now employed in the culture of corn, the country would be able to support a much greater population, and would consequently in a very short time have it.

The happiness of a country does not depend absolutely upon its poverty or its riches, upon its youth or its age, upon its being thinly or fully inhabited, but upon the rapidity with which it is increasing, upon the degree in which the yearly increase of food approaches to the yearly increase of an unrestricted population. This approximation is always the nearest in new colonies, where the knowledge and industry of an old State operate on the fertile unappropriated land of a new one. In other cases, the youth or the age of a State is not in this respect of very great importance. It is probable that the food of Great Britain is divided in as great plenty to the inhabitants at the present period as it was two thousand, three thousand, or four thousand years ago. And there is reason to believe that the poor and thinly inhabited tracts of the Scotch Highlands are as much distressed by an overcharged population as the rich and populous province of Flanders.

Were a country never to be over-run by a people more advanced in arts, but left to its own natural progress in civilization; from the time that its produce might be considered as an unit, to the time that it might be considered as a million, during the lapse of many hundred years there would not be a single period when the mass of the people could be said to be free from distress, either directly or indirectly, for want of food. In every State in Europe, since we have first had accounts of it, millions and millions of human existences have been repressed from this simple cause; though perhaps in some of these States, an absolute famine has never been known.

Famine seems to be the last, the most dreadful resource of nature. The power of population is so superior to the power in the earth to produce subsistence for man, that premature death must in some shape or other visit the human race. The vices of mankind are active and able ministers of depopulation. They are the precursors in the great army of destruction, and often finish the dreadful work themselves. But should they fail in this war of extermination, sickly seasons, epidemics, pestilence, and plague, advance in terrific array and sweep off their thousands and ten thousands. Should success be still incomplete, gigantic inevitable famine stalks in the rear, and with one mighty blow, levels the population with the food of the world.

Must it not then be acknowledged by an attentive examiner of the histories of mankind, that in every age and in every State in which man has existed, or does now exist,

That the increase of population is necessarily limited by the means of subsistence.

That population does invariably increase when the means of subsistence increase. And that the superior power of population is repressed, and the actual population kept equal to the means of subsistence, by misery and vice.

CHAPTER VIII

> *Mr. Wallace—Error of supposing that the difficulty aris- ing from population is at a great distance—Mr. Condor- cet's sketch of the progress of the human mind—Period when the oscillation, mentioned by Mr. Condorcet, ought to be applied to the human race.*

To a person who draws the preceding obvious inferences from a view of the past and present state of mankind, it cannot but be a matter of astonishment that all the writers on the perfectibility of man and of society who have noticed the argument of an over- charged population treat it always very slightly and invariably represent the difficulties arising from it as at a great and almost immeasurable distance. Even Mr. Wallace, who thought the argu- ment itself of so much weight as to destroy his whole system of equality, did not seem to be aware that any difficulty would occur from this cause till the whole earth had been cultivated like a gar- den and was incapable of any further increase of produce. Were this really the case, and were a beautiful system of equality in other respects practicable, I cannot think that our ardour in the pursuit of such a scheme ought to be damped by the contemplation of so remote a difficulty. An event at such a distance might fairly be left to providence; but the truth is that if the view of the argument given in this essay be just, the difficulty, so far from being remote, would be imminent and immediate. At every period during the progress of cultivation, from the present moment to the time when the whole earth was become like a garden, the distress for want of food would be constantly pressing on all mankind, if they were equal. Though the produce of the earth might be increasing every year, population would be increasing much faster, and the redundancy must necessarily be repressed by the periodical or constant action of misery or vice.

Mr. Condorcet's *Esquisse d'un tableau historique des progrès de l'esprit humain* was written, it is said, under the pressure of that cruel proscription which terminated in his death. If he had no hopes of its being seen during his life and of its interesting France in his favour, it is a singular instance of the attachment of a man to principles which every day's experience was so fatally for himself contradicting. To see the human mind in one of the most enlightened nations of the world, and after a lapse of some thousand years, debased by such a fermentation of disgusting passions, of fear, cruelty, malice, revenge, ambition, madness, and folly as would have disgraced the most savage nation in the most barbarous age must have been such a tremendous shock to his ideas of the necessary and inevitable progress of the human mind that nothing but the firmest conviction of the truth of his principles, in spite of all appearances, could have withstood.

This posthumous publication is only a sketch of a much larger work which he proposed should be executed. It necessarily, therefore, wants that detail and application which can alone prove the truth of any theory. A few observations will be sufficient to shew how completely the theory is contradicted when it is applied to the real, and not to an imaginary, state of things.

In the last division of the work, which treats of the future progress of man towards perfection, he says, that comparing, in the different civilized nations of Europe, the actual population with the extent of territory, and observing their cultivation, their industry, their divisions of labour, and their means of subsistence, we shall see that it would be impossible to preserve the same means of subsistence, and, consequently, the same population, without a number of individuals who have no other means of supplying their wants than their industry. Having allowed the necessity of such a class of men, and adverting afterwards to the precarious revenue of those families that would depend so entirely on the life and health of their chief,[6] he says, very justly, "There exists then, a necessary cause of inequality, of dependence, and even of misery, which menaces, without ceasing, the most numerous and active class of our societies." The difficulty is just and well stated, and I am afraid that the mode by which he proposes it should be removed, will be found inefficacious. By the application of calculations to the probabilities of life and the interest of money, he proposes that a fund should be established which should assure to the old an assistance, produced, in part, by their own former savings, and, in part, by the savings of individuals who in making the same sacrifice die before they reap the benefit of it. The same or a similar fund should give assistance to women and children who lose their husbands or fathers and afford a capital to those who were of an age to found a new family, sufficient for the proper development of their industry. These establishments he observes, might be made in the name and under the protection of the society. Going still further, he says that by the just application of calculations, means might be found of more completely preserving a state of equality, by preventing credit from being the exclusive privilege of great fortunes, and yet giving it a basis equally solid, and by rendering the progress of industry, and the activity of commerce, less dependent on great capitalists.

Such establishments and calculations may appear very promising upon paper, but when applied to real life they will be found to be absolutely nugatory. Mr. Condorcet allows that a class of people which maintains itself entirely by industry is necessary to every state. Why does he allow this? No other reason can well be assigned than that he conceives that the labour necessary to procure subsistence for an extended population will not be performed without the goad of necessity. If by establishments of this kind this spur to industry be removed, if the idle and the negligent are placed upon the same footing with regard to their credit, and the future support of their wives and families, as the active and industrious, can we expect to see men exert that animated activity in bettering their condition which now forms the master spring of public prosperity? If an inquisition were to be established to examine the claims of each individual and to determine whether he had or had not exerted himself to the utmost, and to grant or refuse assistance accordingly, this would be little else than a repetition upon a larger scale of the English poor laws and would be completely destructive of the true principles of liberty and equality.

6. To save time and long quotations, I shall here give the substance of some of Mr. Condorcet's sentiments, and hope I shall not misrepresent them, but I refer the reader to the work itself, which will amuse, if it does not convince him.

But independent of this great objection to these establishments, and supposing for a moment that they would give no check to productive industry, by far the greatest difficulty remains yet behind.

Were every man sure of a comfortable provision for a family, almost every man would have one, and were the rising generation free from the "killing frost" of misery, population must rapidly increase. Of this Mr. Condorcet seems to be fully aware himself, and after having described further improvements, he says,

"But in this progress of industry and happiness, each generation will be called to more extended enjoyments, and in consequence, by the physical constitution of the human frame, to an increase in the number of individuals. Must not there arrive a period then, when these laws, equally necessary, shall counteract each other? When the increase of the number of men surpassing their means of subsistence, the necessary result must be either a continual diminution of happiness and population, a movement truly retrograde, or at least a kind of oscillation between good and evil? In societies arrived at this term, will not this oscillation be a constantly subsisting cause of periodical misery? Will it not mark the limit when all further amelioration will become impossible, and point out that term to the perfectibility of the human race which it may reach in the course of ages, but can never pass?"

He then adds,

"There is no person who does not see how very distant such a period is from us, but shall we ever arrive at it? It is equally impossible to pronounce for or against the future realization of an event which cannot take place but at an era when the human race will have attained improvements, of which we can at present scarcely form a conception."

Mr. Condorcet's picture of what may be expected to happen when the number of men shall surpass the means of their subsistence, is justly drawn. The oscillation which he describes will certainly take place and will without doubt be a constantly subsisting cause of periodical misery. The only point in which I differ from Mr. Condorcet with regard to this picture is the period when it may be applied to the human race. Mr. Condorcet thinks that it cannot possibly be applicable but at an era extremely distant. If the proportion between the natural increase of population and food which I have geven be in any degree near the truth, it will appear, on the contrary, that the period when the number of men surpass their means of subsistence has long since arrived, and that this necessary oscillation, this constantly subsisting cause of periodical misery, has existed ever since we have had any histories of mankind, does exist at present, and will for ever continue to exist, unless some decided change take place in the physical constitution of our nature.

Mr. Condorcet, however, goes on to say that should the period which he conceives to be so distant ever arrive, the human race, and the advocates for the perfectibility of man, need not be alarmed at it. He then proceeds to remove the difficulty in a manner which I profess not to understand. Having observed that the ridiculous prejudices of superstition would by that time have ceased to throw over morals a corrupt and degrading austerity, he alludes either to a promiscuous concubinage, which would prevent breeding, or to something else as unnatural. To remove the difficulty in this way will surely, in the opinion of most men, be to destroy that virtue and purity of manners which the advocates of equality and of the perfectibility of man profess to be the end and object of their views.

CHAPTER IX

Mr. Condorcet's conjecture concerning the organic perfectibility of man, and the indefinite prolongation of human life—Fallacy of the argument, which infers an unlimited progress from a partial improvement, the limit of which cannot be ascertained, illustrated in the breeding of animals, and the cultivation of plants.

The last question which Mr. Condorcet proposes for examination is the organic perfectibility of man. He observes that if the proofs which have been already given and which, in their development, will receive greater force in the work itself, are sufficient to establish the indefinite perfectibility of man upon the supposition of the same natural faculties and the same organization which he has at present, what will be the certainty, what the extent of our hope, if this organization, these natural faculties themselves, are susceptible of amelioration?

From the improvement of medicine, from the use of more wholesome food and habitations, from a manner of living which will improve the strength of the body by exercise without impairing it by excess, from the destruction of the two great causes of the degradation of man, misery and too great riches, from the gradual removal of transmissible and contagious disorders by the improvement of physical knowledge, rendered more efficacious by the progress of reason and of social order, he infers that though man will not absolutely become immortal, yet that the duration between his birth and natural death will increase without ceasing, will have no assignable term, and may properly be expressed by the word indefinite. He then defines this word to mean either a constant approach to an unlimited extent, without ever reaching it, or an increase in the immensity of ages to an extent greater than any assignable quantity.

But surely the application of this term in either of these senses to the duration of human life is in the highest degree unphilosophical and totally unwarranted by any appearances in the laws of nature. Variations from different causes are essentially distinct from a regular and unretrograde increase. The average duration of human life will to a certain degree vary from healthy or unhealthy climates, from wholesome or unwholesome food, from virtuous or vicious manners, and other causes, but it may be fairly doubted whether there is really the smallest perceptible advance in the natural duration of human life since first we have had any authentic history of man. The prejudices of all ages have indeed been directly contrary to this supposition, and though I would not lay much stress upon these prejudices, they will in some measure tend to prove that there has been no marked advance in an opposite direction.

It may perhaps be said that the world is yet so young, so completely in its infancy, that it ought not to be expected that any difference should appear so soon.

If this be the case, there is at once an end of all human science. The whole train of reasonings from effects to causes will be destroyed. We may shut our eyes to the book of nature, as it will no longer be of any use to read it. The wildest and most improbable conjectures may be advanced with as much certainty as the most just and sublime theories, founded on careful and reiterated experiments. We may return again to the old mode of philosophizing and make facts bend to systems, instead of establishing systems upon facts. The grand and consistent theory of Newton will be placed upon the same footing as the wild and eccentric hypotheses of Descartes. In short, if the laws of nature are thus fickle and inconstant, if it can be affirmed and be believed that they will change, when for ages and ages they have appeared immutable, the human mind will no longer have any incitements to inquiry, but must remain fixed in inactive torpor, or amuse itself only in bewildering dreams and extravagant fancies.

The constancy of the laws of nature and of effects and causes is the foundation of all human knowledge, though far be it from me to say that the same power which framed and executes the laws of nature, may not change them all "in a moment, in the twinkling of an eye." Such a change may undoubtedly happen. All that I mean to say is that it is impossible to infer it from reasoning. If without any previous observable symptoms or indications of a change, we can infer that a change will take place, we may as well make any assertion whatever and think it as unreasonable to be contradicted in affirming that the moon will come in contact with the earth to-morrow, as in saying that the sun will rise at its usual time.

With regard to the duration of human life, there does not appear to have existed from the earliest ages of the world to the present moment the smallest permanent symptom or indication of increasing prolongation.[7] The observable effects of climate, habit, diet, and other causes, on length of life have furnished the pretext for asserting its indefinite extension; and the sandy foundation on which the argument rests is that because the limit of human life is undefined; because you cannot mark its precise term, and say so far exactly shall it go and no further; that therefore its extent may increase for ever, and be properly termed indefinite or unlimited. But the fallacy and absurdity of this argument will sufficiently appear from a slight examination of what Mr. Condorcet calls the organic perfectibility, or degeneration, of the race of plants and animals, which he says may be regarded as one of the general laws of nature.

I am told that it is a maxim among the improvers of cattle that you may breed to any degree of nicety you please, and they found this maxim upon another, which is that some of the offspring will possess the desirable qualities of the parents in a greater degree. In the famous Leicestershire breed of sheep, the object is to procure

7. Many, I doubt not, will think that the attempting gravely to controvert so absurd a paradox as the immortality of man on earth, or indeed even the perfectibility of man and society, is a waste of time and words, and that such unfounded conjectures are best answered by neglect. I profess, however, to be of a different opinion. When paradoxes of this kind are advanced by ingenious and able men, neglect has no tendency to convince them of their mistakes. Priding themselves on what they conceive to be a mark of the reach and size of their own understandings, of the extent and comprehensiveness of their views; they will look upon this neglect merely as an indication of poverty and narrowness in the mental exertions of their contemporaries; and only think that the world is not yet prepared to receive their sublime truths.

On the contrary, a candid investigation of these subjects, accompanied with a perfect readiness to adopt any theory warranted by sound philosophy, may have a tendency to convince them that in forming improbable and unfounded hypotheses, so far from enlarging the bounds of human science, they are contracting it, so far from promoting the improvement of the human mind, they are obstructing it; they are throwing us back again almost into the infancy of knowledge and weakening the foundations of that mode of philosophising, under the auspices of which, science has of late made such rapid advances. The present rage for wide and unrestrained speculation seems to be a kind of mental intoxication, arising, perhaps, from the great and unexpected discoveries which have been made of late years, in various branches of science. To men elate and giddy with such successes, every thing appeared to be within the grasp of human powers; and under this illusion, they confounded subjects where no real progress could be proved, with those where the progress had been marked, certain, and acknowledged. Could they be persuaded to sober themselves with a little severe and chastized thinking, they would see, that the cause of truth and of sound philosophy cannot but suffer by substituting wild flights and unsupported assertions for patient investigation and well authenticated proofs.

them with small heads and small legs. Proceeding upon these breeding maxims, it is evident that we might go on till the heads and legs were evanescent quantities, but this is so palpable an absurdity that we may be quite sure that the premises are not just and that there really is a limit, though we cannot see it or say exactly where it is. In this case, the point of the greatest degree of improvement, or the smallest size of the head and legs, may be said to be undefined, but this is very different from unlimited, or from indefinite, in Mr. Condorcet's acceptation of the term. Though I may not be able in the present instance to mark the limit at which further improvement will stop, I can very easily mention a point at which it will not arrive. I should not scruple to assert that were the breeding to continue for ever, the head and legs of these sheep would never be so small as the head and legs of a rat.

It cannot be true, therefore, that among animals some of the offspring will possess the desirable qualities of the parents in a greater degree, or that animals are indefinitely perfectible.

The progress of a wild plant to a beautiful garden flower is perhaps more marked and striking than any thing that takes place among animals, yet even here it would be the height of absurdity to assert that the progress was unlimited or indefinite. One of the most obvious features of the improvement is the increase of size. The flower has grown gradually larger by cultivation. If the progress were really unlimited it might be increased ad infinitum, but this is so gross an absurdity that we may be quite sure that among plants as well as among animals there is a limit to improvement, though we do not exactly know where it is. It is probable that the gardeners who contend for flower prizes have often applied stronger dressing without success. At the same time, it would be highly presumptuous in any man to say that he had seen the finest carnation or anemone that could ever be made to grow. He might however assert without the smallest chance of being contradicted by a future fact, that no carnation or anemone could ever by cultivation be increased to the size of a large cabbage; and yet there are assignable quantities much greater than a cabbage. No man can say that he has seen the largest ear of wheat or the largest oak that could ever grow; but he might easily, and with perfect certainty, name a point of magnitude, at which they would not arrive. In all these cases therefore, a careful distinction should be made, between an unlimited progress and a progress where the limit is merely undefined.

It will be said, perhaps, that the reason why plants and animals cannot increase indefinitely in size is that they would fall by their own weight. I answer, how do we know this but from experience? from experience of the degree of strength with which these bodies are formed. I know that a carnation, long before it reached the size of a cabbage, would not be supported by its stalk, but I only know this from my experience of the weakness and want of tenacity in the materials of a carnation stalk. There are many substances in nature of the same size that would support as large a head as a cabbage.

The reasons of the mortality of plants are at present perfectly unknown to us. No man can say why such a plant is annual, another biennial, and another endures for ages. The whole affair in all these cases, in plants, animals, and in the human race, is an affair of experience, and I only conclude that man is mortal because the invariable experience of all ages has proved the mortality of those materials of which his visible body is made.

What can we reason but from what we know.

Sound philosophy will not authorize me to alter this opinion of the mortality of man on earth, till it can be clearly proved that the human race has made, and is making, a decided progress towards an illimitable extent of life. And the chief reason why I adduced the two particular instances from animals and plants was to expose and illustrate, if I could, the fallacy of that argument which infers an unlimited progress, merely because some partial improvement has taken place, and that the limit of this improvement cannot be precisely ascertained.

The capacity of improvement in plants and animals, to a certain degree, no person can possibly doubt. A clear and decided progress has already been made; and yet I think it appears that it would be highly absurd to say that this progress has no limits. In human life, though there are great variations from different causes, it may be doubted whether, since the world began, any organic improvement whatever in the human frame can be clearly ascertained. The foundations therefore, on which the arguments for the organic perfectibility of man rest, are unusually weak and can only be considered as mere conjectures. It does not, however, by any means seem impossible that by an attention to breed, a certain degree of improvement similar to that among animals might take place among men. Whether intellect could be communicated may be a matter of doubt; but size, strength, beauty, complexion, and perhaps even longevity are in a degree transmissible. The error does not seem to lie in supposing a small degree of improvement possible, but in not discriminating between a small improvement, the limit of which is undefined, and an improvement really unlimited. As the human race however could not be improved in this way without condemning all the bad specimens to celibacy, it is not probable that an attention to breed should ever become general; indeed, I know of no well-directed attempts of this kind, except in the ancient family of the Bickerstaffs, who are said to have been very successful in whitening the skins and increasing the height of their race by prudent marriages, particularly by that very judicious cross with Maud, the milk-maid, by which some capital defects in the constitutions of the family were corrected.

It will not be necessary, I think, in order more completely to shew the improbability of any approach in man towards immortality on earth, to urge the very great additional weight that an increase in the duration of life would give to the argument of population.

Mr. Condorcet's book may be considered not only as a sketch of the opinions of a celebrated individual, but of many of the literary men in France at the beginning of the revolution. As such, though merely a sketch, it seems worthy of attention.

CHAPTER X

Mr. Godwin's system of equality—Error of attributing all the vices of mankind to human institutions—Mr. Godwin's first answer to the difficulty arising from population totally insufficient—Mr. Godwin's beautiful system of equality supposed to be realized—Its utter destruction simply from the principle of population in so short a time as thirty years.

In reading Mr. Godwin's ingenious and able work on political justice, it is impossible not to be struck with the spirit and energy of his style, the force and precision of some of his reasonings, the ardent tone of his thoughts, and particularly with that impressive earnestness of manner which gives an air of truth to the whole. At the same time, it must be confessed that he has not proceeded in his enquiries with the caution that sound philosophy seems to require. His conclusions are often unwarranted by his premises. He fails sometimes in removing the objections which he himself brings forward. He relies too much on general and abstract propositions which will not admit of application. And his conjectures certainly far outstrip the modesty of nature.

The system of equality which Mr. Godwin proposes is without doubt by far the most beautiful and engaging of any that has yet appeared. An amelioration of society to be produced merely by reason and conviction wears much more the promise of permanence than any change effected and maintained by force. The unlimited exercise of private judgment is a doctrine inexpressibly grand and captivating and has a vast superiority over those systems where every individual is in a manner the slave of the public. The substitution of benevolence as the master-spring and moving principle of society, instead of self-love, is a consummation devoutly to be wished. In short, it is impossible to contemplate the whole of this fair structure without emotions of delight and admiration, accompanied with ardent longing for the period of its accomplishment. But alas! that moment can never arrive. The whole is little better than a dream, a beautiful phantom of the imagination. These "gorgeous palaces" of happiness and immortality, these "solemn temples" of truth and virtue will dissolve, "like the baseless fabric of a vision," when we awaken to real life and contemplate the true and genuine situation of man on earth.

Mr. Godwin, at the conclusion of the third chapter of his eighth book, speaking of population, says, "There is a principle in human society, by which population is perpetually kept down to the level of the means of subsistence. Thus among the wandering tribes of America and Asia, we never find through the lapse of ages that population has so increased as to render necessary the cultivation of the earth." This principle, which Mr. Godwin thus mentions as some mysterious and occult cause and which he does not attempt to investigate, will be found to be the grinding law of necessity, misery, and the fear of misery.

The great error under which Mr. Godwin labours throughout his whole work is the attributing almost all the vices and misery that are seen in civil society to human institutions. Political regulations and the established administration of property are with him the fruitful sources of all evil, the hotbeds of all the crimes that degrade mankind. Were this really a true state of the case, it would not seem a hopeless task to remove evil completely from the world, and reason seems to be the proper and adequate instrument for effecting so great a purpose. But the truth is, that though human institutions appear to be the obvious and obtrusive causes of much mischief to mankind, yet in reality they are light and superficial, they are mere feathers that float on the surface, in comparison with those deeper seated causes of impurity that corrupt the springs and render turbid the whole stream of human life.

Mr. Godwin, in his chapter on the benefits attendant on a system of equality, says, "The spirit of oppression, the spirit of servility, and the spirit of fraud, these are the immediate growth of the established administration of property. They are alike hostile to intellectual improvement. The other vices of envy, malice, and revenge are their inseparable companions. In a state of society where men lived in the midst of plenty and where all shared alike the bounties of nature, these sentiments would inevitably expire. The narrow principle of selfishness would vanish. No man being obliged to guard his little store or provide with anxiety and pain for his restless wants, each would lose his individual existence in the thought of the general good. No man would be an enemy to his neighbour, for they would have no subject of contention, and, of consequence, philanthropy would resume the empire which reason assigns her. Mind would be delivered from her perpetual anxiety about corporal support, and free to expatiate in the field of thought, which is congenial to her. Each would assist the enquiries of all."

This would indeed be a happy state. But that it is merely an imaginary picture, with scarcely a feature near the truth, the reader, I am afraid, is already too well convinced.

Man cannot live in the midst of plenty. All cannot share alike the bounties of nature. Were there no established administration of property, every man would be obliged to guard with force his little store. Selfishness would be triumphant. The subjects of contention would be perpetual. Every individual mind would be under a constant anxiety about corporal support, and not a single intellect would be left free to expatiate in the field of thought.

How little Mr. Godwin has turned the attention of his penetrating mind to the real state of man on earth will sufficiently appear from the manner in which he endeavours to remove the difficulty of an overcharged population. He says, "The obvious answer to this objection, is, that to reason thus is to foresee difficulties at a great distance. Three fourths of the habitable globe is now uncultivated. The parts already cultivated are capable of immeasureable improvement. Myriads of centuries of still increasing population may pass away, and the earth be still found sufficient for the subsistence of its inhabitants."

I have already pointed out the error of supposing that no distress and difficulty would arise from an overcharged population before the earth absolutely refused to produce any more. But let us imagine for a moment Mr. Godwin's beautiful system of equality realized in its utmost purity, and see how soon this difficulty might be expected to press under so perfect a form of society. A theory that will not admit of application cannot possibly be just.

Let us suppose all the causes of misery and vice in this island removed. War and contention cease. Unwholesome trades and manufactories do not exist. Crowds no longer collect together in great and pestilent cities for purposes of court intrigue, of commerce, and vicious gratifications. Simple, healthy, and rational amusements take place of drinking, gaming, and debauchery. There are no towns sufficiently large to have any prejudicial effects

on the human constitution. The greater part of the happy inhabitants of this terrestrial paradise live in hamlets and farm-houses
scattered over the face of the country. Every house is clean, airy,
sufficiently roomy, and in a healthy situation. All men are equal.
The labours of luxury are at end. And the necessary labours of
agriculture are shared amicably among all. The number of persons,
and the produce of the island, we suppose to be the same as at
present. The spirit of benevolence, guided by impartial justice, will
divide this produce among all the members of the society according to their wants. Though it would be impossible that they should
all have animal food every day, yet vegetable food, with meat
occasionally, would satisfy the desires of a frugal people and
would be sufficient to preserve them in health, strength, and spirits.

Mr. Godwin considers marriage as a fraud and a monopoly. Let
us suppose the commerce of the sexes established upon principles
of the most perfect freedom. Mr. Godwin does not think himself
that this freedom would lead to a promiscuous intercourse, and in
this I perfectly agree with him. The love of variety is a vicious,
corrupt, and unnatural taste and could not prevail in any great
degree in a simple and virtuous state of society. Each man would
probably select himself a partner to whom he would adhere as
long as that adherence continued to be the choice of both parties.
It would be of little consequence, according to Mr. Godwin, how
many children a woman had or to whom they belonged. Provisions
and assistance would spontaneously flow from the quarter in which
they abounded, to the quarter that was deficient.[8] And every
man would be ready to furnish instruction to the rising generation
according to his capacity.

I cannot conceive a form of society so favourable upon the
whole to population. The irremediableness of marriage, as it is at
present constituted, undoubtedly deters many from entering into
that state. An unshackled intercourse on the contrary would be a
most powerful incitement to early attachments, and us we are supposing no anxiety about the future support of children to exist, I
do not conceive that there would be one woman in a hundred, of
twenty three, without a family.

With these extraordinary encouragements to population, and every
cause of depopulation, as we have supposed, removed, the numbers would necessarily increase faster than in any society that has
ever yet been known. I have mentioned, on the authority of a
pamphlet published by a Dr. Styles and referred to by Dr. Price,
that the inhabitants of the back settlements of America doubled

8. *Enquiry concerning Political Justice*, Book 8, p. 504. [Malthus' note. The editor has expanded this and some others of Malthus' notes to include full biblio-graphical information.]

their numbers in fifteen years. England is certainly a more healthy country than the back settlements of America, and as we have supposed every house in the island to be airy and wholesome, and the encouragements to have a family greater even than with the back settlers, no probable reason can be assigned why the population should not double itself in less, if possible, than fifteen years. But to be quite sure that we do not go beyond the truth, we will only suppose the period of doubling to be twenty-five years, a ratio of increase which is well known to have taken place throughout all the Northern States of America.

There can be little doubt that the equalization of property which we have supposed, added to the circumstance of the labour of the whole community being directed chiefly to agriculture, would tend greatly to augment the produce of the country. But to answer the demands of a population increasing so rapidly, Mr. Godwin's calculation of half an hour a day for each man would certainly not be sufficient. It is probable that the half of every man's time must be employed for this purpose. Yet with such, or much greater exertions, a person who is acquainted with the nature of the soil in this country, and who reflects on the fertility of the lands already in cultivation, and the barrenness of those that are not cultivated, will be very much disposed to doubt whether the whole average produce could possibly be doubled in twenty-five years from the present period. The only chance of success would be the ploughing up all the grazing countries and putting an end almost entirely to the use of animal food. Yet a part of this scheme might defeat itself. The soil of England will not produce much without dressing, and cattle seem to be necessary to make that species of manure which best suits the land. In China it is said that the soil in some of the provinces is so fertile as to produce two crops of rice in the year without dressing. None of the lands in England will answer to this description.

Difficult, however, as it might be to double the average produce of the island in twenty-five years, let us suppose it effected. At the expiration of the first period therefore, the food, though almost entirely vegetable, would be sufficient to support in health the doubled population of fourteen millions.

During the next period of doubling, where will the food be found to satisfy the importunate demands of the increasing numbers? Where is the fresh land to turn up? where is the dressing necessary to improve that which is already in cultivation? There is no person with the smallest knowledge of land, but would say that it was impossible that the average produce of the country could be increased during the second twenty-five years by a quantity equal to what it at present yields. Yet we will suppose this increase, however improbable, to take place. The exuberant strength of the argument allows of almost any concession. Even with this concession, however, there would be seven millions at the expiration of the second term, unprovided for. A quantity of food equal to the frugal support of twenty-one millions, would be to be divided among twenty-eight millions.

Alas! what becomes of the picture where men lived in the midst of plenty, where no man was obliged to provide with anxiety and pain for his restless wants, where the narrow principle of self-ishness did not exist, where Mind was delivered from her per-petual anxiety about corporal support and free to expatiate in the field of thought which is congenial to her? This beautiful fabric of imagination vanishes at the severe touch of truth. The spirit of benevolence, cherished and invigorated by plenty, is repressed by the chilling breath of want. The hateful passions that had vanished, reappear. The mighty law of self-preservation expels all the softer and more exalted emotions of the soul. The temptations to evil are too strong for human nature to resist. The corn is plucked before it is ripe, or secreted in unfair proportions, and the whole black train of vices that belong to falsehood are immediately generated. Provisions no longer flow in for the support of the mother with a large family. The children are sickly from insufficient food. The rosy flush of health gives place to the pallid cheek and hollow eye of misery. Benevolence yet lingering in a few bosoms makes some faint expiring struggles, till at length self-love resumes his wonted empire and lords it triumphant over the world.

No human institutions here existed, to the perverseness of which Mr. Godwin ascribes the original sin of the worst men.[9] No opposition had been produced by them between public and private good. No monopoly had been created of those advantages which reason directs to be left in common. No man had been goaded to the breach of order by unjust laws. Benevolence had established her reign in all hearts; and yet in so short a period as within fifty years, violence, oppression, falsehood, misery, every hateful vice, and every form of distress, which degrade and sadden the present state of society, seem to have been generated by the most imperi-ous circumstances, by laws inherent in the nature of man, and absolutely independent of all human regulations.

If we are not yet too well convinced of the reality of this melan-choly picture, let us but look for a moment into the next period of twenty-five years, and we shall see twenty-eight millions of human beings without the means of support; and before the con-clusion of the first century, the population would be one hundred and twelve millions, and the food only sufficient for thirty-five mil-

9. *Ibid.*, p. 340.

lions, leaving seventy-seven millions unprovided for. In these ages want would be indeed triumphant, and rapine and murder must reign at large; and yet all this time we are supposing the produce of the earth absolutely unlimited, and the yearly increase greater than the boldest speculator can imagine.

This is undoubtedly a very different view of the difficulty arising from population from that which Mr. Godwin gives when he says, "Myriads of centuries of still increasing population may pass away, and the earth be still found sufficient for the subsistence of its inhabitants."

I am sufficiently aware that the redundant twenty-eight millions, or seventy-seven millions, that I have mentioned, could never have existed. It is a perfectly just observation of Mr. Godwin that "There is a principle in human society, by which population is perpetually kept down to the level of the means of subsistence." The sole question is, what is this principle? Is it some obscure and occult cause? Is it some mysterious interference of heaven, which at a certain period, strikes the men with impotence, and the women with barrenness? Or is it a cause open to our researches, within our view, a cause which has constantly been observed to operate, though with varied force, in every state in which man has been placed? Is it not a degree of misery, the necessary and inevitable result of the laws of nature, which human institutions, so far from aggravating, have tended considerably to mitigate, though they never can remove?

It may be curious to observe, in the case that we have been supposing, how some of the laws which at present govern civilized society would be successively dictated by the most imperious necessity. As man, according to Mr. Godwin, is the creature of the impressions to which he is subject, the goadings of want could not continue long, before some violations of public or private stock would necessarily take place. As these violations increased in number and extent, the more active and comprehensive intellects of the society would soon perceive that while population was fast increasing, the yearly produce of the country would shortly begin to diminish. The urgency of the case would suggest the necessity of some immediate measures to be taken for the general safety. Some kind of convention would then be called and the dangerous situation of the country stated in the strongest terms. It would be observed that while they lived in the midst of plenty, it was of little consequence who laboured the least, or who possessed the least, as every man was perfectly willing and ready to supply the wants of his neighbour. But that the question was no longer whether one man should give to another that which he did not use himself; but whether he should give to his neighbour the food which was absolutely necessary to his own existence. It would be represented that the number of those that were in want very greatly exceeded the number and means of those who should supply them; that these pressing wants, which from the state of the produce of the country could not all be gratified, had occasioned some flagrant violations of justice; that these violations had already checked the increase of food, and would, if they were not by some means or other prevented, throw the whole community in confusion; that imperious necessity seemed to dictate that a yearly increase of produce should, if possible, be obtained at all events; that in order to effect this first, great, and indispensible purpose, it would be adviseable to make a more complete division of land, and to secure every man's stock against violation by the most powerful sanctions, even by death itself.

It might be urged perhaps by some objectors, that, as the fertility of the land increased and various accidents occurred, the share of some men might be much more than sufficient for their support, and that when the reign of self-love was once established, they would not distribute their surplus produce without some compensation in return. It would be observed in answer, that this was an inconvenience greatly to be lamented, but that it was an evil which bore no comparison to the black train of distresses, that would inevitably be occasioned by the insecurity of property: that the quantity of food which one man could consume was necessarily limited by the narrow capacity of the human stomach; that it was not certainly probable that he should throw away the rest; but that even if he exchanged his surplus food for the labour of others, and made them in some degree dependent on him, this would still be better than that these others should absolutely starve.

It seems highly probable, therefore, that an administration of property, not very different from that which prevails in civilized States at present, would be established as the best, though inadequate, remedy for the evils which were pressing on the society.

The next subject that would come under discussion, intimately connected with the preceding, is the commerce between the sexes. It would be urged by those who had turned their attention to the true cause of the difficulties under which the community laboured, that while every man felt secure that all his children would be well provided for by general benevolence, the powers of the earth would be absolutely inadequate to produce food for the population which would inevitably ensue; that even, if the whole attention and labour of the society were directed to this sole point, and if, by the most perfect security of property and every other encouragement that could be thought of, the greatest possible increase of produce were yearly obtained, yet still, that the increase of food would by no means keep pace with the much more rapid increase of population; that some check to population therefore was imperiously called for; that the most natural and obvious check seemed to be, to make every man provide for his own children; that this would operate in some respect as a measure and guide, in the increase of population; as it might be expected that no man would bring beings into the world for whom he could not find the means of support; that where this notwithstanding was the case, it seemed necessary, for the example of others, that the disgrace and inconvenience attending such a conduct, should fall upon the individual who had thus inconsiderately plunged himself and innocent children in misery and want.

The institution of marriage, or at least of some express or implied obligation on every man to support his own children, seemed to be the natural result of these reasonings in a community under the difficulties that we have supposed.

The view of these difficulties presents us with a very natural origin of the superior disgrace which attends a breach of chastity in the woman, than in the man. It could not be expected that women should have resources sufficient to support their own children. When therefore a woman was connected with a man who had entered into no compact to maintain her children, and aware of the inconveniences that he might bring upon himself, had deserted her, these children must necessarily fall for support upon the society, or starve. And to prevent the frequent recurrence of such an inconvenience, as it would be highly unjust to punish so natural a fault by personal restraint or infliction, the men might agree to punish it with disgrace. The offence is besides more obvious and conspicuous in the woman, and less liable to any mistake. The father of a child may not always be known, but the same uncertainty cannot easily exist with regard to the mother. Where the evidence of the offence was most complete, and the inconvenience to the society at the same time the greatest, there, it was agreed, that the largest share of blame should fall. The obligation on every man to maintain his children, the society would enforce if there were occasion; and the greater degree of inconvenience or labour to which a family would necessarily subject him, added to some portion of disgrace which every human being must incur, who leads another into unhappiness, might be considered as a sufficient punishment for the man.

That a woman should at present be almost driven from society for an offence which men commit nearly with impunity, seems to be undoubtedly a breach of natural justice. But the origin of the custom, as the most obvious and effectual method of preventing the frequent recurrence of a serious inconvenience to a community, appears to be natural, though not perhaps perfectly justifiable. This origin, however, is now lost in the new train of ideas which the custom has since generated. What at first might be dictated by state necessity is now supported by female delicacy; and operates with the greatest force on that part of society where, if the original intention of the custom were preserved, there is the least real occasion for it.

When these two fundamental laws of society, the security of property and the institution of marriage, were once established, inequality of conditions must necessarily follow. Those who were born after the division of property, would come into a world already possessed. If their parents, from having too large a family, could not give them sufficient for their support, what are they to do in a world where every thing is appropriated? We have seen the fatal effects that would result to a society if every man had a valid claim to an equal share of the produce of the earth. The members of a family which was grown too large for the original division of land appropriated to it could not then demand a part of the surplus produce of others, as a debt of justice. It has appeared that from the inevitable laws of our nature, some human beings must suffer from want. These are the unhappy persons who, in the great lottery of life, have drawn a blank. The number of these claimants would soon exceed the ability of the surplus produce to supply. Moral merit is a very difficult distinguishing criterion, except in extreme cases. The owners of surplus produce would in general seek some more obvious mark of distinction. And it seems both natural and just, that except upon particular occasions, their choice should fall upon those who were able, and professed themselves willing, to exert their strength in procuring a further surplus produce; and thus at once benefitting the community and enabling these proprietors to afford assistance to greater numbers. All who were in want of food would be urged by imperious necessity to offer their labour in exchange for this article so absolutely essential to existence. The fund appropriated to the maintenance of labour would be the aggregate quantity of food possessed by the owners of land beyond their own consumption. When the demands upon this fund were great and numerous, it would naturally be divided in very small shares. Labour would be ill paid. Men would offer to work for a bare subsistence, and the rearing of families would be checked by sickness and misery. On the contrary, when this fund was increasing fast, when it was great in proportion to the number of claimants, it would be divided in much larger shares. No man would exchange his labour without receiving an ample quantity of food in return. Labourers would live in ease and comfort and would consequently be able to rear a numerous and vigorous offspring.

On the state of this fund, the happiness or the degree of misery prevailing among the lower classes of people in every known State at present chiefly depends. And on this happiness or degree of misery depends the increase, stationariness, or decrease of population.

And thus it appears that a society constituted according to the most beautiful form that imagination can conceive, with benevolence for its moving principle instead of self-love, and with every evil disposition in all its members corrected by reason and not force, would, from the inevitable laws of nature, and not from any original depravity of man, in a very short period degenerate into a society constructed upon a plan not essentially different from that which prevails in every known State at present; I mean, a society divided into a class of proprietors, and a class of labourers, and with self-love the main-spring of the great machine.

In the supposition I have made, I have undoubtedly taken the increase of population smaller, and the increase of produce greater, than they really would be. No reason can be assigned, why, under the circumstances I have supposed, population should not increase faster than in any known instance. If then we were to take the period of doubling at fifteen years, instead of twenty-five years, and reflect upon the labour necessary to double the produce in so short a time, even if we allow it possible, we may venture to pronounce with certainty that if Mr. Godwin's system of society was established in its utmost perfection, instead of myriads of centuries, not thirty years could elapse before its utter destruction from the simple principle of population.

I have taken no notice of emigration for obvious reasons. If such societies were instituted in other parts of Europe, these countries would be under the same difficulties with regard to population, and could admit no fresh members into their bosoms. If this beautiful society were confined to this island, it must have degenerated strangely from its original purity, and administer but a very small portion of the happiness it proposed; in short, its essential principle must be completely destroyed before any of its members would voluntarily consent to leave it and live under such governments as at present exist in Europe, or submit to the extreme hardships of first settlers in new regions. We well know from repeated experience how much misery and hardship men will undergo in their own country before they can determine to desert it, and how often the most tempting proposals of embarking for new settlements have been rejected by people who appeared to be almost starving.

CHAPTER XI

Mr. Godwin's conjecture concerning the future extinction of the passion between the sexes—Little apparent grounds for such a conjecture—Passion of love not inconsistent either with reason or virtue.

We have supposed Mr. Godwin's system of society once completely established. But it is supposing an impossibility. The same causes in nature which would destroy it so rapidly, were it once established, would prevent the possibility of its establishment. And upon what grounds we can presume a change in these natural causes, I am utterly at a loss to conjecture. No move towards the extinction of the passion between the sexes has taken place in the five or six thousand years that the world has existed. Men in the decline of life have in all ages declaimed a passion which they have ceased to feel, but with as little reason as success. Those who from coldness of constitutional temperament have never felt what love is, will surely be allowed to be very incompetent judges with regard to the power of this passion to contribute to the sum of pleasurable sensations in life. Those who have spent their youth in criminal excesses and have prepared for themselves, as the comforts of their age corporal debility and mental remorse may well inveigh against such pleasures as vain and futile, and unproductive of lasting satisfaction. But the pleasures of pure love will bear the contemplation of the most improved reason, and the most exalted virtue. Perhaps there is scarcely a man who has once experienced the genuine delight of virtuous love, however great his intellectual pleasures may have been, that does not look back to the period as the sunny spot in his whole life, where his imagination loves to bask, which he recollects and contemplates with the fondest regrets, and which he would most wish to live over again. The superiority of intellectual to sensual pleasures consists rather in their filling up more time, in their having a larger range, and in their being less liable to satiety, than in their being more real and essential.

Intemperance in every enjoyment defeats its own purpose. A walk in the finest day through the most beautiful country, if pursued too far, ends in pain and fatigue. The most wholesome and invigorating food, eaten with an unrestrained appetite, produces weakness instead of strength. Even intellectual pleasures, though certainly less liable than others to satiety, pursued with too little intermission, debilitate the body and impair the vigour of the mind. To argue against the reality of these pleasures from their abuse seems to be hardly just. Morality, according to Mr. Godwin, is a calculation of consequences, or, as Archdeacon Paley very justly expresses it, the will of God, as collected from general expediency. According to either of these definitions, a sensual pleasure not attended with the probability of unhappy consequences does not offend against the laws of morality, and if it be pursued with such a degree of temperance as to leave the most ample room for intellectual attainments, it must undoubtedly add to the sum of pleasurable sensations in life. Virtuous love, exalted by friendship, seems to be that sort of mixture of sensual and intellectual enjoyment particularly suited to the nature of man, and most powerfully calculated to awaken the sympathies of the soul and produce the most exquisite gratifications.

Mr. Godwin says, in order to shew the evident inferiority of the pleasures of sense, "Strip the commerce of the sexes of all its attendant circumstances,[1] and it would be generally despised." He might as well say to a man who admired trees: strip them of their spreading branches and lovely foliage, and what beauty can you see in a bare pole? But it was the tree with the branches and foliage, and not without them, that excited admiration. One feature of an object may be as distinct, and excite as different emotions, from the aggregate, as any two things the most remote, as a beautiful woman and a map of Madagascar. It is "the symmetry of person, the vivacity, the voluptuous softness of temper, the affectionate kindness of feelings, the imagination and the wit" of a woman that excite the passion of love, and not the mere distinction of her being a female. Urged by the passion of love, men have been driven into acts highly prejudicial to the general interests of society, but probably they would have found no difficulty in resisting the temptation, had it appeared in the form of a woman with no other attractions whatever but her sex. To strip sensual pleasures of all their adjuncts, in order to prove their inferiority, is to deprive a magnet of some of its most essential causes of attraction, and then to say that it is weak and inefficient.

In the pursuit of every enjoyment, whether sensual or intellectual, Reason, that faculty which enables us to calculate consequences, is the proper corrective and guide. It is probable therefore that improved reason will always tend to prevent the abuse of sensual pleasures, though it by no means follows that it will extinguish them.

I have endeavored to expose the fallacy of that argument which infers an unlimited progress from a partial improvement, the limits of which cannot be exactly ascertained. It has appeared, I think, that there are many instances in which a decided progress

1. *Ibid.*, Book I, Chapter 5, p. 73.

has been observed, where yet it would be a gross absurdity to suppose that progress indefinite. But towards the extinction of the passion between the sexes, no observable progress whatever has hitherto been made. To suppose such an extinction, therefore, is merely to offer an unfounded conjecture, unsupported by any philosophical probabilities.

It is a truth, which history I am afraid makes too clear, that some men of the highest mental powers have been addicted not only to a moderate, but even to an immoderate indulgence in the pleasures of sensual love. But allowing, as I should be inclined to do, notwithstanding numerous instances to the contrary, that great intellectual exertions tend to diminish the empire of this passion over man, it is evident that the mass of mankind must be improved more highly than the brightest ornaments of the species at present before any difference can take place sufficient sensibly to affect population. I would by no means suppose that the mass of mankind has reached its term of improvement, but the principal argument of this essay tends to place in a strong point of view the improbability that the lower classes of people in any country should ever be sufficiently free from want and labour to obtain any high degree of intellectual improvement.

CHAPTER XII

Mr. Godwin's conjecture concerning the indefinite prolongation of human life—Improper inference drawn from the effects of mental stimulants on the human frame, illustrated in various instances—Conjectures not founded on any indications in the past, not to be considered as philosophical conjectures—Mr. Godwin's and Mr. Condorcet's conjecture respecting the approach of man towards immortality on earth, a curious instance of the inconsistency of scepticism.

Mr. Godwin's conjecture respecting the future approach of man towards immortality on earth seems to be rather oddly placed in a chapter which professes to remove the objection to his system of equality from the principle of population. Unless he supposes the passion between the sexes to decrease faster than the duration of life increases, the earth would be more encumbered than ever. But leaving this difficulty to Mr. Godwin, let us examine a few of the appearances from which the probable immortality of man is inferred.

To prove the power of the mind over the body, Mr. Godwin

observes, "How often do we find a piece of good news dissipating a distemper? How common is the remark that those accidents which are to the indolent a source of disease are forgotten and extirpated in the busy and active? I walk twenty miles in an indolent and half determined temper and am extremely fatigued. I walk twenty miles full of ardour, and with a motive that engrosses my soul, and I come in as fresh and as alert as when I began my journey. Emotions excited by some unexpected word, by a letter that is delivered to us, occasions the most extraordinary revolutions in our frame, accelerates the circulation, causes the heart to palpitate, the tongue to refuse its office, and has been known to occasion death by extreme anguish or extreme joy. There is nothing indeed of which the physician is more aware than of the power of the mind in assisting or retarding convalescence."

The instances here mentioned, are chiefly instances of the effects of mental stimulants on the bodily frame. No person has ever for a moment doubted the near, though mysterious connection of mind and body. But it is arguing totally without knowledge of the nature of stimulants to suppose, either that they can be applied continually with equal strength, or if they could be so applied for a time, that they would not exhaust and wear out the subject. In some of the cases here noticed, the strength of the stimulus depends upon its novelty and unexpectedness. Such a stimulus cannot, from its nature, be repeated often with the same effect, as it would by repetition lose that property which gives it its strength.

In the other cases, the argument is from a small and partial effect to a great and general effect, which will in numberless instances be found to be a very fallacious mode of reasoning. The busy and active man may in some degree counteract, or what is perhaps nearer the truth, may disregard those slight disorders of frame, which fix the attention of a man who has nothing else to think of; but this does not tend to prove that activity of mind will enable a man to disregard a high fever, the smallpox, or the plague.

The man who walks twenty miles with a motive that engrosses his soul does not attend to his slight fatigue of body when he comes in; but double his motive, and set him to walk another twenty miles, quadruple it, and let him start a third time, and so on; and the length of his walk will ultimately depend upon muscle and not mind. Powel, for a motive of ten guineas, would have walked further probably than Mr. Godwin, for a motive of half a million. A motive of uncommon power acting upon a frame of moderate strength, would, perhaps, make the man kill himself by his exertions, but it would not make him walk an hundred miles in twenty-four hours. This statement of the case shews the fallacy of supposing that the person was really not at all tired in his first walk of twenty miles, because he did not appear to be so, or, perhaps, scarcely felt any fatigue himself. The mind cannot fix its attention strongly on more than one object at once. The twenty thousand pounds so engrossed his thoughts, that he did not attend to any slight soreness of foot or stiffness of limb. But had he been really as fresh and as alert as when he first set off, he would be able to go the second twenty miles with as much ease as the first, and so on, the third, &c., which leads to a palpable absurdity. When a horse of spirit is nearly half tired, by the stimulus of the spur, added to the proper management of the bit, he may be put so much upon his mettle, that he would appear to a stander-by as fresh and as high spirited as if he had not gone a mile. Nay, probably the horse himself, while in the heat and passion occasioned by this stimulus, would not feel any fatigue; but it would be strangely contrary to all reason and experience to argue from such an appearance that if the stimulus were continued, the horse would never be tired. The cry of a pack of hounds will make some horses, after a journey of forty miles on the road, appear as fresh, and as lively, as when they first set out. Were they then to be hunted, no perceptible abatement would at first be felt by their riders in their strength and spirits, but towards the end of a hard day, the previous fatigue would have its full weight and effect, and make them tire sooner. When I have taken a long walk with my gun and met with no success, I have frequently returned home feeling a considerable degree of uncomfortableness from fatigue. Another day, perhaps, going over nearly the same extent of ground with a good deal of sport, I have come home fresh and alert. The difference in the sensation of fatigue upon coming in, on the different days, may have been very striking, but on the following mornings I have found no such difference. I have not perceived that I was less stiff in my limbs, or less footsore, on the morning after the day of the sport, than on the other morning.

In all these cases, stimulants upon the mind seem to act rather by taking off the attention from the bodily fatigue, than by really and truly counteracting it. If the energy of my mind had really counteracted the fatigue of my body, why should I feel tired the next morning? If the stimulus of the hounds had as completely overcome the fatigue of the journey in reality, as it did in appearance, why should the horse be tired sooner than if he had not gone the forty miles? I happen to have a very bad fit of the toothache at the time I am writing this. In the eagerness of composition, I every now and then, for a moment or two, forget it. Yet I cannot help thinking that the process which causes the pain is still going forwards, and that the nerves which carry the information of it to the brain are even during these moments demanding attention and room for their appropriate vibrations. The multiplicity of vibrations of another kind may perhaps prevent their admission, or overcome them for a time when admitted, till a shoot of extraordinary energy puts all other vibrations to the rout, destroys the vividness of my argumentative conceptions, and rides triumphant in the brain. In this case, as in the others, the mind seems to have little or no power in counteracting, or curing the disorder, but merely possesses a power, if strongly excited, of fixing its attention on other subjects.

I do not, however, mean to say that a sound and vigorous mind has no tendency whatever to keep the body in a similar state. So close and intimate is the union of mind and body that it would be highly extraordinary if they did not mutually assist each other's functions. But, perhaps, upon a comparison, the body has more effect upon the mind, than the mind upon the body. The first object of the mind is to act as purveyor to the wants of the body. When these wants are completely satisfied, an active mind is indeed apt to wander further, to range over the fields of science, or sport in the regions of imagination, to fancy that it has "shuffled off this mortal coil," and is seeking its kindred element. But all these efforts are like the vain exertions of the hare in the fable. The slowly moving tortoise, the body, never fails to overtake the mind, however widely and extensively it may have ranged, and the brightest and most energetic intellects, unwillingly as they may attend to the first or second summons, must ultimately yield the empire of the brain to the calls of hunger, or sink with the exhausted body in sleep.

It seems as if one might say with certainty that if a medicine could be found to immortalize the body, there would be no fear of its being accompanied by the immortality of the mind. But the immortality of the mind by no means seems to infer the immortality of the body. On the contrary, the greatest conceivable energy of mind would probably exhaust and destroy the strength of the body. A temperate vigour of mind appears to be favourable to health, but very great intellectual exertions tend rather, as has been often observed, to wear out the scabbard. Most of the instances which Mr. Godwin has brought to prove the power of the mind over the body, and the consequent probability of the immortality of man, are of this latter description, and could such stimulants be continually applied, instead of tending to immortalize, they would tend very rapidly to destroy the human frame.

The probable increase of the voluntary power of man over his animal frame comes next under Mr. Godwin's consideration, and he concludes by saying that the voluntary power of some men, in this respect, is found to extend to various articles in which other men are impotent. But this is reasoning against an almost universal rule from a few exceptions; and these exceptions seem to be rather tricks, than powers that may be exerted to any good purpose. I have never heard of any man who could regulate his pulse in a fever, and doubt much, if any of the persons here alluded to have made the smallest perceptible progress in the regular correction of the disorders of their frames and the consequent prolongation of their lives.

Mr. Godwin says, "Nothing can be more unphilosophical than to conclude, that, because a certain species of power is beyond the train of our present observation, that it is beyond the limits of the human mind." I own my ideas of philosophy are in this respect widely different from Mr. Godwin's. The only distinction that I see between a philosophical conjecture and the assertions of the Prophet Mr. Brothers is, that one is founded upon indications arising from the train of our present observations, and the other has no foundation at all. I expect that great discoveries are yet to take place in all the branches of human science, particularly in physics; but the moment we leave past experience as the foundation of our conjectures concerning the future; and still more, if our conjectures absolutely contradict past experience, we are thrown upon a wide field of uncertainty, and any one supposition is then just as good as another. If a person were to tell me that men would ultimately have eyes and hands behind them as well as before them, I should admit the usefulness of the addition, but should give as a reason for my disbelief of it, that I saw no indications whatever in the past from which I could infer the smallest probability of such a change. If this be not allowed a valid objection, all conjectures are alike, and all equally philosophical. I own it appears to me that in the train of our present observations, there are no more genuine indications that man will become immortal upon earth, than that he will have four eyes and four hands, or that trees will grow horizontally instead of perpendicularly.

It will be said, perhaps, that many discoveries have already taken place in the world that were totally unforeseen and unexpected. This I grant to be true; but if a person had predicted these discoveries without being guided by any analogies or indications from past facts, he would deserve the name of seer or prophet, but not of philosopher. The wonder that some of our modern discoveries would excite in the savage inhabitants of Europe in the times of Theseus and Achilles proves but little. Persons almost entirely unacquainted with the powers of a machine cannot be expected to guess at its effects. I am far from saying that we are at present by any means fully acquainted with the powers of the human mind; but we certainly know more of this instrument than was known four thousand years ago; and therefore, though not to be called competent judges, we are certainly much better able than savages to say what is, or is not, within its grasp. A watch would strike a Savage with as much surprize as a perpetual motion; yet one is to us a most familiar piece of mechanism and the other has constantly eluded the efforts of the most acute intellects. In many instances we are now able to perceive the causes which prevent an unlimited improvement in those inventions which seemed to promise fairly for it at first. The original improvers of telescopes would probably think that as long as the size of the specula and the length of the tubes could be increased, the powers and advantages of the instrument would increase; but experience has since taught us, that the smallness of the field, the deficiency of light, and the circumstance of the atmosphere being magnified prevent the beneficial results that were to be expected from telescopes of extraordinary size and power. In many parts of knowledge, man has been almost constantly making some progress; in other parts, his efforts have been invariably baffled. The Savage would not probably be able to guess at the causes of this mighty difference. Our further experience has given us some little insight into these causes, and has therefore enabled us better to judge, if not of what we are to expect in future, at least of what we are not to expect, which, though negative, is a very useful piece of information.

As the necessity of sleep seems rather to depend upon the body than the mind, it does not appear how the improvement of the mind can tend very greatly to supersede this "conspicuous infirmity." A man who by great excitements on his mind is able to pass two or three nights without sleep, proportionably exhausts the vigour of his body, and this diminution of health and strength will soon disturb the operations of his understanding, so that by these great efforts he appears to have made no real progress whatever in superseding the necessity of this species of rest.

There is certainly a sufficiently marked difference in the various characters of which we have some knowledge, relative to the energies of their minds, their benevolent pursuits, &c. to enable us to judge whether the operations of intellect have any decided effect in prolonging the duration of human life. It is certain that no decided effect of this kind has yet been observed. Though no attention of any kind has ever produced such an effect as could be construed into the smallest semblance of an approach towards immortality, yet of the two, a certain attention to the body seems to have more effect in this respect than an attention to the mind. The man who takes his temperate meals and his bodily exercise with scrupulous regularity, will generally be found more healthy than the man who, very deeply engaged in intellectual pursuits, often forgets for a time these bodily cravings. The citizen who has retired, and whose ideas, perhaps, scarcely soar above or extend beyond his little garden, puddling all the morning about his borders of box, will, perhaps, live as long as the philosopher whose range of intellect is the most extensive, and whose views are the clearest of any of his contemporaries. It has been positively observed by those who have attended to the bills of mortality that women live longer upon an average than men, and, though I would not by any means say that their intellectual faculties are inferior, yet, I think, it must be allowed that from their different education, there are not so many women as men who are excited to vigorous mental exertion.

As in these and similar instances, or to take a larger range, as in the great diversity of characters that have existed during some thousand years, no decided difference has been observed in the duration of human life from the operation of intellect, the mortality of man on earth seems to be as completely established, and exactly upon the same grounds, as any one, the most constant, of the laws of nature. An immediate act of power in the Creator of the Universe might, indeed, change one or all of these laws, either suddenly or gradually, but without some indications of such a change, and such indications do not exist, it is just as unphilosophical to suppose that the life of man may be prolonged beyond any assignable limits, as to suppose that the attraction of the earth will gradually be changed into repulsion and that stones will ultimately rise instead of fall or that the earth will fly off at a certain period to some more genial and warmer sun.

The conclusion of this chapter presents us, undoubtedly, with a very beautiful and desireable picture, but from fancy and not imagined with truth, it fails of that interest in the heart which nature and probability can alone give.

I cannot quit this subject without taking notice of these conjectures of Mr. Godwin and Mr. Condorcet concerning the indefinite prolongation of human life, as a very curious instance of the longing of the soul after immortality. Both these gentlemen have rejected the light of revelation which absolutely promises eternal life in another state. They have also rejected the light of natural religion, which to the ablest intellects in all ages, has indicated the future existence of the soul. Yet so congenial is the idea of immortality to the mind of man that they cannot consent entirely to throw it out of their systems. After all their fastidious scepticisms concerning the only probable mode of immortality, they introduce a species of immortality of their own, not only completely contradictory to every law of philosophical probability, but in itself in the highest degree, narrow, partial, and unjust. They suppose that all the great, virtuous, and exalted minds that have ever existed or that may exist for some thousands, perhaps millions of years, will be sunk in annihilation, and that only a few beings, not greater in number than can exist at once upon the earth, will be ultimately crowned with immortality. Had such a tenet been advanced as a tenet of revelation I am very sure that all the enemies of religion, and probably Mr. Godwin and Mr. Condorcet among the rest, would have exhausted the whole force of their ridicule upon it, as the most puerile, the most absurd, the poorest, the most pitiful, the most iniquitously unjust, and consequently, the most unworthy of the Deity that the superstitious folly of man could invent.

What a strange and curious proof do these conjectures exhibit of the inconsistency of scepticism! For it should be observed that there is a very striking and essential difference between believing an assertion which absolutely contradicts the most uniform experience, and an assertion which contradicts nothing, but is merely beyond the power of our present observation and knowledge.[2] So diversified are the natural objects around us, so many instances of mighty power daily offer themselves to our view, that we may fairly presume that there are many forms and operations of nature which we have not yet observed, or which, perhaps, we are not capable of observing with our present confined inlets of knowledge. The resurrection of a spiritual body from a natural body does not appear in itself a more wonderful instance of power than the germination of a blade of wheat from the grain, or of an oak from an acorn. Could we conceive an intelligent being so placed as to be conversant only with inanimate or full grown objects, and never to have witnessed the process of vegetation or growth; and were another being to shew him two little pieces of matter, a grain of wheat, and an acorn, to desire him to examine them, to analize them if he pleased, and endeavour to find out their properties and

2. When we extend our view beyond this life, it is evident that we can have no other guides than authority, or conjecture, and perhaps, indeed, an obscure and undefined feeling. What I say here, therefore, does not appear to me in any respect to contradict what I said before, when I observed that it was unphilosophical to expect any specifick event that was not indicated by some kind of analogy in the past. In ranging beyond the bourne from which no traveller returns, we must necessarily quit this rule; but with regard to events that may be expected to happen on earth, we can seldom quit it consistently with true philosophy. Analogy has, however, as I conceive, great latitude. For instance, man has discovered many of the laws of nature: analogy seems to indicate that he will discover many more; but no analogy seems to indicate that he will discover a sixth sense, or a new species of power in the human mind, entirely beyond the train of our present observations.

essences; and then to tell him, that however trifling these little bits of matter might appear to him, that they possessed such curious powers of selection, combination, arrangement, and almost of creation, that upon being put into the ground, they would chuse, amongst all the dirt and moisture that surrounded them, those parts which best suited their purpose, that they would collect and arrange these parts with wonderful taste, judgment, and execution, and would rise up into beautiful forms, scarcely in any respect analogous to the little bits of matter which were first placed in the earth, I feel very little doubt that the imaginary being which I have supposed would hesitate more, would require better authority, and stronger proofs, before he believed these strange assertions, than if he had been told that a being of mighty power, who had been the cause of all that he saw around him, and of that existence of which he himself was conscious, would, by a great act of power upon the death and corruption of human creatures, raise up the essence of thought in an incorporeal, or at least invisible form, to give it a happier existence in another state.

The only difference, with regard to our own apprehensions, that is not in favour of the latter assertion is that the first miracle[3] we have repeatedly seen, and the last miracle we have not seen. I admit the full weight of this prodigious difference, but surely no man can hesitate a moment in saying that, putting Revelation out of the question, the resurrection of a spiritual body from a natural body, which may be merely one among the many operations of nature which we cannot see, is an event indefinitely more probable than the immortality of man on earth, which is not only an event of which no symptoms or indications have yet appeared, but is a positive contradiction to one of the most constant of the laws of nature that has ever come within the observation of man.

I ought perhaps again to make an apology to my readers for dwelling so long upon a conjecture which many, I know, will think too absurd and improbable to require the least discussion. But if it be as improbable and as contrary to the genuine spirit of philosophy

---

3. The powers of selection, combination, and transmutation, which every seed shews, are truely miraculous. Who can imagine that these wonderful faculties are contained in these little bits of matter? To me it appears much more philosophical to suppose that the mighty God of nature is present in full energy in all these operations. To this all powerful Being, it would be equally easy to raise an oak without an acorn as with one. The preparatory process of putting seeds into the ground is merely ordained for the use of man, as one among the various other excitements necessary to awaken matter into mind. It is an idea that will be found consistent equally with the natural phenomena around us, with the various events of human life, and with the successive Revelations of God to man, to suppose that the world is a mighty process for the creation and formation of mind. Many vessels will necessarily come out of this great furnace in wrong shapes. These will be broken and thrown aside as useless; while those vessels whose forms are full of truth, grace, and loveliness will be wafted into happier situations nearer the presence of the mighty maker.

as I own I think it is, why should it not be shewn to be so in a candid examination? A conjecture, however improbable on the first view of it, advanced by able and ingenious men, seems at least to deserve investigation. For my own part I feel no disinclination whatever to give that degree of credit to the opinion of the probable immortality of man on earth, which the appearances that can be brought in support of it deserve. Before we decide upon the utter improbability of such an event, it is but fair impartially to examine these appearances; and from such an examination I think we may conclude that we have rather less reason for supposing that the life of man may be indefinitely prolonged, than that trees may be made to grow indefinitely high, or potatoes indefinitely large.[4]

CHAPTER XIII

Error of Mr. Godwin in considering man too much in the light of a being merely rational—In the compound being, man, the passions will always act as disturbing forces in the decisions of the understanding—Reasonings of Mr. Godwin on the subject of coercion—Some truths of a nature not to be communicated from one man to another.

In the chapter which I have been examining, Mr. Godwin professes to consider the objection to his system of equality from the principle of population. It has appeared, I think clearly, that he is greatly erroneous in his statement of the distance of this difficulty, and that instead of myriads of centuries, it is really not thirty years, or even thirty days, distant from us. The supposition of the approach of man to immortality on earth is certainly not of a kind to soften the difficulty. The only argument, therefore, in the chapter which has any tendency to remove the objection is the conjecture concerning the extinction of the passion between the sexes, but as this is a mere conjecture, unsupported by the smallest shadow of proof, the force of the objection may be fairly said to remain unimpaired, and it is undoubtedly of sufficient weight of itself completely to overturn Mr. Godwin's whole system of equality. I will, however, make one or two observations on a few of the prominent parts of Mr. Godwin's reasonings which will contribute to place in a still clearer point of view the little hope that

4. Though Mr. Godwin advances the idea of the indefinite prolongation of human life merely as a conjecture, yet as he has produced some appearances, which in his conception favour the supposition, he must certainly intend that these appearances should be examined and this is all that I have meant to do.

we can reasonably entertain of those vast improvements in the nature of man and of society which he holds up to our admiring gaze in his political justice.

Mr. Godwin considers man too much in the light of a being merely intellectual. This error, at least such I conceive it to be, pervades his whole work and mixes itself with all his reasonings. The voluntary actions of men may originate in their opinions, but these opinions will be very differently modified in creatures compounded of a rational faculty and corporal propensities from what they would be in beings wholly intellectual. Mr. Godwin in proving that sound reasoning and truth are capable of being adequately communicated, examines the proposition first practically, and then adds, "Such is the appearance which this proposition assumes, when examined in a loose and practical view. In strict consideration it will not admit of debate. Man is a rational being, &c."[5] So far from calling this a strict consideration of the subject, I own I should call it the loosest and most erroneous way possible, of considering it. It is the calculating the velocity of a falling body in vacuo, and persisting in it, that it would be the same through whatever resisting mediums it might fall. This was not Newton's mode of philosophizing. Very few general propositions are just in application to a particular subject. The moon is not kept in her orbit round the earth, nor the earth in her orbit round the sun, by a force that varies merely in the inverse ratio of the squares of the distances. To make the general theory just in application to the revolutions of these bodies, it was necessary to calculate accurately, the disturbing force of the sun upon the moon, and of the moon upon the earth; and till these disturbing forces were properly estimated, actual observations on the motions of these bodies would have proved that the theory was not accurately true.

I am willing to allow that every voluntary act is preceded by a decision of the mind, but it is strangely opposite to what I should conceive to be the just theory upon the subject, and a palpable contradiction to all experience, to say that the corporal propensities of man do not act very powerfully, as disturbing forces, in these decisions. The question, therefore, does not merely depend upon whether a man may be made to understand a distinct proposition or be convinced by an unanswerable argument. A truth may be brought home to his conviction as a rational being, though he may determine to act contrary to it, as a compound being. The cravings of hunger, the love of liquor, the desire of possessing a beautiful woman will urge men to actions, of the fatal consequences of which, to the general interests of society, they are perfectly well convinced, even at the very time they commit them. Remove their

5. *Ibid.*, p. 89.

bodily cravings, and they would not hesitate a moment in determining against such actions. Ask them their opinion of the same conduct in another person, and they would immediately reprobate it. But in their own case, and under all the circumstances of their situation with these bodily cravings, the decision of the compound being is different from the conviction of the rational being.

If this be the just view of the subject, and both theory and experience unite to prove that it is, almost all Mr. Godwin's reasonings on the subject of coercion in his 7th chapter will appear to be founded on error. He spends some time in placing in a ridiculous point of view the attempt to convince a man's understanding and to clear up a doubtful proposition in his mind, by blows. Undoubtedly it is both ridiculous and barbarous, and so is cockfighting, but one has little more to do with the real object of human punishments than the other. One frequent (indeed much too frequent) mode of punishment is death. Mr. Godwin will hardly think this intended for conviction, at least it does not appear how the individual or the society could reap much future benefit from an understanding enlightened in this manner.

The principal objects which human punishments have in view are undoubtedly restraint and example, restraint, or removal of an individual member whose vicious habits are likely to be prejudicial to the society. And example, which by expressing the sense of the community with regard to a particular crime, and by associating more nearly and visibly, crime and punishment, holds out a moral motive to dissuade others from the commission of it.

Restraint, Mr. Godwin thinks, may be permitted as a temporary expedient, though he reprobates solitary imprisonment, which has certainly been the most successful, and, indeed, almost the only attempt towards the moral amelioration of offenders. He talks of the selfish passions that are fostered by solitude and of the virtues generated in society. But surely these virtues are not generated in the society of a prison. Were the offender confined to the society of able and virtuous men he would probably be more improved than in solitude. But is this practicable? Mr. Godwin's ingenuity is more frequently employed in finding out evils than in suggesting practical remedies.

Punishment, for example, is totally reprobated. By endeavouring to make examples too impressive and terrible, nations have indeed been led into the most barbarous cruelties, but the abuse of any practice is not a good argument against its use. The indefatigable pains taken in this country to find out a murder, and the certainty of its punishment, has powerfully contributed to generate that sentiment which is frequent in the mouths of the common people, that a murder will sooner or later come to light; and the habitual horror in which murder is in consequence held, will make a man, in the agony of passion, throw down his knife for fear he should be tempted to use it in the gratification of his revenge. In Italy, where murderers by flying to a sanctuary are allowed more frequently to escape, the crime has never been held in the same detestation and has consequently been more frequent. No man, who is at all aware of the operation of moral motives, can doubt for a moment, that if every murder in Italy had been invariably punished, the use of the stilletto in transports of passion would have been comparatively but little known.

That human laws either do, or can, proportion the punishment accurately to the offence, no person will have the folly to assert. From the inscrutability of motives the thing is absolutely impossible, but this imperfection, though it may be called a species of injustice, is no valid argument against human laws. It is the lot of man, that he will frequently have to chuse between two evils; and it is a sufficient reason for the adoption of any institution, that it is the best mode that suggests itself of preventing greater evils. A continual endeavour should undoubtedly prevail to make these institutions as perfect as the nature of them will admit. But nothing is so easy, as to find fault with human institutions; nothing so difficult, as to suggest adequate practical improvements. It is to be lamented that more men of talents employ their time in the former occupation than in the latter.

The frequency of crime among men, who, as the common saying is, know better, sufficiently proves, that some truths may be brought home to the conviction of the mind without always producing the proper effect upon the conduct. There are other truths of a nature that perhaps never can be adequately communicated from one man to another. The superiority of the pleasures of intellect to those of sense Mr. Godwin considers as a fundamental truth. Taking all circumstances into consideration, I should be disposed to agree with him; but how am I to communicate this truth to a person who has scarcely ever felt intellectual pleasure. I may as well attempt to explain the nature and beauty of colours to a blind man. If I am ever so laborious, patient, and clear, and have the most repeated opportunities of expostulation, any real progress toward the accomplishment of my purpose seems absolutely hopeless. There is no common measure between us. I cannot proceed step by step: it is a truth of a nature absolutely incapable of demonstration. All that I can say is that the wisest and best men in all ages had agreed in giving the preference very greatly to the pleasures of intellect; and that my own experience completely confirmed the truth of their decisions; that I had found sensual pleasures vain, transient, and continually attended with tedium and disgust; but that intellectual pleasures appeared to me ever fresh and young, filled up all my hours satisfactorily, gave a new zest to life, and diffused a lasting serenity over my mind. If he believe me, it can only be from respect and veneration for my authority: it is credulity, and not conviction. I have not said any thing, nor can any thing be said of a nature to produce real conviction. The affair is not an affair of reasoning, but of experience. He would probably observe in reply, what you say may be very true with regard to yourself and many other good men, but for my own part I feel very differently upon the subject. I have very frequently taken up a book, and almost as frequently gone to sleep over it; but when I pass an evening with a gay party, or a pretty woman, I feel alive, and in spirits, and truly enjoy my existence.

Under such circumstances, reasoning and arguments are not instruments from which success can be expected. At some future time perhaps, real satiety of sensual pleasures, or some accidental impressions that awakened the energies of his mind, might effect that, in a month, which the most patient and able expostulations, might be incapable of effecting in forty years.

CHAPTER XIV

Mr. Godwin's five propositions respecting political truth, on which his whole work hinges, not established—Reasons we have for supposing from the distress occasioned by the principle of population, that the vices, and moral weakness of man can never be wholly eradicated—Perfectibility, in the sense in which Mr. Godwin uses the term, not applicable to man—Nature of the real perfectibility of man illustrated.

If the reasonings of the preceding chapter are just, the corollaries respecting political truth, which Mr. Godwin draws from the proposition, that the voluntary actions of men originate in their opinions, will not appear to be clearly established. These corollaries are, "Sound reasoning and truth, when adequately communicated, must always be victorious over error: Sound reasoning and truth are capable of being so communicated: Truth is omnipotent: The vices and moral weakness of man are not invincible: Man is perfectible, or in other words, susceptible of perpetual improvement."

The first three propositions may be considered a complete syllogism. If by adequately communicated, be meant such a conviction as to produce an adequate effect upon the conduct, the major may be allowed and the minor denied. The consequent, or the omnipotence of truth, of course falls to the ground. If by adequately communicated be meant merely the conviction of the rational faculty, the major must be denied, the minor will be only true in cases capable of demonstration, and the consequent equally falls. The fourth proposition, Mr. Godwin calls the preceding proposition, with a slight variation in the statement. If so, it must accompany the preceding proposition in its fall. But it may be worth while to inquire, with reference to the principal argument of this essay, into the particular reasons which we have for supposing that the vices and moral weakness of man can never be wholly overcome in this world.

Man, according to Mr. Godwin, is a creature formed what he is by the successive impressions which he has received, from the first moment that the germ from which he sprung was animated. Could he be placed in a situation where he was subject to no evil impressions whatever, though it might be doubted whether in such a situation virtue could exist, vice would certainly be banished. The great bent of Mr. Godwin's work on political justice, if I understand it rightly, is to shew that the greater part of the vices and weaknesses of men proceed from the injustice of their political and social institutions, and that if these were removed and the understandings of men more enlightened, there would be little or no temptation in the world to evil. As it has been clearly proved, however (at least as I think), that this is entirely a false conception, and that independent of any political or social institutions whatever, the greater part of mankind, from the fixed and unalterable laws of nature, must ever be subject to the evil temptations arising from want, besides other passions; it follows from Mr. Godwin's definition of man that such impressions, and combinations of impressions, cannot be afloat in the world without generating a variety of bad men. According to Mr. Godwin's own conception of the formation of character, it is surely as improbable that under such circumstances all men will be virtuous as that sixes will come up a hundred times following upon the dice. The great variety of combinations upon the dice in a repeated succession of throws appears to me not inaptly to represent the great variety of character that must necessarily exist in the world, supposing every individual to be formed what he is by that combination of impressions which he has received since his first existence. And this comparison will, in some measure, shew the absurdity of supposing, that exceptions will ever become general rules; that extraordinary and unusual combinations will be frequent; or that the individual instances of great virtue which have appeared in all ages of the world will ever prevail universally.

I am aware that Mr. Godwin might say that the comparison is in one respect inaccurate, that in the case of the dice, the preceding causes, or rather the chances respecting the preceding causes, were always the same, and that therefore I could have no good reason for supposing that a greater number of sixes would come up in the next hundred times of throwing than in the preceding same number of throws. But, that man had in some sort a power of influencing those causes that formed character, and that every good and virtuous man that was produced, by the influence which he must necessarily have, rather increased the probability that another such virtuous character would be generated, whereas the coming up of sixes upon the dice once, would certainly not increase the probability of their coming up a second time. I admit this objection to the accuracy of the comparison, but it is only partially valid. Repeated experience has assured us that the influence of the most virtuous character will rarely prevail against very strong temptations to evil. It will undoubtedly affect some, but it will fail with a much greater number. Had Mr. Godwin succeeded in his attempt to prove that these temptations to evil could by the exertions of man be removed, I would give up the comparison; or at least allow that a man might be so far enlightened with regard to the mode of shaking his elbow, that he would be able to throw sixes every time. But as long as a great number of those impressions which form character, like the nice motions of the arm, remain absolutely independent of the will of man; though it would be the height of folly and presumption to attempt to calculate the relative proportions of virtue and vice at the future periods of the world; it may be safely asserted that the vices and moral weakness of mankind, taken in the mass, are invincible.

The fifth proposition is the general deduction from the four former and will consequently fall, as the foundations which support it have given way. In the sense in which Mr. Godwin understands the term perfectible, the perfectibility of man cannot be asserted, unless the preceding propositions could have been clearly established. There is, however, one sense which the term will bear, in which it is, perhaps, just. It may be said with truth that man is always susceptible of improvement, or that there never has been, or will be, a period of his history in which he can be said to have reached his possible acme of perfection. Yet it does not by any means follow from this, that our efforts to improve man will always succeed, or even that he will ever make, in the greatest number of ages, any extraordinary strides towards perfection. The only inference that can be drawn is that the precise limit of his improvement cannot possibly be known. And I cannot help again reminding the reader of a distinction which, it appears to me, ought particularly to be attended to in the present question: I mean, the essential difference there is between an unlimited improvement and an improvement the limit of which cannot be ascertained. The former is an improvement not applicable to man under the present laws of his nature. The latter, undoubtedly, is applicable.

The real perfectibility of man may be illustrated, as I have mentioned before, by the perfectibility of a plant. The object of the enterprising florist is, as I conceive, to unite size, symmetry, and beauty of colour. It would surely be presumptuous in the most successful improver to affirm that he possessed a carnation in which these qualities existed in the greatest possible state of perfection. However beautiful his flower may be, other care, other soil, or other suns might produce one still more beautiful. Yet, although he may be aware of the absurdity of supposing that he has reached perfection; and though he may know by what means he attained that degree of beauty in the flower which he at present possesses, yet he cannot be sure that by pursuing similar means, rather increased in strength, he will obtain a more beautiful blossom. By endeavouring to improve one quality, he may impair the beauty of another. The richer mould which he would employ to increase the size of his plant would probably burst the calyx and destroy at once its symmetry. In a similar manner, the forcing manure used to bring about the French revolution, and to give a greater freedom and energy to the human mind, has burst the calyx of humanity, the restraining bond of all society; and however large the separate petals have grown, however strongly or even beautifully a few of them have been marked, the whole is at present a loose, deformed, disjointed mass, without union, symmetry, or harmony of colouring.

Were it of consequence to improve pinks and carnations, though we could have no hope of raising them as large as cabbages, we might undoubtedly expect, by successive efforts, to obtain more beautiful specimens than we at present possess. No person can deny the importance of improving the happiness of the human species. Every the least advance in this respect is highly valuable. But an experiment with the human race is not like an experiment upon inanimate objects. The bursting of a flower may be a trifle. Another will soon succeed it. But the bursting of the bonds of society is such a separation of parts as cannot take place without giving the most acute pain to thousands, and a long time may elapse, and much misery may be endured, before the wound grows up again.

As the five propositions which I have been examining may be considered as the corner stones of Mr. Godwin's fanciful structure, and, indeed, as expressing the aim and bent of his whole work, however excellent much of his detached reasoning may be, he must be considered as having failed in the great object of his undertaking. Besides the difficulties arising from the compound nature of man, which he has by no means sufficiently smoothed, the principal argument against the perfectibility of man and society remains whole and unimpaired from any thing that he has advanced. And as far as I can trust my own judgment, this argument appears to be conclusive not only against the perfectibility of man, in the enlarged sense in which Mr. Godwin understands the term, but against any very marked and striking change for the better, in the form and structure of general society, by which I mean any great and decided amelioration of the condition of the lower classes of mankind, the most numerous and, consequently, in a general view of the subject, the most important part of the human race. Were I to live a thousand years, and the laws of nature to remain the same, I should little fear, or rather little hope, a contradiction from experience in asserting that no possible sacrifices or exertions of the rich, in a country which had been long inhabited, could for any time place the lower classes of the community in a situation equal, with regard to circumstances, to the situation of the common people about thirty years ago in the northern States of America.

The lower classes of people in Europe may at some future period be much better instructed than they are at present; they may be taught to employ the little spare time they have in many better ways than at the ale-house; they may live under better and more equal laws than they have ever hitherto done, perhaps, in any country; and I even conceive it possible, though not probable, that they may have more leisure; but it is not in the nature of things, that they can be awarded such a quantity of money or subsistence, as will allow them all to marry early, in the full confidence that they shall be able to provide with ease for a numerous family.

CHAPTER XV

*Models too perfect, may sometimes rather impede than
promote improvement—Mr. Godwin's essay on avarice
and profusion—Impossibility of dividing the necessary
labour of a society amicably among all—Invectives
against labour may produce present evil, with little or
no chance of producing future good—An accession to
the mass of agricultural labour must always be an advantage to the labourer.*

Mr. Godwin in the preface to his Enquirer drops a few expres-
sions which seem to hint at some change in his opinions since he
wrote the Political Justice; and as this is a work now of some
years' standing, I should certainly think that I had been arguing
against opinions which the author had himself seen reason to alter,
but that in some of the essays of the Enquirer, Mr. Godwin's
peculiar mode of thinking appears in as striking a light as ever.

It has been frequently observed that though we cannot hope to
reach perfection in any thing, yet that it must always be advantageous to us to place before our eyes the most perfect models.
This observation has a plausible appearance, but is very far from
being generally true. I even doubt its truth in one of the most
obvious exemplifications that would occur. I doubt whether a very
young painter would receive so much benefit from an attempt to
copy a highly finished and perfect picture as from copying one
where the outlines were more strongly marked and the manner of
laying on the colours was more easily discoverable. But in cases
where the perfection of the model is a perfection of a different
and superior nature from that towards which we should naturally
advance, we shall not always fail in making any progress towards
it, but we shall in all probability impede the progress which we
might have expected to make had we not fixed our eyes upon so
perfect a model. A highly intellectual being, exempt from the
infirm calls of hunger or sleep, is undoubtedly a much more perfect
existence than man, but were man to attempt to copy such a model,
he would not only fail in making any advances towards it; but by
unwisely straining to imitate what was inimitable, he would probably destroy the little intellect which he was endeavouring to
improve.

The form and structure of society which Mr. Godwin describes is
as essentially distinct from any forms of society which have
hitherto prevailed in the world, as a being that can live without

food or sleep is from a man. By improving society in its present form, we are making no more advances towards such a state of things as he pictures, than we should make approaches towards a line, with regard to which we were walking parallel. The question therefore is whether, by looking to such a form of society as our polar star, we are likely to advance or retard the improvement of the human species? Mr. Godwin appears to me to have decided this question against himself in his essay on avarice and profusion in the Enquirer.

Dr. Adam Smith has very justly observed that nations as well as individuals grow rich by parsimony and poor by profusion, and that therefore every frugal man was a friend and every spend-thrift an enemy to his country. The reason he gives is that what is saved from revenue is always added to stock, and is therefore taken from the maintenance of labour that is generally unproductive and employed in the maintenance of labour that realizes itself in valuable commodities. No observation can be more evidently just. The subject of Mr. Godwin's essay is a little similar in its first appearance, but in essence is as distinct as possible. He considers the mischief of profusion as an acknowledged truth, and therefore makes his comparison between the avaricious man, and the man who spends his income. But the avaricious man of Mr. Godwin is totally a distinct character, at least with regard to his effect upon the prosperity of the state, from the frugal man of Dr. Adam Smith. The frugal man in order to make more money saves from his income and adds to his capital, and this capital he either employs himself in the maintenance of productive labour, or he lends it to some other person who will probably employ it in this way. He benefits the state because he adds to its general capital, and because wealth employed as capital not only sets in motion more labour, than when spent as income, but the labour is besides of a more valuable kind. But the avaricious man of Mr. Godwin locks up his wealth in a chest and sets in motion no labour of any kind, either productive or unproductive. This is so essential a difference that Mr. Godwin's decision in his essay appears at once as evidently false as Dr. Adam Smith's position is evidently true. It could not, indeed, but occur to Mr. Godwin, that some present inconvenience might arise to the poor, from thus locking up the funds destined for the maintenance of labour. The only way, therefore, he had of weakening this objection was to compare the two characters chiefly with regard to their tendency to accelerate the approach of that happy state of cultivated equality, on which he says we ought always to fix our eyes as our polar star.

I think it has been proved in the former parts of this essay that such a state of society is absolutely impracticable. What consequences then are we to expect from looking to such a point as our guide and polar star in the great sea of political discovery? Reason would teach us to expect no other than winds perpetually adverse, constant but fruitless toil, frequent shipwreck, and certain misery. We shall not only fail in making the smallest real approach towards such a perfect form of society; but by wasting our strength of mind and body in a direction in which it is impossible to proceed, and by the frequent distress which we must necessarily occasion by our repeated failures, we shall evidently impede that degree of improvement in society which is really attainable.

It has appeared that a society constituted according to Mr. Godwin's system must, from the inevitable laws of our nature, degenerate into a class of proprietors and a class of labourers, and that the substitution of benevolence for self-love as the moving principle of society, instead of producing the happy effects that might be expected from so fair a name, would cause the same pressure of want to be felt by the whole of society which is now felt only by a part. It is to the established administration of property and to the apparently narrow principle of self-love that we are indebted for all the noblest exertions of human genius, all the finer and more delicate emotions of the soul, for everything, indeed, that distinguishes the civilized from the savage state; and no sufficient change has as yet taken place in the nature of civilized man, to enable us to say that he either is, or ever will be, in a state when he may safely throw down the ladder by which he has risen to this eminence.

If in every society that has advanced beyond the savage state, a class of proprietors and a class of labourers[6] must necessarily exist, it is evident that, as labour is the only property of the class of labourers, every thing that tends to diminish the value of this property must tend to diminish the possessions of this part of society. The only way that a poor man has of supporting himself in independence is by the exertion of his bodily strength. This is the only commodity he has to give in exchange for the necessaries of life. It would hardly appear then that you benefit him by narrowing the market for this commodity, by decreasing the demand for labour, and lessening the value of the only property that he possesses.

6. It should be observed that the principal argument of this essay only goes to prove the necessity of a class of proprietors and a class of labourers, but by no means infers that the present great inequality of property is either necessary or useful to society. On the contrary, it must certainly be considered as an evil, and every institution that promotes it is essentially bad and impolitic. But whether a government could with advantage to society actively interfere to repress inequality of fortunes, may be a matter of doubt. Perhaps the generous system of perfect liberty adopted by Dr. Adam Smith and the French economists would be ill exchanged for any system of restraint.

Mr. Godwin would perhaps say that the whole system of barter and exchange is a vile and iniquitous traffic. If you would essentially relieve the poor man, you should take a part of his labour upon yourself, or give him your money without exacting so severe a return for it. In answer to the first method proposed, it may be observed that even if the rich could be persuaded to assist the poor in this way, the value of the assistance would be comparatively trifling. The rich, though they think themselves of great importance, bear but a small proportion in point of numbers to the poor, and would therefore relieve them but of a small part of their burdens by taking a share. Were all those that are employed in the labours of luxuries, added to the number of those employed in producing necessaries; and could these necessary labours be amicably divided among all, each man's share might indeed be comparatively light; but desirable as such an amicable division would undoubtedly be, I cannot conceive any practical principle[7] according to which it could take place. It has been shewn that the spirit of benevolence, guided by the strict impartial justice that Mr. Godwin describes, would, if vigorously acted upon, depress in want and misery the whole human race. Let us examine what would be the consequence if the proprietor were to retain a decent share for himself, but to give the rest away to the poor without exacting a task from them in return. Not to mention the idleness and the vice that such a proceeding, if general, would probably create in the present state of society, and the great risk there would be of diminishing the produce of land, as well as the labours of luxury, another objection yet remains.

It has appeared that from the principle of population more will always be in want than can be adequately supplied. The surplus of the rich man might be sufficient for three, but four will be desirous to obtain it. He cannot make this selection of three out of the four without conferring a great favour on those that are the objects of his choice. These persons must consider themselves as under a great obligation to him and as dependent upon him for their support. The rich man would feel his power and the poor man his dependence, and the evil effects of these two impressions on the human heart are well known. Though I perfectly agree with Mr. Godwin therefore in the evil of hard labour, yet I still think it a less evil, and less calculated to debase the human mind, than dependence, and every history of man that we have ever read,

7. Mr. Godwin seems to have but little respect for practical principles; but I own it appears to me, that he is a much greater benefactor to mankind, who points out how an inferior good may be attained, than he who merely expatiates on the deformity of the present state of society and the beauty of a different state, without pointing out a practical method, that might be immediately applied, of accelerating our advances from the one to the other.

places in a strong point of view the danger to which that mind is exposed, which is intrusted with constant power.

In the present state of things, and particularly when labour is in request, the man who does a day's work for me confers full as great an obligation upon me as I do upon him. I possess what he wants, he possesses what I want. We make an amicable exchange. The poor man walks erect in conscious independence; and the mind of his employer is not vitiated by a sense of power.

Three or four hundred years ago, there was undoubtedly much less labour in England, in proportion to the population, than at present, but there was much more dependence, and we probably should not now enjoy our present degree of civil liberty if the poor, by the introduction of manufactures, had not been enabled to give something in exchange for the provisions of the great Lords, instead of being dependent upon their bounty. Even the greatest enemies of trade and manufactures, and I do not reckon myself a very determined friend to them, must allow that when they were introduced into England, liberty came in their train.

Nothing that has been said tends in the most remote degree to undervalue the principle of benevolence. It is one of the noblest and most godlike qualities of the human heart, generated perhaps, slowly and gradually from self-love, and afterwards intended to act as a general law, whose kind office it should be to soften the partial deformities, to correct the asperities, and to smooth the wrinkles of its parent; and this seems to be the analogy of all nature. Perhaps there is no one general law of nature that will not appear, to us at least, to produce partial evil; and we frequently observe at the same time, some bountiful provision, which acting as another general law, corrects the inequalities of the first.

The proper office of benevolence is to soften the partial evils arising from self-love, but it can never be substituted in its place. If no man were to allow himself to act till he had completely determined that the action he was about to perform was more conducive than any other to the general good, the most enlightened minds would hesitate in perplexity and amazement; and the unenlightened would be continually committing the grossest mistakes.

As Mr. Godwin, therefore, has not laid down any practical principle according to which the necessary labours of agriculture might be amicably shared among the whole class of labourers, by general invectives against employing the poor he appears to pursue an unattainable good through much present evil. For if every man who employs the poor ought to be considered as their enemy, and as adding to the weight of their oppressions, and if the miser is for this reason to be preferred to the man who spends his income, it follows that any number of men who now spend their incomes might, to the advantage of society, be converted into misers. Suppose then that a hundred thousand persons who now employ ten men each were to lock up their wealth from general use, it is evident, that a million of working men of different kinds would be completely thrown out of all employment. The extensive misery that such an event would produce in the present state of society, Mr. Godwin himself could hardly refuse to acknowledge, and I question whether he might not find some difficulty in proving that a conduct of this kind tended more than the conduct of those who spend their incomes to "place human beings in the condition in which they ought to be placed."

But Mr. Godwin says that the miser really locks up nothing, that the point has not been rightly understood, and that the true development and definition of the nature of wealth have not been applied to illustrate it. Having defined therefore wealth, very justly, to be the commodities raised and fostered by human labour, he observes that the miser locks up neither corn, nor oxen, nor clothes, nor houses. Undoubtedly he does not really lock up these articles, but he locks up the power of producing them, which is virtually the same. These things are certainly used and consumed by his contemporaries, as truly and to as great an extent, as if he were a beggar; but not to as great an extent, as if he had employed his wealth in turning up more land, in breeding more oxen, in employing more taylors, and in building more houses. But supposing, for a moment, that the conduct of the miser did not tend to check any really useful produce, how are all those who are thrown out of employment to obtain patents which they may shew in order to be awarded a proper share of the food and raiment produced by the society? This is the unconquerable difficulty.

I am perfectly willing to concede to Mr. Godwin that there is much more labour in the world than is really necessary, and that, if the lower classes of society could agree among themselves never to work more than six or seven hours in the day, the commodities essential to human happiness might still be produced in as great abundance as at present. But it is almost impossible to conceive that such an agreement could be adhered to. From the principle of population, some would necessarily be more in want than others. Those that had large families would naturally be desirous of exchanging two hours more of their labour for an ampler quantity of subsistence. How are they to be prevented from making this exchange? It would be a violation of the first and most sacred property that a man possesses, to attempt, by positive institutions, to interfere with his command over his own labour.

Till Mr. Godwin, therefore, can point out some practical plan according to which the necessary labour in a society might be equitably divided, his invectives against labour, if they were attended to, would certainly produce much present evil without approximating us to that state of cultivated equality to which he looks forward as his polar star, and which, he seems to think, should at present be our guide in determining the nature and tendency of human actions. A mariner guided by such a polar star is in danger of shipwreck.

Perhaps there is no possible way in which wealth could in general be employed so beneficially to a state, and particularly to the lower orders of it, as by improving and rendering productive that land which to a farmer would not answer the expence of cultivation. Had Mr. Godwin exerted his energetic eloquence in painting the superior worth and usefulness of the character who employed the poor in this way, to him who employed them in narrow luxuries, every enlightened man must have applauded his efforts. The increasing demand for agricultural labour must always tend to better the condition of the poor; and if the accession of work be of this kind, so far is it from being true that the poor would be obliged to work ten hours for the same price that they before worked eight, that the very reverse would be the fact; and a labourer might then support his wife and family as well by the labour of six hours, as he could before by the labour of eight.

The labour created by luxuries, though useful in distributing the produce of the country without vitiating the proprietor by power or debasing the labourer by dependence, has not, indeed, the same beneficial effects on the state of the poor. A great accession of work from manufacturers, though it may raise the price of labour even more than an increasing demand for agricultural labour; yet, as in this case, the quantity of food in the country may not be proportionably increasing, the advantage to the poor will be but temporary, as the price of provisions must necessarily rise in proportion to the price of labour. Relative to this subject, I cannot avoid venturing a few remarks on a part of Dr. Adam Smith's *Wealth of Nations*, speaking at the same time with that diffidence which I ought certainly to feel in differing from a person so justly celebrated in the political world.

CHAPTER XVI

Probable error of Dr. Adam Smith in representing every increase of the revenue or stock of a society as an increase in the funds for the maintenance of labour— Instances where an increase of wealth can have no tendency to better the condition of the labouring poor—England has increased in riches without a proportional increase in the funds for the maintenance of labour—The state of the poor in China would not be improved by an increase of wealth from manufactures.

The professed object of Dr. Adam Smith's inquiry is the nature and causes of the wealth of nations. There is another inquiry, however, perhaps still more interesting, which he occasionally mixes with it, I mean an inquiry into the causes which affect the happiness of nations or the happiness and comfort of the lower orders of society, which is the most numerous class in every nation. I am sufficiently aware of the near connection of these two subjects, and that the causes which tend to increase the wealth of a State tend also, generally speaking, to increase the happiness of the lower classes of the people. But perhaps Dr. Adam Smith has considered these two inquiries as still more nearly connected than they really are; at least he has not stopped to take notice of those instances where the wealth of a society may increase (according to his definition of wealth) without having any tendency to increase the comforts of the labouring part of it. I do not mean to enter into a philosophical discussion of what constitutes the proper happiness of man, but shall merely consider two universally acknowledged ingredients, health, and the command of the necessaries and conveniences of life.

Little or no doubt can exist that the comforts of the labouring poor depend upon the increase of the funds destined for the maintenance of labour, and will be very exactly in proportion to the rapidity of this increase. The demand for labour which such increase would occasion, by creating a competition in the market, must necessarily raise the value of labour, and, till the additional number of hands required were reared, the increased funds would be distributed to the same number of persons as before the increase, and therefore every labourer would live comparatively at his ease. But perhaps Dr. Adam Smith errs in representing every increase of the revenue or stock of a society as an increase of these funds. Such surplus stock or revenue will, indeed, always be considered by the individual possessing it as an additional fund from which he may maintain more labour; but it will not be a real and effectual fund for the maintenance of an additional number of labourers, unless the whole, or at least a great part of this increase of the stock or revenue of the society, be convertible into a proportional quantity of provisions; and it will not be so convertible where the increase has arisen merely from the produce of labour, and not from the produce of land. A distinction will in this case occur, between the number of hands which the stock of the society could employ, and the number which its territory can maintain.

To explain myself by an instance. Dr. Adam Smith defines the wealth of a nation to consist in the annual produce of its land and labour. This definition evidently includes manufactured produce, as well as the produce of the land. Now supposing a nation for a course of years was to add what it saved from its yearly revenue to its manufacturing capital solely, and not to its capital employed upon land, it is evident that it might grow richer according to the above definition, without a power of supporting a greater number of labourers, and therefore, without an increase in the real funds for the maintenance of labour. There would, notwithstanding, be a demand for labour from the power which each manufacturer would possess, or at least think he possessed, of extending his old stock in trade or of setting up fresh works. This demand would of course raise the price of labour, but if the yearly stock of provisions in the country was not increasing, this rise would soon turn out to be merely nominal, as the price of provisions must necessarily rise with it. The demand for manufacturing labourers might, indeed, entice many from agriculture and thus tend to diminish the annual produce of the land, but we will suppose any effect of this kind to be compensated by improvements in the instruments of agriculture, and the quantity of provisions therefore to remain the same. Improvements in manufacturing machinery would of course take place, and this circumstance, added to the greater number of hands employed in manufactures, would cause the annual produce of the labour of the country to be upon the whole greatly increased. The wealth therefore of the country would be increasing annually, according to the definition, and might not, perhaps, be increasing very slowly.

The question is whether wealth, increasing in this way, has any tendency to better the condition of the labouring poor. It is a self-evident proposition that any general rise in the price of labour, the stock of provisions remaining the same, can only be a nominal rise, as it must very shortly be followed by a proportional rise in provisions. The increase in the price of labour therefore, which we have supposed, would have little or no effect in giving the labouring poor a greater command over the necessaries and conveniences of life. In this respect they would be nearly in the same state as before. In one other respect they would be in a worse state. A greater proportion of them would be employed in manufactures, and fewer, consequently, in agriculture. And this exchange of professions will be allowed, I think, by all, to be very unfavourable in respect of health, one essential ingredient of happiness, besides the greater uncertainty of manufacturing labour, arising from the capricious taste of man, the accidents of war, and other causes.

It may be said, perhaps, that such an instance as I have supposed could not occur, because the rise in the price of provisions would immediately turn some additional capital into the channel of agriculture. But this is an event which may take place very slowly, as it should be remarked that a rise in the price of labour had preceded the rise of provisions, and would therefore impede the good effects upon agriculture, which the increased value of the produce of the land might otherwise have occasioned.

It might also be said, that the additional capital of the nation would enable it to import provisions sufficient for the maintenance of those whom its stock could employ. A small country with a large navy, and great inland accommodations for carriage, such as Holland, may indeed import and distribute an effectual quantity of provisions; but the price of provisions must be very high to make such an importation and distribution answer in large countries less advantageously circumstanced in this respect.

An instance, accurately such as I have supposed, may not, perhaps, ever have occurred, but I have little doubt that instances nearly approximating to it may be found without any very laborious search. Indeed I am strongly inclined to think that England herself, since the revolution, affords a very striking elucidation of the argument in question.

The commerce of this country, internal as well as external, has certainly been rapidly advancing during the last century. The exchangeable value in the market of Europe of the annual produce of its land and labour has, without doubt, increased very considerably. But upon examination it will be found that the increase has been chiefly in the produce of labour and not in the produce of land, and therefore, though the wealth of the nation has been advancing with a quick pace, the effectual funds for the maintenance of labour have been increasing very slowly, and the result is such as might be expected. The increasing wealth of the nation has had little or no tendency to better the condition of the labouring poor. They have not, I believe, a greater command of the necessaries and conveniences of life, and a much greater proportion of them than at the period of the revolution is employed in manufactures and crowded together in close and unwholesome rooms.

Could we believe the statement of Dr. Price that the population of England has decreased since the revolution, it would even appear that the effectual funds for the maintenance of labour had been declining during the progress of wealth in other respects. For I conceive that it may be laid down as a general rule that if the effectual funds for the maintenance of labour are increasing, that is, if the territory can maintain as well as the stock employ a greater number of labourers, this additional number will quickly spring up, even in spite of such wars as Dr. Price enumerates. And consequently, if the population of any country has been stationary or declining, we may safely infer that however it may have advanced in manufacturing wealth, its effectual funds for the maintenance of labour cannot have increased.

It is difficult, however, to conceive that the population of England has been declining since the revolution, though every testimony concurs to prove that its increase, if it has increased, has been very slow. In the controversy which the question has occasioned, Dr. Price undoubtedly appears to be much more completely master of his subject, and to possess more accurate information than his opponents. Judging simply from this controversy, I think one should say that Dr. Price's point is nearer being proved than Mr. Howlett's. Truth probably lies between the two statements, but this supposition makes the increase of population since the revolution to have been very slow in comparison with the increase of wealth.

That the produce of the land has been decreasing, or even that it has been absolutely stationary during the last century, few will be disposed to believe. The inclosure of commons and waste lands certainly tends to increase the food of the country, but it has been asserted with confidence that the inclosure of common fields has frequently had a contrary effect, and that large tracts of land which formerly produced great quantities of corn, by being converted into pasture, both employ fewer hands and feed fewer mouths than before their inclosure. It is, indeed, an acknowledged truth, that pasture land produces a smaller quantity of human subsistence than corn land of the same natural fertility, and could it be clearly ascertained that from the increased demand for butcher's meat of the best quality, and its increased price in consequence, a greater quantity of good land has annually been employed in grazing, the diminution of human subsistence, which this circumstance would occasion, might have counterbalanced the advantages derived from the inclosure of waste lands and the general improvements in husbandry.

It scarcely need be remarked that the high price of butcher's meat at present, and its low price formerly, were not caused by the scarcity in the one case or the plenty in the other, but by the different expence sustained at the different periods, in preparing cattle for the market. It is, however, possible that there might have been more cattle a hundred years ago in the country than at present; but no doubt can be entertained that there is much more meat of a superior quality brought to market at present than ever there was. When the price of butcher's meat was very low, cattle were reared chiefly upon waste lands; and except for some of the principal markets, were probably killed with but little other fatting. The veal that is sold so cheap in some distant counties at present, bears little other resemblance than the name to that which is bought in London. Formerly, the price of butcher's meat would not pay for rearing, and scarcely for feeding cattle on land that would answer in tillage; but the present price will not only pay for fatting cattle on the very best land, but will even allow of the rearing many on land that would bear good crops of corn. The same number of cattle, or even the same weight of cattle at the different periods when killed, will have consumed (if I may be allowed the expression) very different quantities of human subsistence. A fatted beast may in some respects be considered, in the language of the French economists, as an unproductive labourer: he has added nothing to the value of the raw produce that he has consumed. The present system of grazing undoubtedly tends more than the former system to diminish the quantity of human subsistence in the country, in proportion to the general fertility of the land.

I would not by any means be understood to say that the former system either could or ought to have continued. The increasing price of butcher's meat is a natural and inevitable consequence of the general progress of cultivation; but I cannot help thinking, that the present great demand for butcher's meat of the best quality, and the quantity of good land that is in consequence annually employed to produce it, together with the great number of horses at present kept for pleasure, are the chief causes that have prevented the quantity of human food in the country from keeping pace with the generally increased fertility of the soil; and a change of custom in these respects would, I have little doubt, have a very sensible effect on the quantity of subsistence in the country, and consequently on its population.

The employment of much of the most fertile land in grazing, the improvements in agricultural instruments, the increase of large farms, and particularly the diminution of the number of cottages throughout the kingdom, all concur to prove that there are not probably so many persons employed in agricultural labour now as at the period of the revolution. Whatever increase of population, therefore, has taken place, must be employed almost wholly in manufactures, merely from the caprice of fashion, such as the adoption of muslins instead of silks, or of shoe-strings and covered buttons, instead of buckles and metal buttons, combined with the restraints in the market of labour arising from corporation and parish laws, have frequently driven thousands on charity for support. The great increase of the poor rates is, indeed, of itself a strong evidence that the poor have not a greater command of the necessaries and conveniences of life, and if to the consideration that their condition in this respect is rather worse than better, be added the circumstance that a much greater proportion of them is employed in large manufactories, unfavourable both to health and virtue, it must be acknowledged that the increase of wealth of late years, has had no tendency to increase the happiness of the labouring poor.

That every increase of the stock of revenue of a nation cannot be considered as an increase of the real funds for the maintenance of labour and, therefore, cannot have the same good effect upon the condition of the poor will appear in a strong light if the argument be applied to China.

Dr. Adam Smith observes that China has probably long been as rich as the nature of her laws and institutions will admit, but that with other laws and institutions, and if foreign commerce were had in honour, she might still be much richer. The question is, would such an increase of wealth be an increase of the real funds for the maintenance of labour, and consequently, tend to place the lower classes of people in China in a state of greater plenty?

It is evident, that if trade and foreign commerce were held in great honour in China, from the plenty of labourers, and the cheapness of labour she might work up manufactures for foreign sale to an immense amount. It is equally evident that from the great bulk of provisions and the amazing extent of her inland territory she could not in return import such a quantity as would be any sensible addition to the annual stock of subsistence in the country. Her immense amount of manufactures, therefore, she would exchange chiefly for luxuries collected from all parts of the world. At present it appears that no labour whatever is spared in the production of food. The country is rather over peopled in proportion to what its stock can employ, and labour is, therefore, so abundant, that no pains are taken to abridge it. The consequence of this is, probably, the greatest production of food that the soil can possibly afford, for it will be generally observed that processes for abridging labour, though they may enable a farmer to bring a certain quantity of grain cheaper to market, tend rather to diminish than increase the whole produce; and in agriculture, therefore, may in some respects be considered rather as private, than public advantages.

An immense capital could not be employed in China in preparing manufactures for foreign trade without taking off so many labourers from agriculture as to alter this state of things, and in some degree to diminish the produce of the country. The demand for manufacturing labourers would naturally raise the price of labour, but as the quantity of subsistence would not be increased, the price of provisions would keep pace with it, or even more than keep pace with it if the quantity of provisions were really decreasing. The country would be evidently advancing in wealth, the exchangeable value of the annual produce of its land and labour would be annually augmented, yet the real funds for the maintenance of labour would be stationary, or even declining, and, consequently, the increasing wealth of the nation would rather tend to depress than to raise the condition of the poor. With regard to the command over the necessaries and comforts of life, they would be in the same or rather worse state than before; and a great part of them would have exchanged the healthy labours of agriculture, for the unhealthy occupations of manufacturing industry.

The argument, perhaps, appears clearer when applied to China, because it is generally allowed that the wealth of China has been long stationary. With regard to any other country it might be always a matter of dispute at which of the two periods compared, wealth was increasing the fastest, as it is upon the rapidity of the increase of wealth at any particular period that Dr. Adam Smith says the condition of the poor depends. It is evident, however, that two nations might increase exactly with the same rapidity in the exchangeable value of the annual produce of their land and labour, yet if one had applied itself chiefly to agriculture, and the other chiefly to commerce, the funds for the maintenance of labour, and consequently the effect of the increase of wealth in each nation, would be extremely different. In that which had applied itself chiefly to agriculture, the poor would live in great plenty, and population would rapidly increase. In that which had applied itself chiefly to commerce, the poor would be comparatively but little benefited and consequently population would increase slowly.

CHAPTER XVII

*Question of the proper definition of the wealth of a state
—Reason given by the French Economists for considering
all manufacturers as unproductive labourers, not the true
reason—The labour of artificers and manufacturers sufficiently productive to individuals, though not to the state
—A remarkable passage in Dr. Price's two volumes of
observations—Error of Dr. Price in attributing the happiness and rapid population of America, chiefly, to its
peculiar state of civilization—No advantage can be
expected from shutting our eyes to the difficulties in the
way to the improvement of society.*

A question seems naturally to arise here whether the exchangeable value of the annual produce of the land and labour be the
proper definition of the wealth of a country, or whether the gross
produce of the land, according to the French economists, may not
be a more accurate definition. Certain it is that every increase of
wealth, according to the definition of the economists, will be an
increase of the funds for the maintenance of labour, and consequently will always tend to ameliorate the condition of the labouring poor, though an increase of wealth, according to Dr. Adam
Smith's definition, will by no means invariably have the same
tendency. And yet it may not follow from this consideration that
Dr. Adam Smith's definition is not just. It seems in many respects
improper to exclude the clothing and lodging of a whole people
from any part of their revenue. Much of it may, indeed, be of
very trivial and unimportant value in comparison with the food of
the country, yet still it may be fairly considered as a part of its
revenue, and, therefore, the only point in which I should differ
from Dr. Adam Smith, is where he seems to consider every increase
of the revenue or stock of a society as an increase of the funds for
the maintenance of labour, and consequently as tending always
to ameliorate the condition of the poor.

The fine silks and cottons, the laces, and other ornamental
luxuries of a rich country may contribute very considerably to augment the exchangeable value of its annual produce; yet they contribute but in a very small degree to augment the mass of happiness
in the society, and it appears to me that it is with some view to the
real utility of the produce that we ought to estimate the productiveness or unproductiveness of different sorts of labour. The French

economists consider all labour employed in manufactures as unproductive. Comparing it with the labour employed upon land, I should be perfectly disposed to agree with them, but not exactly for the reasons which they give. They say that labour employed upon land is productive because the produce, over and above completely paying the labourer and the farmer, affords a clear rent to the landlord, and that the labour employed upon a piece of lace is unproductive because it merely replaces the provisions that the workman had consumed, and the stock of his employer, without affording any clear rent whatever. But supposing the value of the wrought lace to be such, as that besides paying in the most complete manner the workman and his employer, it could afford a clear rent to a third person; it appears to me that in comparison with the labour employed upon land, it would be still as unproductive as ever. Though according to the reasoning used by the French economists, the man employed in the manufacture of lace would, in this case, seem to be a productive labourer; yet according to their definition of the wealth of a state, he ought not to be considered in that light. He will have added nothing to the gross produce of the land: he has consumed a portion of this gross produce, and has left a bit of lace in return; and though he may sell this bit of lace for three times the quantity of provisions that he consumed whilst he was making it, and thus be a very productive labourer with regard to himself; yet he cannot be considered as having added by his labour to any essential part of the riches of the state. The clear rent, therefore, that a certain produce can afford, after paying the expences of procuring it, does not appear to be the sole criterion by which to judge of the productiveness or unproductiveness to a state of any particular species of labour.

Suppose that two hundred thousand men, who are now employed in producing manufactures that only tend to gratify the vanity of a few rich people, were to be employed upon some barren and uncultivated lands, and to produce only half the quantity of food that they themselves consumed; they would be still more productive labourers with regard to the state than they were before, though their labour, so far from affording a rent to a third person, would but half replace the provisions used in obtaining the produce. In their former employment they consumed a certain portion of the food of the country and left in return some silks and laces. In their latter employment they consumed the same quantity of food and left in return provision for a hundred thousand men. There can be little doubt which of the two legacies would be the most really beneficial to the country, and it will, I think, be allowed that the wealth which supported the two hundred thousand men while they were producing silks and laces would have been more usefully employed in supporting them while they were producing the additional quantity of food.

A capital employed upon land may be unproductive to the individual that employs it and yet be highly productive to the society. A capital employed in trade, on the contrary, may be highly productive to the individual and yet be almost totally unproductive to the society; and this is the reason why I should call manufacturing labour unproductive in comparison of that which is employed in agriculture, and not for the reason given by the French economists. It is indeed almost impossible to see the great fortunes that are made in trade, and the liberality with which so many merchants live, and yet agree in the statement of the economists, that manufacturers can only grow rich by depriving themselves of the funds destined for their support. In many branches of trade the profits are so great as would allow of a clear rent to a third person; but as there is no third person in the case, and as all the profits centre in the master manufacturer or merchant, he seems to have a fair chance of growing rich without much privation; and we consequently see large fortunes acquired in trade by persons who have not been remarked for their parsimony.

Daily experience proves that the labour employed in trade and manufactures is sufficiently productive to individuals, but it certainly is not productive in the same degree to the state. Every accession to the food of a country tends to the immediate benefit of the whole society; but the fortunes made in trade tend but in a remote and uncertain manner to the same end, and in some respects have even a contrary tendency. The home trade of consumption is by far the most important trade of every nation. China is the richest country in the world, without any other. Putting then, for a moment, foreign trade out of the question, the man who by an engenious manufacture obtains a double portion out of the old stock of provisions will certainly not be so useful to the state as the man who, by his labour, adds a single share to the former stock. The consumable commodities of silks, laces, trinkets, and expensive furniture are undoubtedly a part of the revenue of the society; but they are the revenue only of the rich, and not of the society in general. An increase in this part of the revenue of a state, cannot therefore be considered of the same importance as an increase of food, which forms the principal revenue of the great mass of the people.

Foreign commerce adds to the wealth of a state, according to Dr. Adam Smith's definition, though not according to the definition of the economists. Its principal use, and the reason probably that it has in general been held in such high estimation, is that it adds greatly to the external power of a nation or to its power of commanding the labour of other countries; but it will be found, upon a near examination, to contribute but little to the increase of the internal funds for the maintenance of labour, and consequently but little to the happiness of the greatest part of society. In the natural progress of a state towards riches, manufactures and foreign commerce would follow, in their order, the high cultivation of the soil. In Europe, this natural order of things has been inverted, and the soil has been cultivated from the redundancy of manufacturing capital, instead of manufactures rising from the redundancy of capital employed upon land. The superior encouragement that has been given to the industry of the towns, and the consequent higher price that is paid for the labour of artificers, than for the labour of those employed in husbandry, are probably the reasons why so much soil in Europe remains uncultivated. Had a different policy been pursued throughout Europe, it might undoubtedly have been much more populous than at present, and yet not be more incumbered by its population.

I cannot quit this curious subject of the difficulty arising from population, a subject that appears to me to deserve a minute investigation and able discussion much beyond my power to give it, without taking notice of an extraordinary passage in Dr. Price's two volumes of Observations. Having given some tables on the probabilities of life in towns and in the country, he says,[8] "From this comparison, it appears with how much truth great cities hae been called the graves of mankind. It must also convince all who consider it, that according to the observation at the end of the fourth essay in the former volume, it is by no means strictly proper to consider our diseases as the original intention of nature. They are, without doubt, in general our own creation. *Were there a country where the inhabitants led lives entirely natural and virtuous, few of them would die without measuring out the whole period of present existence allotted to them; pain and distemper would be unknown among them, and death would come upon them like a sleep, in consequence of no other cause than gradual and unavoidable decay.*"

I own that I felt myself obliged to draw a very opposite conclusion from the facts advanced in Dr. Price's two volumes. I had for some time been aware that population and food increased in different ratios, and a vague opinion had been floating in my mind that they could only be kept equal by some species of misery or vice, but the perusal of Dr. Price's two volumes of Observations, after that opinion had been conceived, raised it at once to convic-

8. Richard Price, *Observations on Reversionary Payments* (1771), Volume 2, p. 243.

tion. With so many facts in his view to prove the extraordinary rapidity with which population increases when unchecked, and with such a body of evidence before him to elucidate even the manner by which the general laws of nature repress a redundant population, it is perfectly inconceivable to me how he could write the passage that I have quoted. He was a strenuous advocate for early marriages as the best preservative against vicious manners. He had no fanciful conceptions about the extinction of the passion between the sexes, like Mr. Godwin, nor did he ever think of eluding the difficulty in the ways hinted at by Mr. Condorcet. He frequently talks of giving the prolifick powers of nature room to exert themselves. Yet with these ideas, that his understanding could escape from the obvious and necessary inference that an unchecked population would increase beyond comparison faster than the earth, by the best directed exertions of man, could produce food for its support, appears to me as astonishing as if he had resisted the conclusion of one of the plainest propositions of Euclid.

Dr. Price, speaking of the different stages of the civilized state, says, "The first, or simple stages of civilization, are those which favour most the increase and the happiness of mankind." He then instances the American colonies, as being at that time in the first and happiest of the states that he had described, and as affording a very striking proof of the effects of the different stages of civilization on population. But he does not seem to be aware that the happiness of the Americans depended much less upon their peculiar degree of civilization than upon the peculiarity of their situation as new colonies, upon their having a great plenty of fertile uncultivated land. In parts of Norway, Denmark, or Sweden, or in this country two or three hundred years ago, he might have found perhaps nearly the same degree of civilization, but by no means the same happiness or the same increase of population. He quotes himself a statute of Henry the Eighth, complaining of the decay of tillage, and the enhanced price of provisions, "whereby a marvellous number of people were rendered incapable of maintaining themselves and families." The superior degree of civil liberty which prevailed in America contributed, without doubt, its share to promote the industry, happiness, and population of these states, but even civil liberty, all powerful as it is, will not create fresh land. The Americans may be said, perhaps, to enjoy a greater degree of civil liberty, now they are an independent people, than while they were in subjection to England, but we may be perfectly sure that population will not long continue to increase with the same rapidity as it did then.

A person who contemplated the happy state of the lower classes of people in America twenty years ago, would naturally wish to retain them for ever in that state, and might think, perhaps, that by preventing the introduction of manufactures and luxury he might effect his purpose; but he might as reasonably expect to prevent a wife or mistress from growing old by never exposing her to the sun or air. The situation of new colonies, well governed, is a bloom of youth that no efforts can arrest. There are, indeed, many modes of treatment in the political, as well as animal body, that contribute to accelerate or retard the approaches of age, but there can be no chance of success, in any mode that could be divised, for keeping either of them in perpetual youth. By encouraging the industry of the towns more than the industry of the country, Europe may be said, perhaps, to have brought on a premature old age. A different policy in this respect would infuse fresh life and vigour into every state. While from the law of primogeniture, and other European customs, land bears a monopoly price, a capital can never be employed in it with much advantage to the individual; and therefore it is not probable that the soil should be properly cultivated. And though in every civilized state, a class of proprietors and a class of labourers must exist; yet one permanent advantage would always result from a nearer equalization of property. The greater the number of proprietors, the smaller must be the number of labourers; a greater part of society would be in the happy state of possessing property, and a smaller part in the unhappy state of possessing no other property than their labour. But the best directed exertions, though they may alleviate, can never remove the pressure of want, and it will be difficult for any person who contemplates the genuine situation of man on earth, and the general laws of nature, to suppose it possible that any, the most enlightened efforts, could place mankind in a state where "few would die without measuring out the whole period of present existence allotted to them; where pain and distemper would be unknown among them; and death would come upon them like a sleep, in consequence of no other cause than gradual and unavoidable decay."

It is undoubtedly a most disheartening reflection that the great obstacle in the way to any extraordinary improvement in society is of a nature that we can never hope to overcome. The perpetual tendency in the race of man to increase beyond the means of subsistence is one of the general laws of animated nature which we can have no reason to expect will change. Yet discouraging as the contemplation of this difficulty must be to those whose exertions are laudably directed to the improvement of the human species, it is evident that no possible good can arise from any endeavours to slur it over or keep it in the back ground. On the contrary, the most baleful mischiefs may be expected from the unmanly conduct of not daring to face truth because it is unpleasing. Independently of what relates to this great obstacle, sufficient yet remains to be done for mankind to animate us to the most unremitted exertion. But if we proceed without a thorough knowledge and accurate comprehension of the nature, extent, and magnitude of the difficulties we have to encounter, or if we unwisely direct our efforts towards an object in which we cannot hope for success, we shall not only exhaust our strength in fruitless exertions and remain at as great a distance as ever from the summit of our wishes, but we shall be perpetually crushed by the recoil of this rock of Sisyphus.

CHAPTER XVIII

The constant pressure of distress on man, from the principle of population, seems to direct our hopes to the future—State of trial inconsistent with our ideas of the foreknowledge of God—The world, probably, a mighty process for awakening matter into mind—Theory of the formation of mind—Excitements from the wants of the body—Excitements from the operation of general laws—Excitements from the difficulties of life arising from the principle of population.

The view of human life which results from the contemplation of the constant pressure of distress on man from the difficulty of subsistence, by shewing the little expectation that he can reasonably entertain of perfectibility on earth, seems strongly to point his hopes to the future. And the temptations to which he must necessarily be exposed from the operation of those laws of nature which we have been examining, would seem to represent the world in the light in which it has been frequently considered, as a state of trial and school of virtue preparatory to a superior state of happiness. But I hope I shall be pardoned if I attempt to give a view in some degree different of the situation of man on earth, which appears to me to be more consistent with the various phenomena of nature which we observe around us and more consonant to our ideas of the power, goodness, and foreknowledge of the Deity.

It cannot be considered as an unimproving exercise of the human mind to endeavour to "Vindicate the ways of God to man" if we proceed with a proper distrust of our own understandings and a just sense of our insufficiency to comprehend the reason of all that we see, if we hail every ray of light with gratitude, and when no light appears, think that the darkness is from within and not from without, and bow with humble deference to the supreme wisdom of him whose "thoughts are above our thoughts" "as the heavens are high above the earth."

In all our feeble attempts, however, to "find out the Almighty to perfection," it seems absolutely necessary that we should reason from nature up to nature's God and not presume to reason from God to nature. The moment we allow ourselves to ask why some things are not otherwise, instead of endeavouring to account for them as they are, we shall never know where to stop; we shall be led into the grossest and most childish absurdities; all progress in the knowledge of the ways of Providence must necessarily be at an end; and the study will even cease to be an improving exercise of the human mind. Infinite power is so vast and incomprehensible an idea that the mind of man must necessarily be bewildered in the contemplation of it. With the crude and puerile conceptions which we sometimes form of this attribute of the Deity, we might imagine that God could call into being myriads and myriads of existences, all free from pain and imperfection, all eminent in goodness and wisdom, all capable of the highest enjoyments, and unnumbered as the points throughout infinite space. But when from these vain and extravagant dreams of fancy, we turn our eyes to the book of nature, where alone we can read God as he is, we see a constant succession of sentient beings, rising apparently from so many specks of matter, going through a long and sometimes painful process in this world, but many of them attaining, ere the termination of it, such high qualities and powers as seem to indicate their fitness for some superior state. Ought we not then to correct our crude and puerile ideas of Infinite Power from the contemplation of what we actually see existing? Can we judge of the Creator but from his creation? And unless we wish to exalt the power of God at the expence of his goodness, ought we not to conclude that even to the Great Creator, Almighty as he is, a certain process may be necessary, a certain time (or at least what appears to us as time) may be requisite, in order to form beings with those exalted qualities of mind which will fit them for his high purposes?

A state of trial seems to imply a previously formed existence that does not agree with the appearance of man in infancy and indicates something like suspicion and want of foreknowledge, inconsistent with those ideas which we wish to cherish of the Supreme Being. I should be inclined, therefore, as I have hinted before in a note, to consider the world and this life as the mighty process of God, not for the trial, but for the creation and formation of mind, a process necessary to awaken inert, chaotic matter into spirit, to sublimate the dust of the earth into soul, to elicit an ethereal spark from the clod of clay. And in this view of the subject, the various impressions and excitements which man receives through life may be considered as the forming hand of his Creator, acting by general laws, and awakening his sluggish existence, by the animating touches of the Divinity, into a capacity of superior enjoyment. The original sin of man is the torpor and corruption of the chaotic matter in which he may be said to be born.

It could answer no good purpose to enter into the question whether mind be a distinct substance from matter, or only a finer form of it. The question is, perhaps, after all, a question merely of words. Mind is as essentially mind, whether formed from matter or any other substance. We know from experience that soul and body are most intimately united, and every appearance seems to indicate that they grow from infancy together. It would be a supposition attended with very little probability to believe that a complete and full formed spirit existed in every infant, but that it was clogged and impeded in its operations during the first twenty years of life by the weakness, or hebetude, of the organs in which it was enclosed. As we shall all be disposed to agree that God is the creator of mind as well as of body, and as they both seem to be forming and unfolding themselves at the same time, it cannot appear inconsistent either with reason or revelation, if it appear to be consistent with phenomena of nature, to suppose that God is constantly occupied in forming mind out of matter and that the various impressions that man receives through life is the process for that purpose. The employment is surely worthy of the highest attributes of the Deity.

This view of the state of man on earth will not seem to be unattended with probability, if, judging from the little experience we have of the nature of mind, it shall appear upon investigation that the phenomena around us, and the various events of human life, seem peculiarly calculated to promote this great end, and especially if, upon this supposition, we can account, even to our own narrow understandings, for many of those roughnesses and inequalities in life which querulous man too frequently makes the subject of his complaint against the God of nature.

The first great awakeners of the mind seem to be the wants of the body.[9] They are the first stimulants that rouse the brain of infant man into sentient activity, and such seems to be the sluggishness of original matter that unless by a peculiar course of

9. It was my intention to have entered at some length into this subject as a kind of second part to the essay. A long interruption, from particular business, has obliged me to lay aside this intention, at least for the present. I shall now, therefore, only give a sketch of a few of the leading circumstances that appear to me to favour the general supposition that I have advanced.

excitements other wants, equally powerful, are generated, these stimulants seem, even afterwards, to be necessary to continue that activity which they first awakened. The savage would slumber for ever under his tree unless he were roused from his torpor by the cravings of hunger or the pinchings of cold, and the exertions that he makes to avoid these evils, by procuring food and building himself a covering, are the exercises which form and keep in motion his faculties, which otherwise would sink into listless inactivity. From all that experience has taught us concerning the structure of the human mind, if those stimulants to exertion, which arise from the wants of the body, were removed from the mass of mankind, we have much more reason to think that they would be sunk to the level of brutes, from a deficiency of excitements, than that they would be raised to the rank of philosophers by the possession of leisure. In those countries where nature is the most redundant in spontaneous produce the inhabitants will not be found the most remarkable for acuteness of intellect. Necessity has been with great truth called the mother of invention. Some of the noblest exertions of the human mind have been set in motion by the necessity of satisfying the wants of the body. Want has not unfrequently given wings to the imagination of the poet, pointed the flowing periods of the historian, and added acuteness to the researches of the philosopher, and though there are undoubtedly many minds at present so far improved by the various excitements of knowledge or of social sympathy that they would not relapse into listlessness if their bodily stimulants were removed, yet it can scarcely be doubted that these stimulants could not be withdrawn from the mass of mankind without producing a general and fatal torpor, destructive of all the germs of future improvement.

Locke, if I recollect, says that the endeavour to avoid pain rather than the pursuit of pleasure is the great stimulus to action in life, and that in looking to any particular pleasure, we shall not be roused into action in order to obtain it, till the contemplation of it has continued so long as to amount to a sensation of pain or uneasiness under the absence of it. To avoid evil and to pursue good seem to be the great duty and business of man, and this world appears to be peculiarly calculated to afford opportunity of the most unremitted exertion of this kind, and it is by this exertion, by these stimulants, that mind is formed. If Locke's idea be just, and there is great reason to think that it is, evil seems to be necessary to create exertion, and exertion seems evidently necessary to create mind.

The necessity of food for the support of life gives rise, probably, to a greater quantity of exertion than any other want, bodily or mental. The supreme Being has ordained that the earth shall not produce food in great quantities till much preparatory labour and ingenuity has been exercised upon its surface. There is no conceivable connection to our comprehensions, between the seed and the plant or tree that rises from it. The Supreme Creator might, undoubtedly, raise up plants of all kinds for the use of his creatures without the assistance of those little bits of matter, which we call seed, or even without the assisting labour and attention of man. The processes of ploughing and clearing the ground, of collecting and sowing seeds, are not surely for the assistance of God in his creation, but are made previously necessary to the enjoyment of the blessings of life, in order to rouse man into action and form his mind to reason.

To furnish the most unremitted excitements of this kind, and to urge man to further the gracious designs of Providence by the full cultivation of the earth, it has been ordained that population should increase much faster than food. This general law (as it has appeared in the former parts of this essay) undoubtedly produces much partial evil, but a little reflection may perhaps satisfy us that it produces a great overbalance of good. Strong excitements seem necessary to create exertion, and to direct this exertion, and form the reasoning faculty, it seems absolutely necessary that the Supreme Being should act always according to general laws. The constancy of the laws of nature, or the certainty with which we may expect the same effect from the same causes, is the foundation of the faculty of reason. If in the ordinary course of things, the finger of God were frequently visible, or to speak more correctly, if God were frequently to change his purpose (for the finger of God is, indeed, visible in every blade of grass that we see), a general and fatal torpor of the human faculties would probably ensue, even the bodily wants of mankind would cease to stimulate them to exertion, could they not reasonably expect that if their efforts were well directed they would be crowned with success. The constancy of the laws of nature is the foundation of the industry and foresight of the husbandman, the indefatigable ingenuity of the artificer, the skilful researches of the physician and anatomist, and the watchful observation and patient investigation of the natural philosopher. To this constancy we owe all the greatest and noblest efforts of intellect. To this constancy we owe the immortal mind of a Newton.

As the reasons, therefore, for the constancy of the laws of nature seem, even to our understandings, obvious and striking, if we return to the principle of population and consider man as he really is, inert, sluggish, and averse from labour unless compelled by necessity (and it is surely the height of folly to talk of man, according to our crude fancies, of what he might be), we may pronounce with certainty that the world would not have been peopled but for the superiority of the power of population to the means of subsistence. Strong and constantly operative as this stimulus is on man to urge him to the cultivation of the earth, if we still see that cultivation proceeds very slowly, we may fairly conclude that a less stimulus would have been insufficient. Even under the operation of this constant excitement, savages will inhabit countries of the greatest natural fertility for a long period before they betake themselves to pasturage or agriculture. Had population and food increased in the same ratio, it is probable that man might never have emerged from the savage state. But supposing the earth once well peopled, an Alexander, a Julius Caesar, a Tamerlane, or a bloody revolution might irrecoverably thin the human race and defeat the great designs of the Creator. The ravages of a contagious disorder would be felt for ages, and an earthquake might unpeople a region for ever. The principle according to which population increases prevents the vices of mankind or the accidents of nature, the partial evils arising from general laws, from obstructing the high purpose of the creation. It keeps the inhabitants of the earth always fully up to the level of the means of subsistence, and is constantly acting upon man as a powerful stimulus, urging him to the further cultivation of the earth, and to enable it consequently to support a more extended population. But it is impossible that this law can operate and produce the effects apparently intended by the Supreme Being without occasioning partial evil. Unless the principle of population were to be altered, according to the circumstances of each separate country (which would not only be contrary to our universal experience, with regard to the laws of nature, but would contradict even our own reason, which sees the absolute necessity of general laws, for the formation of intellect), it is evident that the same principle which, seconded by industry, will people a fertile region in a few years must produce distress in countries that have been long inhabited.

It seems, however, every way probable that even the acknowledged difficulties occasioned by the law of population tend rather to promote than impede the general purpose of Providence. They excite universal exertion and contribute to that infinite variety of situations, and consequently of impressions, which seems upon the whole favourable to the growth of mind. It is probable that too great or too little excitement, extreme poverty, or too great riches may be alike unfavourable in this respect. The middle regions of society seem to be best suited to intellectual improvement, but it is contrary to the analogy of all nature to expect that the whole of society can be a middle region. The temperate zones of the earth seem to be the most favourable to the mental and corporeal energies of man, but all cannot be temperate zones. A world warmed and enlightened but by one sun must from the laws of matter have some parts chilled by perpetual frosts and others scorched by perpetual heats. Every piece of matter lying on a surface must have an upper and an under side; all the particles cannot be in the middle. The most valuable parts of an oak to a timber merchant are not either the roots or the branches, but these are absolutely necessary to the existence of the middle part, or stem, which is the object in request. The timber merchant could not possibly expect to make an oak grow without roots or branches, but if he could find out a mode of cultivation which would cause more of the substance to go to stem, and less to root and branch, he would be right to exert himself in bringing such a system into general use.

In the same manner, though we cannot possibly expect to exclude riches and poverty from society, yet if we could find out a mode of government by which the numbers in the extreme regions would be lessened and the numbers in the middle regions increased, it would be undoubtedly our duty to adopt it. It is not, however, improbable that as in the oak, the roots and branches could not be diminished very greatly without weakening the vigorous circulation of the sap in the stem, so in society the extreme parts could not be diminished beyond a certain degree without lessening that animated exertion throughout the middle parts which is the very cause that they are the most favourable to the growth of intellect. If no man could hope to rise or fear to fall in society, if industry did not bring with it its reward and idleness its punishment, the middle parts would not certainly be what they now are. In reasoning upon this subject, it is evident that we ought to consider chiefly the mass of mankind and not individual instances. There are undoubtedly many minds, and there ought to be many, according to the chances, out of so great a mass that, having been vivified early by a peculiar course of excitements, would not need the constant action of narrow motives to continue them in activity. But if we were to review the various useful discoveries, the valuable writings, and other laudable exertions of mankind, I believe we should find that more were to be attributed to the narrow motives that operate upon the many than to the apparently more enlarged motives that operate upon upon the few.

Leisure is without doubt highly valuable to man, but taking man as he is, the probability seems to be that in the greater number of instances it will produce evil rather than good. It has been not unfrequently remarked that talents are more common among younger brothers than among elder brothers, but it can scarcely be imagined that younger brothers are, upon an average, born with a greater original susceptibility of parts. The difference, if there really is any observable difference, can only arise from their different situations. Exertion and activity are in general absolutely necessary in the one case and are only optional in the other.

That the difficulties of life contribute to generate talents, every day's experience must convince us. The exertions that men find it necessary to make in order to support themselves or families, frequently awaken faculties that might otherwise have lain for ever dormant, and it has been commonly remarked that new and extraordinary situations generally create minds adequate to grapple with the difficulties in which they are involved.

CHAPTER XIX

The sorrows of life necessary to soften and humanize the heart—The excitements of social sympathy often produce characters of a higher order than the mere possessors of talents—Moral evil probably necessary to the production of moral excellence—Excitements from intellectual wants continually kept up by the infinite variety of nature, and the obscurity that involves metaphysical subjects—The difficulties in Revelation to be accounted for upon this principle—The degree of evidence which the scriptures contain, probably, best suited to the improvement of the human faculties, and the moral amelioration of mankind—The idea that mind is created by excitements, seems to account for the existence of natural and moral evil.

The sorrows and distresses of life form another class of excitements which seem to be necessary, by a peculiar train of impressions, to soften and humanize the heart, to awaken social sympathy, to generate all the Christian virtues, and to afford scope for the ample exertion of benevolence. The general tendency of an uniform course of prosperity is rather to degrade than exalt the character. The heart that has never known sorrow itself will seldom be feelingly alive to the pains and pleasures, the wants and wishes, of its fellow beings. It will seldom be overflowing with that warmth of brotherly love, those kind and amiable affections, which dignify the human character even more than the possession of the highest talents. Talents, indeed, though undoubtedly a very prominent and fine feature of mind, can by no means be considered as constituting the whole of it. There are many minds which have not been exposed to those excitements that usually form talents, that have yet been vivified to a high degree by the excitements of social sympathy. In every rank of life, in the lowest as frequently as in the highest, characters are to be found overflowing with the milk of human kindness, breathing love towards God and man, and though without those peculiar powers of mind called talents, evidently holding a higher rank in the scale of beings than many who possess them. Evangelical charity, meekness, piety, and all that class of virtues distinguished particularly by the name of Christian virtues do not seem necessarily to include abilities, yet a soul possessed of these amiable qualities, a soul awakened and vivified by these delightful sympathies, seems to hold a nearer commerce with the skies than mere acuteness of intellect.

The greatest talents have been frequently misapplied and have produced evil proportionate to the extent of their powers. Both reason and revelation seem to assure us that such minds will be condemned to eternal death, but while on earth, these vicious instruments performed their part in the great mass of impressions, by the disgust and abhorrence which they excited. It seems highly probable that moral evil is absolutely necessary to the production of moral excellence. A being with only good placed in view may be justly said to be impelled by a blind necessity. The pursuit of good in this case can be no indication of virtuous propensities. It might be said, perhaps, that Infinite Wisdom cannot want such an indication as outward action, but would foreknow with certainty whether the being would chuse good or evil. This might be a plausible argument against a state of trial, but will not hold against the supposition that mind in this world is in a state of formation. Upon this idea, the being that has seen moral evil and has felt disapprobation and disgust at it is essentially different from the being that has seen only good. They are pieces of clay that have received distinct impressions: they must, therefore, necessarily be in different shapes; or, even if we allow them both to have the same lovely form of virtue, it must be acknowledged that one has undergone the further process, necessary to give firmness and durability to its substance, while the other is still exposed to injury, and liable to be broken by every accidental impulse. An ardent love and admiration of virtue seems to imply the existence of something opposite to it, and it seems highly probable that the same beauty of form and substance, the same perfection of character, could not be generated without the impressions of disapprobation which arise from the spectacle of moral evil.

When the mind has been awakened into activity by the passions and the wants of the body, intellectual wants arise; and the desire of knowledge and the impatience under ignorance form a new and important class of excitements. Every part of nature seems peculiarly calculated to furnish stimulants to mental exertion of this kind, and to offer inexhaustible food for the most unremitted inquiry. Our immortal Bard says of Cleopatra—

> Custom cannot stale
> Her infinite variety.

the expression, when applied to any one object, may be considered as a poetical amplification, but it is accurately true when applied to nature. Infinite variety seems, indeed, eminently her characteristic feature. The shades that are here and there blended in the picture give spirit, life, and prominence to her exuberant beauties, and those roughnesses and inequalities, those inferior parts that support the superior, though they sometimes offend the fastidious microscopic eye of short sighted man, contribute to the symmetry, grace, and fair proportion of the whole.

The infinite variety of the forms and operations of nature, besides tending immediately to awaken and improve the mind by the variety of impressions that it creates, opens other fertile sources of improvement by offering so wide and extensive a field for investigation and research. Uniform, undiversified perfection could not possess the same awakening powers. When we endeavour then to contemplate the system of the universe, when we think of the stars as the suns of other systems scattered throughout infinite space, when we reflect that we do not probably see a millionth part of those bright orbs that are beaming light and life to unnumbered worlds, when our minds unable to grasp the immeasurable conception sink, lost and confounded, in admiration at the mighty incomprehensible power of the Creator, let us not querulously complain that all climates are not equally genial, that perpetual spring does not reign throughout the year, that all God's creatures do not possess the same advantages, that clouds and tempests sometimes darken the natural world and vice and misery the moral world, and that all the works of the creation are not formed with equal perfection. Both reason and experience seem to indicate to us that the infinite variety of nature (and variety cannot exist without inferior parts, or apparent blemishes) is admirably adapted to further the high purpose of the creation and to produce the greatest possible quantity of good.

The obscurity that involves all metaphysical subjects appears to me in the same manner peculiarly calculated to add to that class of excitements which arise from the thirst of knowledge. It is probable that man, while on earth, will never be able to attain complete satisfaction on these subjects; but this is by no means a reason that he should not engage in them. The darkness that surrounds these interesting topics of human curiosity may be intended to furnish endless motives to intellectual activity and exertion. The constant effort to dispel this darkness, even if it fail of success, invigorates and improves the thinking faculty. If the subjects of human inquiry were once exhausted, mind would probably stagnate; but the infinitely diversified forms and operations of nature, together with the endless food for speculation which metaphysical subjects offer, prevent the possibility that such a period should ever arrive.

It is by no means one of the wisest sayings of Solomon that "there is no new thing under the sun." On the contrary, it is probable that were the present system to continue for millions of years, continual additions would be making to the mass of human knowledge, and yet perhaps it may be a matter of doubt whether what may be called the capacity of mind be in any marked and decided manner increasing. A Socrates, a Plato, or an Aristotle, however confessedly inferior in knowledge to the philosophers of the present day, do not appear to have been much below them in intellectual capacity. Intellect rises from a speck, continues in vigour only for a certain period, and will not perhaps admit while on earth of above a certain number of impressions. These impressions may, indeed, be infinitely modified, and from these various modifications, added probably to a difference in the susceptibility of the original germs,[1] arise the endless diversity of character that we see in the world; but reason and experience seem both to assure us, that the capacity of individual minds does not increase in proportion to the mass of existing knowledge. The finest minds seem to be formed rather by efforts at original thinking, by endeavours to form new combinations, and to discover new truths, than by passively receiving the impressions of other men's ideas. Could we suppose the period arrived, when there was no further hope of future discoveries, and the only employment of mind was to acquire pre-existing knowledge, without any efforts to form new and original combinations; though the mass of human knowledge were a thousand times greater than it is at present, yet it is evident that one of the noblest stimulants to mental exertion would have ceased; the finest feature of intellect would be lost; every thing allied to genius would be at an end; and it appears to be impossible, that, under such circumstances, any individuals could possess the same intellectual energies as were possessed by a Locke, a Newton, or a Shakespear, or even by a Socrates, a Plato, an Aristotle, or a Homer.

1. It is probable that no two grains of wheat are exactly alike. Soil undoubtedly makes the principal difference in the blades that spring up, but probably not all. It seems natural to suppose some sort of difference in the original germs that are afterwards awakened into thought, and the extraordinary difference of susceptibility in very young children seems to confirm the supposition.

If a revelation from heaven of which no person could feel the smallest doubt were to dispel the mists that now hang over metaphysical subjects, were to explain the nature and structure of mind, the affections and essences of all substances, the mode in which the Supreme Being operates in the works of the creation, and the whole plan and scheme of the Universe, such an accession of knowledge so obtained, instead of giving additional vigour and activity to the human mind, would in all probability tend to repress future exertion and to damp the soaring wings of intellect.

For this reason I have never considered the doubts and difficulties that involve some parts of the sacred writings as any argument against their divine original. The Supreme Being might undoubtedly have accompanied his revelations to man by such a succession of miracles, and of such a nature, as would have produced universal overpowering conviction and have put an end at once to all hesitation and discussion. But weak as our reason is to comprehend the plans of the Great Creator, it is yet sufficiently strong to see the most striking objections to such a revelation. From the little we know of the structure of the human understanding, we must be convinced that an overpowering conviction of this kind, instead of tending to the improvement and moral amelioration of man, would act like the touch of a torpedo on all intellectual exertion and would almost put an end to the existence of virtue. If the scriptural denunciations of eternal punishment were brought home with the same certainty to every man's mind as that the night will follow the day, this one vast and gloomy idea would take such full possession of the human faculties as to leave no room for any other conceptions, the external actions of men would be all nearly alike, virtuous conduct would be no indication of virtuous disposition, vice and virtue would be blended together in one common mass, and though the all-seeing eye of God might distinguish them they must necessarily make the same impressions on man, who can judge only from external appearances. Under such a dispensation, it is difficult to conceive how human beings could be formed to a detestation of moral evil, and a love and admiration of God, and of moral excellence.

Our ideas of virtue and vice are not, perhaps, very accurate and well-defined; but few, I think, would call an action really virtuous which was performed simply and solely from the dread of a very great punishment or the expectation of a very great reward. The fear of the Lord is very justly said to be the beginning of wisdom, but the end of wisdom is the love of the Lord and the admiration of moral good. The denunciations of future punishment contained in the scriptures seem to be well calculated to arrest the progress of the vicious and awaken the attention of the careless, but we see from repeated experience that they are not accompanied with evidence of such a nature as to overpower the human will and to make men lead virtuous lives with vicious dispositions, merely from a dread of hereafter. A genuine faith, by which I mean a faith that shews itself in all the virtues of a truly christian life, may generally be considered as an indication of an amiable and virtuous disposition, operated upon more by love than by pure unmixed fear.

When we reflect on the temptations to which man must necessarily be exposed in this world, from the structure of his frame, and the operation of the laws of nature, and the consequent moral certainty that many vessels will come out of this mighty creative furnace in wrong shapes, it is perfectly impossible to conceive that any of these creatures of God's hand can be condemned to eternal suffering. Could we once admit such an idea, all our natural conceptions of goodness and justice would be completely overthrown, and we could no longer look up to God as a merciful and righteous Being. But the doctrine of life and immortality which was brought to light by the gospel, the doctrine that the end of righteousness is everlasting life, but that the wages of sin are death, is in every respect just and merciful, and worthy of the Great Creator. Nothing can appear more consonant to our reason than that those beings which come out of the creative process of the world in lovely and beautiful forms, should be crowned with immortality, while those which come out misshapen, those whose minds are not suited to a purer and happier state of existence, should perish and be condemned to mix again with their original clay. Eternal condemnation of this kind may be considered as a species of eternal punishment, and it is not wonderful that it should be represented sometimes under images of suffering. But life and death, salvation and destruction, are more frequently opposed to each other in the New Testament than happiness and misery. The Supreme Being would appear to us in a very different view if we were to consider him as pursuing the creatures that had offended him with eternal hate and torture, instead of merely condemning to their original insensibility those beings that, by the operation of general laws, had not been formed with qualities suited to a purer state of happiness.

Life is, generally speaking, a blessing independent of a future state. It is a gift which the vicious would not always be ready to throw away, even if they had no fear of death. The partial pain, therefore, that is inflicted by the Supreme Creator, while he is forming numberless beings to a capacity of the highest enjoyments, is but as the dust of the balance in comparison of the happiness that is communicated, and we have every reason to think that there is no more evil in the world than what is absolutely necessary as one of the ingredients in the mighty process.

The striking necessity of general laws for the formation of intellect will not in any respect be contradicted by one or two exceptions, and these evidently not intended for partial purposes, but calculated to operate upon a great part of mankind, and through many ages. Upon the idea that I have given of the formation of mind, the infringement of the general laws of nature, by a divine revelation, will appear in the light of the immediate hand of God mixing new ingredients in the mighty mass, suited to the particular state of the process, and calculated to give rise to a new and powerful train of impressions, tending to purify, exalt, and improve the human mind. The miracles that accompanied these revelations when they had once excited the attention of mankind, and rendered it a matter of most interesting discussion, whether the doctrine was from God or man, had performed their part, had answered the purpose of the Creator; and these communications of the divine will were afterwards left to make their way by their own intrinsic excellence and by operating as moral motives, gradually to influence and improve, and not to overpower and stagnate the faculties of man.

It would be undoubtedly presumptuous to say that the Supreme Being could not possibly have effected his purpose in any other way than that which he has chosen; but as the revelation of the divine will which we possess is attended with some doubts and difficulties, and as our reason points out to us the strongest objections to a revelation which would force immediate, implicit, universal belief, we have surely just cause to think that these doubts and difficulties are no argument against the divine origin of the scriptures, and that the species of evidence which they possess is best suited to the improvement of the human faculties and the moral amelioration of mankind.

The idea that the impressions and excitements of this world are the instruments with which the Supreme Being forms matter into mind, and that the necessity of constant exertion to avoid evil and to pursue good is the principal spring of these impressions and excitements, seems to smooth many of the difficulties that occur in a contemplation of human life, and appears to me to give a satisfactory reason for the existence of natural and moral evil, and, consequently, for that part of both, and it certainly is not a very small part, which arises from the principle of population. But, though upon this supposition, it seems highly improbable that evil should ever be removed from the world, yet it is evident that this impression would not answer the apparent purpose of the Creator, it would not act so powerfully as an excitement to exertion, if the quantity of it did not diminish or increase with the activity or the indolence of man. The continual variations in the weight and in the distribution of this pressure keep alive a constant expectation of throwing it off.

> Hope springs eternal in the human breast,
> Man never is, but always to be blest.

Evil exists in the world not to create despair but activity. We are not patiently to submit to it, but to exert ourselves to avoid it. It is not only the interest but the duty of every individual to use his utmost efforts to remove evil from himself and from as large a circle as he can influence, and the more he exercises himself in this duty, the more wisely he directs his efforts, and the more successful these efforts are, the more he will probably improve and exalt his own mind and the more completely does he appear to fulfil the will of his Creator.

An Essay on the Principle of Population: From the Revised Edition (1803–) †

Preface

* * *

Throughout the whole of the present work I have so far differed in principle from the former, as to suppose the action of another check to population which does not come under the head either of vice or misery; and, in the latter part I have endeavoured to soften some of the harshest conclusions of the first Essay. In doing this, I hope that I have not violated the principles of just reasoning; nor expressed any opinion respecting the probable improvement of society, in which I am not borne out by the experience of the past. To those who still think that any check to population whatever would be worse than the evils which it would relieve, the conclusions of the former Essay will remain in full force: and if we adopt this opinion we shall be compelled to acknowledge, that the poverty and misery which prevailed among the lower classes of society are absolutely irremediable.

* * *

† The *Essay* was greatly enlarged in its second edition (see Introduction) and went through six editions in Malthus' lifetime. The present text is from the seventh edition, which appeared posthumously but was Malthus' work.

Book IV. Of Our Future Prospects Respecting the Removal or Mitigation of the Evils Arising from the Principle of Population

CHAPTER 1. OF MORAL RESTRAINT, AND OUR OBLIGATION TO PRACTISE THIS VIRTUE

As it appears that, in the actual state of every society which has come within our review, the natural progress of population has been constantly and powerfully checked; and as it seems evident that no improved form of government, no plans of emigration, no benevolent institutions, and no degree or direction of national industry, can prevent the continued action of a great check to population in some form or other; it follows that we must submit to it as an inevitable law of nature; and the only inquiry that remains is, how it may take place with the least possible prejudice to the virtue and happiness of human society.

All the immediate checks to population, which have been observed to prevail in the same and different countries, seem to be resolvable into moral restraint, vice and misery; and if our choice be confined to these three, we cannot long hesitate in our decision respecting which it would be most eligible to encourage.

In the first edition of this essay I observed, that as from the laws of nature it appeared, that some check to population must exist, it was better that this check should arise from a foresight of the difficulties attending a family and the fear of dependent poverty, than from the actual presence of want and sickness. This idea will admit of being pursued farther; and I am inclined to think that, from the prevailing opinions respecting population, which undoubtedly originated in barbarous ages, and have been continued and circulated by that part of every community which may be supposed to be interested in their support, we have been prevented from attending to the clear dictates of reason and nature on this subject.

Natural and moral evil seem to be the instruments employed by the Deity in admonishing us to avoid any mode of conduct which is not suited to our being, and will consequently injure our happiness. If we are intemperate in eating and drinking, our health is disordered; if we indulge the transports of anger, we seldom fail to commit acts of which we afterwards repent; if we multiply too fast, we die miserably of poverty and contagious diseases. The laws of nature in all these cases are similar and uniform. They indicate to us that we have followed these impulses too far, so as to trench upon some other law, which equally demands attention. * * *

From the inattention of mankind hitherto to the consequences of increasing too fast, it must be presumed, that these consequences are not so immediately and powerfully connected with the conduct which leads to them, as in the other instances; but the delayed knowledge of particular effects does not alter their nature, or our obligation to regulate our conduct accordingly, as soon as we are satisfied of what this conduct ought to be. * * *

* * * It is of the very utmost importance to the happiness of mankind, that population should not increase too fast; but it does not appear, that the object to be accomplished would admit of any considerable diminution in the desire of marriage. It is clearly the duty of each individual not to marry till he has a prospect of supporting his children; but it is at the same time to be wished that he should retain undiminished his desire of marriage, in order that he may exert himself to realise this prospect, and be stimulated to make provision for the support of greater numbers.

It is evidently therefore regulation and direction which are required with regard to the principle of population, not diminution or alteration. And if moral restraint be the only virtuous mode of avoiding the incidental evils arising from this principle, our obligation to practise it will evidently rest exactly upon the same foundation as our obligation to practise any of the other virtues.

Whatever indulgence we may be disposed to allow to occasional failures in the discharge of a duty of acknowledged difficulty, yet of the strict line of duty we cannot doubt. Our obligation not to marry till we have a fair prospect of being able to support our children will appear to deserve the attention of the moralist, if it can be proved that an attention to this obligation is of most powerful effect in the prevention of misery; and that, if it were the general custom to follow the first impulse of nature, and marry at the age of puberty, the universal prevalence of every known virtue in the greatest conceivable degree, would fail of rescuing society from the most wretched and desperate state of want, and all the diseases and famines which usually accompany it.

* * *

CHAPTER III. OF THE ONLY EFFECTUAL MODE OF IMPROVING THE CONDITION OF THE POOR

* * *

The object of those who really wish to better the condition of the lower classes of society must be to raise the relative proportion between the price of labour and the price of provisions, so as to enable the labourer to command a larger share of the necessaries and comforts of life. We have hitherto principally attempted to attain this end by encouraging the married poor and consequently increasing the number of labourers, and overstocking the market with a commodity which we still say that we wish to be dear. It would seem to have required no great spirit of divination to foretell the certain failure of such a plan of proceeding. There is nothing however like experience. It has been tried in many different countries, and for many hundred years, and the success has always been answerable to the nature of the scheme. It is really time now to try something else.

When it was found that oxygen, or pure vital air, would not cure consumptions as was expected, but rather aggravated their symptoms, trial was made of an air of the most opposite kind. I wish we had acted with the same philosophical spirit in our attempts to cure the disease of poverty; and having found that the pouring in of fresh supplies of labour only tended to aggravate the symptoms, had tried what would be the effect of withholding a little these supplies.

In all old and fully-peopled states it is from this method, and this alone, that we can rationally expect any essential and permanent melioration in the condition of the labouring classes of the people.

In an endeavour to raise the proportion of the quantity of provisions to the number of consumers in any country, our attention would naturally be first directed to the increasing of the absolute quantity of provisions; but finding that, as fast as we did this, the number of consumers more than kept pace with it, and that with all our exertions we were still as far as ever behind, we should be convinced that our efforts directed only in this way would never succeed. It would appear to be setting the tortoise to catch the hare. Finding, therefore, that from the laws of nature we could not proportion the food to the population, our next attempt should naturally be to proportion the population to the food. If we can persuade the hare to go to sleep the tortoise may have some chance of overtaking her.

We are not, however, to relax our efforts in increasing the quantity of provisions, but to combine another effort with it; that of keeping the population, when once it has been overtaken, at such a distance behind as to effect the relative proportion which we desire; and thus unite the two grand *desiderata*, a great actual population and a state of society in which abject poverty and dependence are comparatively but little known; two objects which are far from being incompatible.

If we be really serious in what appears to be the object of such general research, the mode of essentially and permanently bettering the condition of the poor, we must explain to them the true nature of their situation, and show them that the withholding of the supplies of labour is the only possible way of really raising its price, and that they themselves, being the possessors of this commodity, have alone the power to do this.

* * *

CHAPTER VIII. PLAN OF THE GRADUAL ABOLITION OF THE POOR LAWS PROPOSED

If the principles in the preceding chapters should stand the test of examination, and we should ever feel the obligation of endeavouring to act upon them, the next inquiry would be in what way we ought practically to proceed. The first grand obstacle which presents itself in this country is the system of the poor-laws, which has been justly stated to be an evil in comparison of which the national debt, with all its magnitude of terror, is of little moment.[1] The rapidity with which the poor's rates have increased of late years presents us indeed with the prospect of such an extraordinary proportion of paupers in the society as would seem to be incredible in a nation flourishing in arts, agriculture, and commerce, and with a government which has generally been allowed to be the best that has hitherto stood the test of experience.[2]

* * *

I have reflected much on the subject of the poor-laws, and hope therefore that I shall be excused in venturing to suggest a mode of their gradual abolition to which I confess that at present I can see no material objection. Of this indeed I feel nearly convinced that, should we ever become so fully sensible of the widespreading tyranny, dependence, indolence, and unhappiness which they create as seriously to make an effort to abolish them, we shall be compelled by a sense of justice to adopt the principle, if not the plan, which I shall mention. It seems impossible to get rid of so extensive a system of support, consistently with humanity, without applying ourselves directly to its vital principle, and endeavouring to counteract that deeply-seated cause which occasions the rapid growth of all such establishments and invariably renders them inadequate to their object.

As a previous step even to any considerable alteration in the present system, which would contract or stop the increase of the

1. *Reports of the Society for bettering the Condition of the Poor.*
2. If the poor's rates continue increasing as rapidly as they have done on the average of the last ten years, how melancholy are our future prospects! The system of the poor-laws has been justly stated by the French to be *la plaie politique de l'Angleterre la plus devorante.* (Comté de Mendicité.)

relief to be given, it appears to me that we are bound in justice and honour formally to disclaim the *right* of the poor to support.

To this end, I should propose a regulation to be made, declaring that no child born from any marriage, taking place after the expiration of a year from the date of the law, and no illegitimate child born two years from the same date, should ever be entitled to parish assistance. And to give a more general knowledge of this law, and to enforce it more strongly on the minds of the lower classes of people, the clergyman of each parish should, after the publication of banns, read a short address stating the strong obligation on every man to support his own children; the impropriety, and even immorality, of marrying without a prospect of being able to do this; the evils which had resulted to the poor themselves from the attempt which had been made to assist by public institutions in a duty which ought to be exclusively appropriated to parents; and the absolute necessity which had at length appeared of abandoning all such institutions, on account of their producing effects totally opposite to those which were intended.

This would operate as a fair, distinct, and precise notice, which no man could well mistake; and, without pressing hard on any particular individuals, would at once throw off the rising generation from that miserable and helpless dependence upon the government and the rich, the moral as well as physical consequences of which are almost incalculable.

After the public notice which I have proposed had been given, and the system of poor-laws had ceased with regard to the rising generation, if any man chose to marry, without a prospect of being able to support a family, he should have the most perfect liberty so to do. Though to marry, in this case, is, in my opinion, clearly an immoral act, yet it is not one which society can justly take upon itself to prevent or punish; because the punishment provided for it by the laws of nature falls directly and most severely upon the individual who commits the act, and through him, only more remotely and feebly, on the society. When nature will govern and punish for us, it is a very miserable ambition to wish to snatch the rod from her hand and draw upon ourselves the odium of executioner. To the punishment therefore of nature he should be left, the punishment of want. He has erred in the face of a most clear and precise warning, and can have no just reason to complain of any person but himself when he feels the consequences of his error. All parish assistance should be denied him; and he should be left to the uncertain support of private charity. He should be taught to know that the laws of nature, which are the laws of God, had doomed him and his family to suffer for disobeying their repeated admonitions; that he had no claim of *right* on society for the smallest portion of food, beyond that which his labour would fairly purchase; and that if he and his family were saved from feeling the natural consequences of his imprudence he would owe it to the pity of some kind benefactor, to whom, therefore, he ought to be bound by the strongest ties of gratitude.

If this system were pursued, we need be under no apprehensions that the number of persons in extreme want would be beyond the power and the will of the benevolent to supply. The sphere for the exercise of private charity would, probably, not be greater than it is at present; and the principal difficulty would be to restrain the hand of benevolence from assisting those in distress in so indiscriminate a manner as to encourage indolence and want of foresight in others.

With regard to illegitimate children, after the proper notice had been given, they should not be allowed to have any claim to parish assistance,. but be left entirely to the support of private charity. If the parents desert their child, they ought to be made answerable for the crime. The infant is, comparatively speaking, of little value to the society, as others will immediately supply its place. * * *

CHAPTER IX. OF THE MODES OF CORRECTING THE PREVAILING OPINIONS ON POPULATION

It is not enough to abolish all the positive institutions which encourage population; but we must endeavour, at the same time, to correct the prevailing opinions which have the same, or perhaps even a more powerful effect. This must necessarily be a work of time; and can only be done by circulating juster notions on these subjects in writing and conversation; and by endeavouring to impress as strongly as possible on the public mind that it is not the duty of man simply to propagate his species, but to propagate virtue and happiness; and that, if he has not a tolerably fair prospect of doing this, he is by no means called upon to leave descendants.

* * *

The fairest chance of accomplishing this end would probably be by the establishment of a system of parochial education upon a plan similar to that proposed by Adam Smith.[3] In addition to the usual subjects of instruction, and those which he has mentioned, I should be disposed to lay considerable stress on the frequent explanation of the real state of the lower classes of society as affected

3. *Wealth of Nations.*

by the principle of population, and their consequent dependence on themselves for the chief part of their happiness or misery. * * *

The principal argument which I have heard advanced against a system of national education in England is, that the common people would be put in a capacity to read such works as those of Paine, and that the consequences would probably be fatal to government. But on this subject I agree most cordially with Adam Smith in thinking that an instructed and well-informed people would be much less likely to be led away by inflammatory writings, and much better able to detect the false declamation of interested and ambitious demagogues, than an ignorant people. * * *

In most countries, among the lower classes of people, there appears to be something like a standard of wretchedness, a point below which they will not continue to marry and propagate their species. This standard is different in different countries, and is formed by various concurring circumstances of soil, climate, government, degree of knowledge, and civilisation, etc. The principal circumstances which contribute to raise it are liberty, security of property, the diffusion of knowledge, and a taste for the conveniences and the comforts of life. Those which contribute principally to lower it are despotism and ignorance.

In an attempt to better the condition of the labouring classes of society our object should be to raise this standard as high as possible, by cultivating a spirit of independence, a decent pride, and a taste for cleanliness and comfort. The effect of a good government in increasing the prudential habits and personal respectability of the lower classes of society has already been insisted on; but certainly this effect will always be incomplete without a good system of education; and, indeed, it may be said that no government can approach to perfection that does not provide for the instruction of the people. The benefits derived from education are among those which may be enjoyed without restriction of numbers; and, as it is in the power of governments to confer these benefits, it is undoubtedly their duty to do it.

CHAPTER XIV. OF OUR RATIONAL EXPECTATIONS RESPECTING THE
FUTURE IMPROVEMENT OF SOCIETY

* * *

It is less the object of the present work to propose new plans of improving society than to inculcate the necessity of resting contented with that mode of improvement which already has in part been acted upon as dictated by the course of nature, and of not obstructing the advances which would otherwise be made in this way.

It would be undoubtedly highly advantageous that all our positive institutions, and the whole tenour of our conduct to the poor, should be such as actively to co-operate with that lesson of prudence inculcated by the common course of human events; and if we take upon ourselves sometimes to mitigate the natural punishments of imprudence, that we could balance it by increasing the rewards of an opposite conduct. But much would be done if merely the institutions which directly tend to encourage marriage were gradually changed, and we ceased to circulate opinions and inculcate doctrines which positively counteract the lessons of nature.

The limited good which it is sometimes in our power to effect, is often lost by attempting too much, and by making the adoption of some particular plan essentially necessary even to a partial degree of success. In the practical application of the reasonings of this work, I hope that I have avoided this error. I wish to press on the recollection of the reader that, though I may have given some new views of old facts, and may have indulged in the contemplation of a considerable degree of *possible* improvement, that I might not shut out that prime cheerer hope; yet in my expectations of probable improvement and in suggesting the means of accomplishing it, I have been very cautious. * * *

From a review of the state of society in former periods compared with the present, I should certainly say that the evils resulting from the principle of population have rather diminished than increased, even under the disadvantage of an almost total ignorance of the real cause. And if we can indulge the hope that this ignorance will be gradually dissipated, it does not seem unreasonable to expect that they will be still further diminished. The increase of absolute population, which will of course take place, will evidently tend but little to weaken this expectation, as everything depends upon the relative proportion between population and food, and not on the absolute number of people. In the former part of this work it appeared that the countries which possessed the fewest people often suffered the most from the effects of the principle of population; and it can scarcely be doubted that, taking Europe throughout, fewer famines and fewer diseases arising from want have prevailed in the last century than in those which preceded it.

On the whole, therefore, though our future prospects respecting the mitigation of the evils arising from the principle of population may not be so bright as we could wish, yet they are far from being entirely disheartening, and by no means preclude that gradual and progressive improvement in human society which, before the late wild speculations on this subject, was the object of rational expectation. To the laws of property and marriage, and to the apparent narrow principle of self-interest which prompts each individual to exert himself in bettering his condition, we are indebted for all the noblest exertions of human genius, for everything that distinguishes the civilised from the savage state. A strict inquiry into the principle of population obliges us to conclude that we shall never be able to throw down the ladder by which we have risen to this eminence; but it by no means proves that we may not rise higher by the same means. The structure of society, in its great features, will probably always remain unchanged. We have every reason to believe that it will always consist of a class of proprietors and a class of labourers; but the condition of each, and the proportion which they bear to each other, may be so altered as greatly to improve the harmony and beauty of the whole. It would indeed be a melancholy reflection that, while the views of physical science are daily enlarging, so as scarcely to be bounded by the most distant horizon, the science of moral and political philosophy should be confined within such narrow limits, or at best be so feeble in its influence, as to be unable to counteract the obstacles to human happiness arising from a single cause. But however formidable these obstacles may have appeared in some parts of this work, it is hoped that the general result of the inquiry is such as not to make us give up the improvement of human society in despair. The partial good which seems to be attainable is worthy of all our exertions; is sufficient to direct our efforts, and animate our prospects. And although we cannot expect that the virtue and happiness of mankind will keep pace with the brilliant career of physical discovery; yet, if we are not wanting to ourselves, we may confidently indulge the hope that, to no unimportant extent, they will be influenced by its progress and will partake in its success.

PART III

Nineteenth-Century
Comment

WILLIAM GODWIN

Of Population (1820) †

Preface

When I wrote my Enquiry concerning Political Justice, I flattered myself that there was no mean probability that I should render an important service to mankind. * * *

The book I produced seemed for some time fully to answer in its effects the most sanguine expectations I had conceived from it. I could not complain that it "fell dead-born from the press," or that it did not awaken a considerable curiosity among my countrymen. * * * Among other phenomena of the kind, I hailed the attack of Mr. Malthus. I believed, that the Essay on Population, like other erroneous and exaggerated representations of things, would soon find its own level.

In this I have been hitherto disappointed. * * * Finding therefore, that whatever arguments have been produced against it by others, it still holds on its prosperous career, and has not long since appeared in the impressive array of a Fifth Edition, I cannot be contented to go out of the world, without attempting to put into a permanent form what has occurred to me on the subject. * * *

Between the advantages and disadvantages attendant on the state of man on earth there is one thing that seems decisively to turn the balance in favour of the former. Man is to a considerable degree the artificer of his own fortune. We can apply our reflections and our ingenuity to the remedy of whatever we regret. Speaking in a general way, and within certain liberal and expansive limitations, it should appear that there is no evil under which the human species can labour, that man is not competent to cure. * * * Man, in the most dejected condition in which a human being can be placed, has still something within him which whispers him, "I belong to a world that is worth living in."

Such was, and was admitted to be the state of the human species, previously to the appearance of the Essay on Population. Now let us see how, under the ascendancy of Mr. Malthus's theory, all this is completely reversed.

The great error of those who sought to encourage and console their fellow-beings in this vale of tears, was, we are told, in suppos-

† William Godwin (1756–1836), British social philosopher. The present text is from his *Of Population: An Enquiry* *concerning the Power of Increase in the Numbers of Mankind.*

ing that any thing that we could do, could be of substantial benefit in remedying the defects of our social existence. "Human institutions are light and superficial, mere feathers that float upon the surface." The enemy that hems us in, and reduces our condition to despair, is no other than "the laws of Nature, which are the laws of God."

Nor is this by any means the worst of the case. The express object of Mr. Malthus's writing was to prove how pernicious was their error, who aimed at any considerable and essential improvement in human society. The only effectual checks upon that excess of population, which, if unchecked, would be sufficient in no long time to people all the stars, are vice and misery. The main and direct moral and lesson of the Essay on Population, is passiveness. * * *

Till Mr. Malthus wrote, political writers and sages had courage. They said, "The evils we suffer are from ourselves; let us apply ourselves with assiduity and fortitude to the cure of them." This courage was rapidly descending, by the progress of illumination and intellect, to a very numerous portion of mankind; and the sober and considerate began deliberately to say, "Let us endeavour to remedy the evils of political society, and mankind may then be free and contented and happy." Mr. Malthus has placed himself in the gap. He has proclaimed, with a voice that has carried astonishment and terror into the hearts of thousands, the accents of despair. He has said, The evils of which you complain, do not lie within your reach to remove: they come from the laws of nature, and the unalterable impulse of human kind.

But Mr. Malthus does not stop here. He presents us with a code of morality conformable to his creed.

This code consists principally of negatives.

We must not preach up private charity. For charity, "if exerted at all, will necessarily lead" to pernicious consequences.

We must not preach up frugality. For the "waste among the rich, and the horses kept by them merely for their pleasure, operate like granaries, and tend rather to benefit than to injure the lower classes of society."

We must deny that the poor, whatever may be the causes of degree or their distress, "have a right to support."

We must maintain that every man "has a right to do what he will with his own."

We must preach down marriage. We must affirm that no man has a right to marry, without a fair "prospect of being able to support a family." "They should not have families, if they cannot support them." And this rule is strictly to govern our treatment of the married man in distress. "To the punishment of Nature he should be left, the punishment of want. He should be taught to know that the laws of Nature, which are the laws of God, have doomed him and his family to suffer for disobeying their repeated admonitions."

What havock do these few maxims make with the old received notions of morality!

It has not been enough attended to, how complete a revolution the Essay on Population proposes to effect in human affairs. Mr. Malthus is the most daring and gigantic of all innovators.

To omit all other particulars, if we embrace his creed, we must have a new religion, and a new God.

NASSAU W. SENIOR

Two Lectures on Population (1829) †

* * * In my introductory Lecture I sketched what appeared to me an outline of those laws in the following proposition:—"That the population of a given district is limited only by moral or physical evil, or by deficiency in the means of obtaining those articles of wealth; or, in other words, those necessaries, decencies, and luxuries, which the habits of the individuals of each class of the inhabitants of that district lead them to require."

The only modification which subsequent reflection induces me to apply to this proposition is, to substitute for the word "deficiency," the words, "the apprehension of a deficiency." My reasons for this substitution are: first, that the actual deficiency of necessaries is a branch of physical evil; and, secondly, that it is not the existence of a deficiency, but the *fear* of its existence which is the principal check to population, so far as necessaries are concerned, and the sole check as respects decencies and luxuries.

But before I take this proposition in detail, I feel that I ought to explain, as precisely as I can, what I mean by the words, necessaries, decencies, and luxuries; terms which have been used ever since the moral sciences first attracted attention in this country, but have never, within my knowledge, been defined.

It is scarcely necessary to remind you, that they are relative terms, and that some person must always be assigned, with reference to whom a given commodity or service is a luxury, a decency, or a necessary.

By *necessaries* then, I express those things, the use of which is

† Nassau William Senior (1790–1864), British political economist. The present text is from Senior's *Selected Writings on Economics*.

requisite to keep a given individual in the health and strength essential to his going through his habitual occupations.

By *decencies*, those things which a given individual must use in order to preserve his existing rank in society.

Every thing else of which a given individual makes use; or, in other words, all that portion of his consumption which is not essential to his health and strength, or to the preservation of his existing rank in society, I term *luxury*.

* * *

The check from an apprehended deficiency of luxuries is but slight. The motives, perhaps I might say the instincts, that prompt the human race to marriage, are too powerful to be much restrained by the fear of losing conveniences, unconnected with health or station in society.

The fear of losing decencies, or perhaps more frequently the hope to acquire, by a longer accumulation during celibacy the means of purchasing the decencies of a higher social rank, is a check of far more importance. Want of actual necessaries is seldom apprehended by any except the poorest classes in any country. And in England, though it sometimes is felt, it probably is anticipated by none. When an Englishman stands hesitating between love and prudence, a family really starving is not among his terrors. Against actual want he knows that he has the fence of the poor laws. But, however humble his desires, he cannot contemplate, without anxiety, a probability that the income which supported his social rank while single, may be insufficient to maintain it when he is married; that he may be unable to give to his children the advantages of education which he enjoyed himself; in short, that he may lose his caste. * * *

Supposing our population to have increased, as would be the case by the beginning of the next century, to one hundred millions, about an acre and a half would be allotted to each family; and, as I before observed, I think that allotment might be sufficient. But it can scarcely be supposed, that three roods would be enough, which would be their allotment in twenty-five years more, or granting that to be enough, it cannot be supposed that at the end of a further term of doubling a family of four persons could live on the produce of a rood and a half.

* * * Where the evil is the loss of luxuries, or even of decencies, it is trifling in the first instance, and bearable in the second. But in the case which I am supposing, the only prudential check would be an apprehended deficiency of necessaries; and that deficiency, in the many instances in which it would be incurred, would be the positive check in its most frightful form. It would be incurred not only in consequence of that miscalculation of chances to which all men are subject, and certainly those not the least so, who are anxious to marry, but through accidents against which no human prudence can guard. A *single* bad harvest may be provided against, but a succession of unfavourable seasons, and such successions do occur, must reduce such a people to absolute famine. When such seasons affect a nation indulging in considerable superfluous expenditure, they are relieved by a temporary sacrifice of that superfluity. The grain consumed in ordinary years by our breweries and distilleries is a store always at hand to supply a scarcity, and the same may be said of the large quantity of food used for the support of domestic animals, but applicable to human subsistence. To these resources may be added the importation from abroad of necessaries instead of luxuries, and the materials of luxury; of corn, for instance, instead of wine.

It appears, therefore, that habits of considerable superfluous expenditure afford the only permanent protection against a population pressing so closely on the means of subsistence, as to be continually incurring the misery of the positive checks. And as these habits can exist only in an opulent society, it appears to me equally clear, that as a nation advances in opulence, the positive checks are likely to be superseded by the preventive. If this be true, the evil of a redundant population, or to speak more intelligibly, of a population too numerous to be adequately and regularly supplied with necessaries, is likely to diminish in the progress of improvement. As wealth increases, what were the luxuries of one generation become the decencies of their successors. Not only a taste for additional comfort and convenience, but a feeling of degradation in their absence becomes more and more widely diffused. The increase, in many respects, of the productive powers of labour, must enable increased comforts to be enjoyed by increased numbers, and as it is the more beneficial, so it appears to me to be the more natural course of events, that increased comfort should not only accompany, but rather precede, increase of numbers.

* * *

If it be conceded, that there exists in the human race a natural tendency to rise from barbarism to civilization, and that the means of subsistence are proportionally more abundant in a civilized than in a savage state, and neither of these propositions can be denied, it must follow that there is a natural tendency in subsistence to increase in a greater ratio than population.

But, although Mr. Malthus has perhaps fallen into the exaggeration which is natural to a discoverer, his error, if it be one, does not affect the practical conclusions which place him, as a benefactor to mankind, on a level with Adam Smith. Whether, in the absence of disturbing causes, it be the tendency of subsistence or of population to advance with greater rapidity, is a question of slight importance, if it be acknowledged that human happiness or misery depend principally on their relative advance, and that there are causes, and causes within human control, by which that advance can be regulated.

These are propositions which Mr. Malthus has established by facts and reasonings, which, opposed as they were to long-rooted prejudice, and assailed by every species of sophistry and clamour, are now so generally admitted, that they have become rather matter of allusion than of formal statement. * * *

FRIEDRICH ENGELS

Outlines of a Critique of Political Economy (1844) †

Malthus * * * asserts that population constantly exerts pressure on the means of subsistence; that as production is increased, population increases in the same proportion; and that the inherent tendency of population to multiply beyond the available means of subsistence is the cause of all poverty and all vice. For if there are too many people, then in one way or another they must be eliminated; they must die, either by violence or through starvation. When this has happened, however, a gap appears once more, and this is immediately filled by other propagators of population, so that the old poverty begins anew. Moreover, this is the case under all conditions—not only in the civilized but also in the natural state of man. The savages of New Holland, who live *one* to the square mile, suffer just as much from overpopulation as England. In short, if we want to be logical, we have to recognize *that the earth was already overpopulated when only one man existed.* Now the consequence of this theory is that since it is precisely the poor who constitute this surplus population, nothing ought to be done for them, except to make it as easy as possible for them to starve to death; to convince them that this state of affairs cannot be altered and that there is no salvation for their entire class other than that they should propagate as little as possible * * *.

Is it necessary for me to give any more details of this vile and infamous doctrine, this repulsive blasphemy against man and nature, or to follow up its consequences any further? Here, brought

† Friedrich Engels (1820–1895), German socialist. The present translation is from Ronald L. Meek, ed., *Marx and Engels on the Population Bomb* (Berkeley, Calif., 1971).

before us at last, is the immorality of the economists in its highest form. What were all the wars and horrors of the monopoly system when compared with this theory? And it is precisely this theory which is the cornerstone of the liberal system of free trade, whose fall will bring the whole edifice down with it. For once competition has here been proved to be the cause of misery, poverty and crime, who will still dare to say a word in its defense?

* * * If, however, it is a fact that every adult produces more than he can himself consume, that children are like trees, returning abundantly the expenditure laid out on them—and surely these are facts?—one would imagine that every worker ought to be able to produce far more than he needs, and that the community ought therefore to be glad to furnish him with everything that he requires; one would imagine that a large family would be a most desirable gift to the community. But the economists, with their crude outlook, know no other equivalent apart from that which is paid over to them in tangible hard cash. They are so firmly entangled in their contradictions that they are just as little concerned with the most striking facts as they are with the most scientific principles.

We shall destroy the contradiction simply by resolving it. With the fusion of those interests which now conflict with one another, there will disappear the antithesis between surplus population in one place and surplus wealth in another, and also the wonderful phenomenon—more wonderful than all the wonders of all the religions put together—that a nation must starve to death from sheer wealth and abundance; and there will disappear too the crazy assertion that the earth does not possess the power to feed mankind. * * *

The Malthusian theory, however, was an absolutely necessary transitional stage, which has taken us infinitely further forward. Thanks to this theory, as also thanks to economics in general, our attention has been drawn to the productive power of the soil and of humanity, so that now, having triumphed over this economic despair, we are forever secure from the fear of overpopulation. From this theory we derive the most powerful economic arguments in favor of a social reorganization; for even if Malthus were altogether right, it would still be necessary to carry out this reorganization immediately, since only this reorganization, only the enlightenment of the masses which it can bring with it, can make possible that moral restraint upon the instinct for reproduction which Malthus himself puts forward as the easiest and most effective countermeasure against overpopulation. Thanks to this theory we have come to recognize in the dependence of man upon competitive conditions his most complete degradation. It has shown us that in the last analysis private property has turned man into a commodity, whose production and consumption also depend only on demand; that the system of competition has thereby slaughtered, and is still slaughtering today, millions of people—all this we have seen, and all this impels us to do away with this degradation of humanity by doing away with private property, competition and conflicting interests.

However, in order to deprive the general fear of overpopulation of all foundation, let us return once again to the question of the relation of productive power to population. Malthus puts forward a calculation upon which his whole system is based. Population increases in geometrical progression—$1+2+4+8+16+32$, etc. The productive power of the land increases in arithmetical progression —$1+2+3+4+5+6$. The difference is obvious and horrifying— but is it correct? Where has it been proved that the productivity of the land increases in arithmetical progression? The area of land is limited—that is perfectly true. But the labor power to be employed on this area increases together with the population; and even if we assume that the increase of output associated with this increase of labor is not always proportionate to the latter, there still remains a third element—which the economists, however, never consider as important—namely, science, the progress of which is just as limitless and at least as rapid as that of population. For what great advances is the agriculture of this century obliged to chemistry alone—and indeed to two men alone, Sir Humphry Davy and Justus Liebig? But science increases at least as fast as population; the latter increases in proportion to the size of the previous generation, and science advances in proportion to the body of knowledge passed down to it by the previous generation, that is, in the most normal conditions it also grows in geometrical progression—and what is impossible for science? But it is ridiculous to speak of overpopulation while "the valley of the Mississippi alone contains enough waste land to accommodate the whole population of Europe," while altogether only one-third of the earth can be described as cultivated, and while the productivity of this third could be increased sixfold and more merely by applying improvements which are already known.

JOHN STUART MILL

Principles of Political Economy (1848) †

In all countries which have passed a very early stage in the progress of agriculture, every increase in the demand for food, occasioned by increased population, will always, unless there is a simultaneous improvement in production, diminish the share which on a fair division would fall to each individual. An increased production, in default of unoccupied tracts of fertile land, or of fresh improvements tending to cheapen commodities, can never be obtained but by increasing the labor in more than the same proportion. The population must either work harder, or eat less, or obtain their usual food by sacrificing a part of their other customary comforts. Whenever this necessity is postponed, it is because the improvements which facilitate production continue progressive; because the contrivances of mankind for making their labor more effective, keep up an equal struggle with nature, and extort fresh resources from her reluctant powers as fast as human necessities occupy and engross the old.

From this, results the important corollary, that the necessity of restraining population is not, as many persons believe, peculiar to a condition of great inequality of property. A greater number of people cannot, in any given state of civilization, be collectively so well provided for as a smaller. The niggardliness of nature, not the injustice of society, is the cause of the penalty attached to overpopulation. An unjust distribution of wealth does not even aggravate the evil, but, at most, causes it to be somewhat earlier felt. It is in vain to say, that all mouths which the increase of mankind calls into existence, bring with them hands. The new mouths require as much food as the old ones, and the hands do not produce as much. If all instruments of production were held in joint property by the whole people, and the produce divided with perfect equality among them, and if in a society thus constituted, industry were as energetic and the produce as ample as at present, there would be enough to make all the existing population extremely comfortable; but when that population had doubled itself, as, with the existing habits of the people, under such an encouragement, it undoubtedly would, in little more than twenty years, what would then be their condition? Unless the arts of pro-

† John Stuart Mill (1806–1873), British philosopher and political economist. In the present text, the first excerpt is from Book I, Chapter 13, Section 2; the subsequent excerpts are from Book II, Chapters 11–13.

duction were in the same time improved in so unexampled a degree as to double the productive power of labor—the inferior soils which must be resorted to, and the more laborious and scantily remunerative cultivation which must be employed on the superior soils, to procure food for so much larger a population, would, by an insuperable necessity, render every individual in the community poorer than before. If the population continued to increase at the same rate, a time would soon arrive when no one would have more than mere necessaries, and, soon after, a time when no one would have a sufficiency of those, and the further increase of population would be arrested by death.

* * *

Chapter XI. Of Wages

Wages, like other things, may be regulated either by competition or by custom. In this country there are few kinds of labor of which the remuneration would not be lower than it is, if the employer took the full advantage of competition. Competition, however, must be regarded, in the present state of society, as the principal regulator of wages, and custom or individual character only as a modifying circumstance, and that in a comparatively slight degree.

Wages, then, depend mainly upon the demand and supply of labor; or as it is often expressed, on the proportion between population and capital. * * *

* * * But dearness or cheapness of food, when of a permanent character, and capable of being calculated on beforehand, may affect wages. In the first place, if the laborers have, as if often the case, no more than enough to keep them in working condition, and enable them barely to support the ordinary number of children, it follows that if food grows permanently dearer without a rise of wages, a greater number of the children will prematurely die; and thus wages will ultimately be higher, but only because the number of people will be smaller, than if food had remained cheap. But, secondly, even though wages were high enough to admit of food's becoming more costly without depriving the laborers and their families of necessaries; though they could bear, physically speaking, to be worse off, perhaps they would not consent to be so. They might have habits of comfort which were to them as necessaries, and sooner than forego which, they would put an additional restraint on their power of multiplication; so that wages would rise, not by increase of deaths but by diminution of births. In these cases, then, wages do adapt themselves to the price of food, though after an interval of almost a generation. * * *

The converse case occurs when, by improvements in agriculture, the repeal of corn laws, or other such causes, the necessaries of the laborers are cheapened, and they are enabled with the same wages, to command greater comforts than before. Wages will not fall immediately; it is even possible that they may rise; but they will fall at last, so as to leave the laborers no better off than before, unless, during this interval of prosperity, the standard of comfort regarded as indispensable by the class, is permanently raised. * * *

§ 3. Wages depend, then, on the proportion between the number of the laboring population, and the capital or other funds devoted to the purchase of labor; we will say, for shortness, the capital. If wages are higher at one time or place than at another, if the subsistence and comfort of the class of hired laborers are more ample, it is for no other reason than because capital bears a greater proportion to population. It is not the absolute amount of accumulation or of production, that is of importance to the laboring class; it is not the amount even of the funds destined for distribution among the laborers: it is the proportion between those funds and the numbers among whom they are shared. The condition of the class can be bettered in no other way than by altering that proportion to their advantage: and every scheme for their benefit, which does not proceed on this as its foundation, is, for all permanent purposes, a delusion.

* * *

Except, therefore, in the very peculiar cases which I have just noticed, of which the only one of any practical importance is that of a new colony, or a country in circumstances equivalent to it; it is impossible that population should increase at its utmost rate without lowering wages. Nor will the fall be stopped at any point, short of that which either by its physical or its moral operation, checks the increase of population. In no old country, therefore, does population increase at anything like its utmost rate; in most, at a very moderate rate: in some countries not at all. These facts are only to be accounted for in two ways. Either the whole number of births which nature admits of, and which happen in some circumstances, do not take place; or if they do, a large proportion of those who are born, die. The retardation of increase results either from mortality or prudence; from Mr. Malthus's positive, or from his preventive check: and one or the other of these must and does exist, and very powerfully too, in all old societies. Wherever population is not kept down by the prudence either of individuals or of the state, it is kept down by starvation or disease.

* * * [W]hile there is a growing sensitiveness to the hardships of the poor, and a ready disposition to admit claims in them upon

the good offices of other people, there is an all but universal unwillingness to face the real difficulty of their position, or advert at all to the conditions which nature has made indispensable to the improvement of their physical lot. Discussions on the condition of the laborers, lamentations over its wretchedness, denunciations of all who are supposed to be indifferent to it, projects of one kind or another for improving it, were in no country and in no time of the world so rife as in the present generation; but there is a tacit agreement to ignore totally the law of wages, or to dismiss it in a parenthesis, with such terms as "hard-hearted Malthusianism;" as if it were not a thousand times more hard-hearted to tell human beings that they may, than that they may not, call into existence swarms of creatures who are sure to be miserable, and most likely to be depraved; and forgetting that the conduct, which it is reckoned so cruel to disapprove, is a degrading slavery to a brute instinct in one of the persons concerned, and most commonly, in the other, helpless submission to a revolting abuse of power.

* * * I ask, then, is it true, or not, that if their numbers were fewer they would obtain higher wages? This is the question, and no other: and it is idle to divert attention from it, by attacking any incidental position of Malthus or some other writer, and pretending that to refute that, is to disprove the principle of population. Some, for instance, have achieved an easy victory over a passing remark of Mr. Malthus, hazarded chiefly by way of illustration, that the increase of food may perhaps be assumed to take place in an arithmetical ratio, while population increases in a geometrical: when every candid reader knows that Mr. Malthus laid no stress on this unlucky attempt to give numerical precision to things which do not admit of it, and every person capable of reasoning must see that it is wholly superfluous to his argument. * * *

Chapter XIII. The Remedies for Low Wages Further Considered

§ 1. By what means, then, is poverty to be contended against? How is the evil of low wages to be remedied? * * * Poverty, like most social evils, exists because men follow their brute instincts without due consideration. But society is possible, precisely because man is not necessarily a brute. Civilization in every one of its aspects is a struggle against the animal instincts. Over some even of the strongest of them, it has shown itself capable of acquiring abundant control. It has artificialized large portions of mankind to such an extent, that of many of their most natural inclinations they have scarcely a vestige or a remembrance left. If it has not brought the instinct of population under as much restraint as is needful, we must remember that it has never seriously tried. What efforts it has made, have mostly been in the contrary direction. Religion, morality, and statesmanship have vied with one another in incitements to marriage, and to the multiplication of the species, so it be but in wedlock. Religion has not even yet discontinued its encouragements. The Roman Catholic clergy (of any other clergy it is unnecessary to speak, since no other have any considerable influence over the poorer classes) everywhere think it their duty to promote marriage, in order to prevent fornication. * * * While a man who is intemperate in drink, is discountenanced and despised by all who profess to be moral people, it is one of the chief grounds made use of in appeals to the benevolent, that the applicant has a large family and is unable to maintain them.[1]

One cannot wonder that silence on this great department of human duty should produce unconsciousness of moral obligations, when it produces oblivion of physical facts. That it is possible to delay marriage, and to live in abstinence while unmarried, most people are willing to allow: but when persons are once married, the idea, in this country, never seems to enter anyone's mind that having or not having a family, or the number of which it shall consist, is amenable to their own control. One would imagine that children were rained down upon married people, direct from heaven, without their being art or part in the matter; that it was really, as the common phrases have it, God's will, and not their own, which decided the numbers of their offspring. * * *

§ 2. Those who think it hopeless that the laboring classes should be induced to practise a sufficient degree of prudence in regard to the increase of their families, because they have hitherto stopped short of that point, show an inability to estimate the ordinary principles of human action. Nothing more would probably be necessary to secure that result, than an opinion generally diffused that it was desirable. As a moral principle, such an opinion has never yet existed in any country: it is curious that it does not so exist in countries in which, from the spontaneous operation of individual forethought, population is, comparatively speaking, efficiently repressed. What is practised as prudence, is still not recognized as duty; the talkers and writers are mostly on the other side, even in France, where a sentimental horror of Malthus is almost as rife as in this country. * * *

But let us try to imagine what would happen if the idea became general among the laboring class, that the competition of too great numbers was the principal cause of their poverty; so that every

1. Little improvement can be expected in morality until the producing large families is regarded with the same feelings as drunkenness or any other physical excess. But while the aristocracy and clergy are foremost to set the example of this kind of incontinence what can be expected from the poor?

laborer looked (with Sismondi) upon every other who had more than the number of children which the circumstances of society allowed to each, as doing him a wrong—as filling up the place which he was entitled to share. Anyone who supposes that this state of opinion would not have a great effect on conduct, must be profoundly ignorant of human nature; can never have considered how large a portion of the motives which induce the generality of men to take care even of their own interests, is derived from regard for opinion—from the expectation of being disliked or despised for not doing it. * * *

If the opinion were once generally established among the laboring class that their welfare required a due regulation of the numbers of families, the respectable and well-conducted of the body would conform to the prescription, and only those would exempt themselves from it, who were in the habit of making light of social obligations generally; and there would be then an evident justification for converting the moral obligation against bringing children into the world who are a burden to the community, into a legal one; just as in many other cases of the progress of opinion, the law ends by enforcing against recalcitrant minorities, obligations which to be useful must be general, and which, from a sense of their utility, a large majority have voluntarily consented to take upon themselves. There would be no need, however, of legal sanctions, if women were admitted, as on all other grounds they have the clearest title to be, to the same rights of citizenship with men. Let them cease to be confined by custom to one physical function as their means of living and their source of influence, and they would have for the first time an equal voice with men in what concerns that function: and of all the improvements in reserve for mankind which it is now possible to foresee, none might be expected to be so fertile as this in almost every kind of moral and social benefit.

* * *

§ 3. For the purpose therefore of altering the habits of the laboring people, there is need of a twofold action, directed simultaneously upon their intelligence and their poverty. An effective national education of the children of the laboring class, is the first thing needful: and, coincidently with this, a system of measures which shall (as the Revolution did in France) extinguish extreme poverty for one whole generation.

CHARLES DARWIN

The Origin of Species (1859) †

Geometrical Ratio of Increase

A struggle for existence inevitably follows from the high rate at which all organic beings tend to increase. Every being, which during its natural lifetime produces several eggs or seeds, must suffer destruction during some period of its life, and during some season or occasional year, otherwise, on the principle of geometrical increase, its numbers would quickly become so inordinately great that no country could support the product. Hence, as more individuals are produced than can possibly survive, there must in every case be a struggle for existence, either one individual with another of the same species, or with the individuals of distinct species, or with the physical conditions of life. It is the doctrine of Malthus applied with manifold force to the whole animal and vegetable kingdoms; for in this case there can be no artificial increase of food, and no prudential restraint from marriage. Although some species may be now increasing, more or less rapidly, in numbers, all cannot do so, for the world would not hold them.[1]

There is no exception to the rule that every organic being naturally increases at so high a rate, that, if not destroyed, the earth would soon be covered by the progeny of a single pair. Even slow-breeding man has doubled in twenty-five years, and at this rate, in less than a thousand years, there would literally not be standing-room for his progeny. Linnæus has calculated that if an annual plant produced only two seeds—and there is no plant so unproductive as this—and their seedlings next year produced two, and so on, then in twenty years there should be a million plants. The elephant is reckoned the slowest breeder of all known animals, and I have taken some pains to estimate its probable minimum rate of natural increase; it will be safest to assume that it begins breeding when

† Charles Robert Darwin (1809–1882), British scientist. The present text is from Chapter 3 of the seventh edition of *The Origin of Species*.
1. Compare Darwin's remark in his autobiography: "In October 1838, that is, fifteen months after I had begun my systematic enquiry, I happened to read for amusement Malthus on *Population*, and being well prepared to appreciate the struggle for existence which everywhere goes on from long-continued observation of the habits of animals and plants, it at once struck me that under these circumstances favourable variations would tend to be preserved, and unfavourable ones to be destroyed. The result of this would be the formation of new species. Here, then, I had at last got a theory by which to work. . . ." (*The Autobiography of Charles Darwin, 1809–1882*, Nora Barlow, ed., [New York, 1969,] p. 120) [*Editor*].

thirty years old, and goes on breeding till ninety years old, bringing forth six young in the interval, and surviving till one hundred years old, if this be so, after a period of from 740 to 750 years there would be nearly nineteen million elephants alive, descended from the first pair.

But we have better evidence on this subject than mere theoretical calculations, namely, the numerous recorded cases of the astonishingly rapid increase of various animals in a state of nature, when circumstances have been favourable to them during two or three following seasons. Still more striking is the evidence from our domestic animals of many kinds which have run wild in several parts of the world; if the statements of the rate of increase of slow-breeding cattle and horses in South America, and latterly in Australia, had not been well authenticated, they would have been incredible. So it is with plants; cases could be given of introduced plants which have become common throughout whole islands in a period of less than ten years. Several of the plants, such as the cardoon and a tall thistle, which are now the commonest over the whole plains of La Plata, clothing square leagues of surface almost to the exclusion of every other plant, have been introduced from Europe; and there are plants which now range in India, as I hear from Dr. Falconer, from Cape Comorin to the Himalaya, which have been imported from America since its discovery. In such cases, and endless others could be given, no one supposes, that the fertility of the animals or plants has been suddenly and temporarily increased in any sensible degree. The obvious explanation is that the conditions of life have been highly favourable, and that there has consequently been less destruction of the old and young, and that nearly all the young have been enabled to breed. Their geometrical ratio of increase, the result of which never fails to be surprising, simply explains their extraordinarily rapid increase and wide diffusion in their new homes.

In a state of nature almost every full-grown plant annually produces seed, and amongst animals there are very few which do not annually pair. Hence we may confidently assert, that all plants and animals are tending to increase at a geometrical ratio,—that all would rapidly stock every station in which they could anyhow exist,—and that this geometrical tendency to increase must be checked by destruction at some period of life. Our familiarity with the larger domestic animals tends, I think, to mislead us: we see no great destruction falling on them, but we do not keep in mind that thousands are annually slaughtered for food, and that in a state of nature an equal number would have somehow to be disposed of.

The only difference between organisms which annually produce eggs or seeds by the thousand, and those which produce extremely few, is, that the slow-breeders would require a few more years to people, under favourable conditions, a whole district, let it be ever so large. The condor lays a couple of eggs and the ostrich a score, and yet in the same country the condor may be the more numerous of the two; the Fulmar petrel lays but one egg, yet it is believed to be the most numerous bird in the world. One fly deposits hundreds of eggs, and another, like the hippobosca, a single one; but this difference does not determine how many individuals of the two species can be supported in a district. A large number of eggs is of some importance to those species which depend on a fluctuating amount of food, for it allows them rapidly to increase in number. But the real importance of a large number of eggs or seeds is to make up for much destruction at some period of life; and this period in the great majority of cases is an early one. If an animal can in any way protect its own eggs or young, a small number may be produced, and yet the average stock be fully kept up; but if many eggs or young are destroyed, many must be produced, or the species will become extinct. It would suffice to keep up the full number of a tree, which lived on an average for a thousand years, if a single seed were produced once in a thousand years, supposing that this seed were never destroyed, and could be ensured to germinate in a fitting place. So that, in all cases, the average number of any animal or plant depends only indirectly on the number of its eggs or seeds.

In looking at Nature, it is most necessary to keep the foregoing considerations always in mind—never to forget that every single organic being may be said to be striving to the utmost to increase in numbers; that each lives by a struggle at some period of its life; that heavy destruction inevitably falls either on the young or old, during each generation or at recurrent intervals. Lighten any check, mitigate the destruction ever so little, and the number of the species will almost instantaneously increase to any amount. * * *

KARL MARX

Capital (1867) †

If the reader reminds me of Malthus, whose "Essay on Population" appeared in 1798, I remind him that this work in its first form is nothing more than a schoolboyish, superficial plagiary of De Foe, Sir James Steuart, Townsend, Franklin, Wallace, &c., and

† Karl Marx (1818–1883), German economist. The present text is from a footnote to Part VII, Chapter 25, Section I.

does not contain a single sentence thought out by himself. The great sensation this pamphlet caused, was due solely to party interest. The French Revolution had found passionate defenders in the United Kingdom; the "principle of population," slowly worked-out in the eighteenth century, and then, in the midst of a great social crisis, proclaimed with drums and trumpets as the infallible antidote to the teachings of Condorcet, &c., was greeted with jubilance by the English oligarchy as the great destroyer of all hankerings after human development. Malthus, hugely astonished at his success, gave himself to stuffing into his book materials superficially compiled, and adding to it new matter, not discovered but annexed by him. Note further: Although Malthus was a parson of the English State Church, he had taken the monastic vow of celibacy—one of the conditions of holding a Fellowship in Protestant Cambridge University: "Socios collegiorum maritos esse non permittimus, sed statim postquam quis uxorem duxerit, socius collegii desinat esse." (Reports of Cambridge University Commission, p. 172.) This circumstance favourably distinguishes Malthus from the other Protestant parsons, who have shuffled off the command enjoining celibacy of the priesthood and have taken, "Be fruitful and multiply," as their special Biblical mission in such a degree that they generally contribute to the increase of population to a really unbecoming extent, whilst they preach at the same time to the labourers the "principle of population." It is characteristic that the economic fall of man, the Adam's apple, the urgent appetite, "the checks which tend to blunt the shafts of Cupid," as Parson Townsend waggishly puts it, that this delicate question was and is monopolised by the Reverends of Protestant Theology, or rather of the Protestant Church. With the exception of the Venetian monk, Ortes, an original and clever writer, most of the population-theory teachers are Protestant parsons. For instance, Bruckner, "Théorie du Système animal," Leyden, 1767, in which the whole subject of the modern population theory is exhausted, and to which the passing quarrel between Quesnay and his pupil, the elder Mirabeau, furnished ideas on the same topic; then Parson Wallace, Parson Townsend, Parson Malthus and his pupil, the arch-Parson Thomas Chalmers, to say nothing of lesser reverend scribblers in this line. Originally, political economy was studied by philosophers like Hobbes, Locke, Hume; by business men and statesmen, like Thomas More, Temple, Sully, De Witt, North, Law, Vanderlint, Cantillon, Franklin; and especially, and with the greatest success, by medical men like Petty, Barbon, Mandeville, Quesnay. Even in the middle of the eighteenth century, the Rev. Mr. Tucker, a notable economist of his time, excused himself for meddling with the things of Mammon. Later on, and in truth with this very "principle of population," struck the hour of the Protestant parsons. Petty, who regarded the population as the basis of wealth, and was, like Adam Smith, an outspoken foe to parsons, says, as if he had a presentiment of their bungling interference, "that Religion best flourishes when the Priests are most mortified, as was before said of the Law, which best flourisheth when lawyers have least to do." He advises the Protestant priests, therefore if they once for all, will not follow the Apostle Paul and "mortify" themselves by celibacy, "not to breed more Churchmen than the Benefices, as they now stand shared out, will receive, that is to say, if there be places for about twelve thousand in England and Wales, it will not be safe to breed up 24,000 ministers, for then the twelve thousand which are unprovided for, will seek ways how to get themselves a livelihood, which they cannot do more easily than by persuading the people that the twelve thousand incumbents do poison or starve their souls, and misguide them in their way to Heaven." (Petty; "A Treatise on Taxes and Contributions, London, 1667," p. 57.) * * *

GEORGE BERNARD SHAW

Fabian Essays (1889) †

All economic analyses begin with the cultivation of the earth. To the mind's eye of the astronomer the earth is a ball spinning in space without ulterior motives. To the bodily eye of the primitive cultivator it is a vast green plain, from which, by sticking a spade into it, wheat and other edible matters can be made to spring. * * *

According to our hypothesis, the inland sea of cultivation has now spread into the wilderness so far that at its margin the return to a man's labour for a year is only £500. But as there is always a flood tide in that sea, caused by the incessant increase of population, the margin will not stop there: it will at last encroach upon every acre of cultivable land, rising to the snow line on the mountains and falling to the coast of the actual salt water sea, but always reaching the barrenest places last of all, because the cultivators are still, as ever, on the make, and will not break bad land when better is to be had. * * *

* * * In current economic terms the price is regulated by supply and demand. As the demand for land intensifies by the advent of

† George Bernard Shaw (1856–1950), British playwright and Fabian Socialist. The present text is from his contribution, titled "Economic," to the *Fabian Essays,* Shaw, ed., (London, 1889).

fresh proletarians, the price goes up; and the bargains are made more stringent. Tenants' rights, instead of being granted in perpetuity, and so securing for ever to the tenant the increase due to unforeseen improvements in production, are granted on leases for finite terms, at the expiration of which the landlord can revise the terms or eject the tenant. The payments rise until the original head rents and quit rents appear insignificant in comparison with the incomes reaped by the intermediate tenant right holders or middlemen. Sooner or later the price of tenant right will rise so high that the actual cultivator will get no more of the produce than suffices him for subsistence. At that point there is an end of sub-letting tenant rights. The land's absorption of the proletarians as tenants paying more than the economic rent stops.

And now, what is the next proletarian to do? For all his forerunners we have found a way of escape: for him there seems none. The board is at the door, inscribed 'Only standing room left'; and it might well bear the more poetic legend, *Lasciate ogni speranza, voi ch' entrate*. This man, born a proletarian, must die a proletarian, and leave his destitution as an only inheritance to his son. It is not yet clear that there is ten days life in him; for whence is his subsistence to come if he cannot get at the land? Food he must have, and clothing; and both promptly. There is food in the market, and clothing also; but not for nothing: hard money must be paid for it, and paid on the nail too; for he who has no property gets no credit. Money then is a necessity of life; and money can only be procured by selling commodities. This presents no difficulty to the cultivators of the land, who can raise commodities by their labour; but the proletarian, being landless, has neither commodities nor means of producing them. Sell something he must. Yet he has nothing to sell—except himself. The idea seems a desperate one; but it proves quite easy to carry out. The tenant cultivators of the land have not strength enough or time enough to exhaust the productive capacity of their holdings. If they could buy men in the market for less than these men's labour would add to the produce, then the purchase of such men would be a sheer gain. It would indeed be only a purchase in form: the men would literally cost nothing, since they would produce their own price, with a surplus for the buyer. Never in the history of buying and selling was there so splendid a bargain for buyers as this. Aladdin's uncle's offer of new lamps for old ones was in comparison a catchpenny. Accordingly, the proletarian no sooner offers himself for sale than he finds a rush of bidders for him, each striving to get the better of the others by offering to give him more and more of the produce of his labour, and to content themselves with less and less surplus. But even the highest bidder must have some surplus, or he will not buy. The proletarian, in accepting the highest bid, sells himself openly into bondage. He is not the first man who has done so; for it is evident that his fore-runners, the purchasers of tenant right, had been enslaved by the proprietors who lived on the rents paid by them. But now all the disguise falls off; the proletarian renounces not only the fruit of his labour, but also his right to think for himself and to direct his industry as he pleases. The economic change is merely formal: the moral change is enormous. Soon the new direct traffic in men overspreads the whole market, and takes the place formerly held by the traffic in tenant rights. * * *

* * * It was the increase of population that spread cultivation and civilization from the centre to the snow line, and at last forced men to sell themselves to the lords of the soil: it is the same force that continues to multiply men so that their exchange value falls slowly and surely until it disappears altogether—until even black chattel slaves are released as not worth keeping in a land where men of all colours are to be had for nothing. This is the con-dition of our English labourers today: they are no longer even dirt cheap: they are valueless, and can be had for nothing. * * * That is just the case of every member of the proletariat who could be replaced by one of the unemployed today. Their wage is not the price of themselves: for they are worth nothing: it is only their keep. For bare subsistence wages you can get as much common labour as you want, and do what you please with it within the limits of a criminal code which is sure to be interpreted by a proprietary-class judge in your favour. * * *

Over Population

The introduction of the capitalistic system is a sign that the exploitation of the labourer toiling for a bare subsistence wage has become one of the chief arts of life among the holders of tenant rights. It also produces a delusive promise of endless employment which blinds the proletariat to those disastrous consequences of rapid multiplication which are obvious to the small cultivator and peasant proprietor. But indeed the more you degrade the workers, robbing them of all artistic enjoyment, and all chance of respect and admiration from their fellows, the more you throw them back, reckless, on the one pleasure and the one human tie left to them—the gratification of their instinct for producing fresh supplies of men. You will applaud this instinct as divine until at last the excessive supply becomes a nuisance: there comes a plague of men; and you suddenly discover that the instinct is diabolic, and set up a cry of 'over population'. But your slaves are beyond caring for your cries: they breed like rabbits; and their poverty breeds filth, ugliness, dishonesty, disease, obscenity, drunkenness, and murder. In the midst of the riches which their labour piles up for you, their misery rises up too and stifles you. You withdraw in disgust to the other end of the town from them; you appoint special carriages on your railways and special seats in your churches and theatres for them; you set your life apart from theirs by every class barrier you can devise; and yet they swarm about you still: your face gets stamped with your habitual loathing and suspicion of them: your ears get so filled with the language of the vilest of them that you break into it when you lose your self-control: they poison your life as remorselessly as you have sacrified theirs heartlessly. You begin to believe intensely in the devil. Then comes the terror of their revolting; the drilling and arming of bodies of them to keep down the rest; the prison, the hospital, paroxysms of frantic coercion, followed by paroxysms of frantic charity. And in the meantime, the population continues to increase!

PART IV

Malthus in the Twentieth Century

Analysis of Malthus' Argument

SCOTT GORDON

The Basic Analytical Structure of Malthusian Theory (1975) †

The most striking passage in Malthus' *Essay on Population* is his comparison of arithmetic and geometric ratios, but this is not the analytical core of the theory. It *is* true that an arithmetic growth function cannot keep up with a geometric one, but Malthus' illustration only dramatises the problem of population, it does not provide a *theory* of it.

The core of Malthus' theory is his view that population change is governed by the relation between two factors: (1) the human "subsistence" requirement of food; and (2) the actual supply of food available. If we represent the population size by P; the change in population (its growth or decline) by ΔP; the per capita "subsistence" requirement by R; and the actual per capita food supply by S, then Malthus' basic assertion is a function:

$$\Delta P = f(S - R)$$

such that ΔP is positive when $S > R$ and negative when $R > S$. The population size will be in stable equilibrium only when $R = S$. This function is the core of Malthus' theory but, in itself, it does not lead necessarily to Malthus' conclusion that population will outstrip food supply, since there is nothing in this function which forbids S from exceeding R in perpetuity. To arrive at Malthus' equilibrium model, we must examine the determinants of S, the food supply; and to expand the model in the way in which Malthus did by his addition of "moral restraint" we must examine the determinants of R, the "subsistence" requirement.

Consider, first, the determinants of the actual food supply. If S were a function of *only* the amount of labor devoted to food production, L, i.e.,

$$S = g(L)$$

then, since each increase in population may bring with it a corresponding increase in L, there would be no reason for per capita

† Scott Gordon (b. 1924) is professor of economics at Indiana University, Bloomington, and at Queen's University, Kingston, Ontario. The present essay has not been previously published.

food output to fall as population increased. As one nineteenth-century critic of Malthus remarked "God sends two hands with every stomach." Similarly, there would be no "population problem" arising from the fact that agriculture requires farm machinery, buildings, etc. because labor can make these things too. The difficulty is that one of the necessary inputs is *land* and this is fixed in amount. So the food supply function of Malthus' theory is one with numerous inputs, including land. Using A to indicate the available land acreage, the proper food supply function is:

$$S = h(L, \ldots A, \ldots)$$

Since A is fixed, then as population grows the ratio of A to L necessarily falls; the function, h, is non-linear (i.e., it is not "arithmetic!") and the per capita supply of food falls as population increases. The non-linearity of the function h represents the Law of Diminishing Returns, which Malthus did not discover explicitly until twenty years after he wrote the *Essay*, but which he may have had vaguely in mind even in 1897. At any rate, the Law of Diminishing Returns is necessary to the kind of equilibrium population model that Malthus depicted in the first edition of his *Essay*.

Now consider the determinants of the "subsistence" requirement, R. If R is a reflection of purely physiological necessities, then it is an exogenously determined constant to which the food supply, S, gravitates as an equilibrium condition; that is, population will ineluctably grow (or decline) until S equals the *given* value of R. But if we suppose that R is a sociological rather than a physiological datum, then population growth may be constrained by a rise in R. Anything, then, which raises man's view of what is a "minimum" standard of living will act as a constraint on population growth. Through this door Malthus' "moral restraint," and numerous other sociological factors, may enter as determinants of population.

In this brief exposition of Malthus' analytics I have treated S and R as independent of one another. The actual food supply is one thing; the food requirement is quite another. It is possible however that they are not independent. For example, the actual standard of living (per capita S in Malthus' model) may well be a factor in determining what people regard as the minimal "requirement," if R is a sociological rather than a physiological datum. This possibility requires one to develop a more dynamic theory of population than Malthus' static equilibrium model. That is, however, not only a more interesting, but a much longer story . . .

ANTONY FLEW

The Structure of Malthus' Population Theory (1957) †

(a) The foundation of the whole structure [of Malthus' theory] is in every successive treatment substantially the same, but it is presented most powerfully in the *Summary*.[1] "In taking a view of animated nature, we cannot fail to be struck with a prodigious power of increase in plants and animals" (p. 119). "Elevated as man is above all other animals by his intellectual faculties, it is not to be supposed that the physical laws to which he is subjected should be essentially different from those which are observed to prevail in other parts of animated nature" (*Ibid.*, pp. 121–122). ". . . all animals, according to the known laws by which they are produced, must have a capacity of increasing in a geometrical progression" (*Ibid.*, p. 123).

This contention is then supported and made more precise as far as the human animal is concerned by examining what has in fact happened with practically isolated human populations in peculiarly favourable although not of course ideal conditions. So "It may be safely asserted, . . . that population, when unchecked, increases in geometrical progression of such a nature as to double itself every twenty-five years" (*Ibid.*, p. 138).

(b) At this stage in every statement of his theory Malthus argues for the conclusion that: ". . . the means of subsistence, under circumstances the most favourable to human industry, could not possibly be made to increase faster than in an arithmetical ratio" (*Second Essay*, Vol. I, p. 10);[2] that "by the laws of nature in respect to the powers of a limited territory, the additions which can be made in equal periods to the food which it produces must, after a short time, either be constantly decreasing, which is what would really take place; or, at the very most, must remain stationary, so as to increase the means of subsistence only in arithmetical progression" (*Summary*, p. 143).

(c) He next compares these two powers, of reproduction and production, noticing the utter disproportion between the geometrical progression of the one (1, 2, 4, 8, 16, 32 . . .) and the

† Antony Flew (b. 1923) is professor of philosophy at the University of Reading. The present essay was published in the *Australasian Journal of Philosophy*, 35 (1957), 1–20. Footnotes for this selection are by the editor. Editorial additions appear in brackets.

1. Malthus, *A Summary View of the*

Principle of Population (1830); references are to pagination of the reprint of this essay in D. V. Glass, ed., *Introduction to Malthus* (London, 1953).

2. Page references to the *Second Essay* are to the substantially unaltered and more accessible sixth edition (London, 1826).

arithmetical progression of the other (1, 2, 3, 4, 5, 6 . . .). In every statement of his position it is with the help of the observation of this disproportion that he tries to derive the conclusion that there must always be some check or checks operating against the power of reproduction. "By that law of our nature which makes food necessary for the life of man, the effects of these two unequal powers must be kept equal. This implies a strong and constantly operating check on population from the difficulty of subsistence" (*First Essay*, p. 14).[3] So ". . . the power of population being in every period so much superior, the increase of the human species can only be kept down to the level of the means of subsistence by the constant operation of the strong law of necessity, acting as a check upon the greater power" (*Second Essay*, Vol. I, p. 11). But in the *Summary* he is much more cautious: "it follows necessarily that the average rate of the *actual* increase of population over the greatest part of the globe . . . must be totally of a different character from the rate at which it would increase, if *unchecked* (p. 143; italics original).

(d) "The great question, which remains to be considered, is the manner in which this constant and necessary check on population practically operates" (*Summary*, p. 143). "The natural tendency to increase is everywhere so great that it will generally be easy to account for the height at which the population is found in any country. The more difficult, as well as the more interesting part of the enquiry is, to trace the immediate causes which stop its further progress. . . . What becomes of this mighty power . . . what are the kinds of restraint, and the forms of premature death, which keep the population down to the level of the means of subsistence?" (*Second Essay*, Vol. I, p. 218). * * *

But of course in addition to this speculative interest in discovering what the checks are and how they have operated Malthus always had a practical concern to find out and advocate what they ought to be and how they ought to operate. It is this concern which directs the whole of the *First Essay* and the second part of the *Second Essay*, and which shows itself repeatedly, not always fortunately, elsewhere. There is no suitably short passage to quote from the former (cf. however pp. 346 ff); but at the beginning of the fourth book of the latter Malthus wrote that taking the operation of some great check as "an inevitable law of nature, . . . the only enquiry that remains is, how it may take place with the least possible prejudice to the virtue and happiness of human society" (Vol. II, p. 255).

(e) In the next stage of his argument Malthus' second were

3. References to the *First Essay* are to the pagination of the first edition (or, of course, the facsimile edition; London, 1926).

importantly different from his first thoughts. While in both cases the duality of his interests leads him to mix two quite different systems of classification.

In the *First Essay* the categories "preventive check" and "positive check" are presented as the most important but not as together exhaustive: "a foresight of the difficulties attending the rearing of a family, acts as a preventive check; and the actual distresses of some of the lower classes, by which they are disabled from giving the proper food and attention to their children, acts as a positive check" (pp. 62–3); but "to these two great checks to population . . . may be added, vicious customs with respect to women, great cities, unwholesome manufactures, luxury, pestilence, and war" (pp. 99–100). In the *Second Essay* and after "positive checks" and "preventive checks" are the labels of two, supposedly, mutually elusive and together exhaustive categories. The former "include every cause [e.g. wars, pestilences, and famines—A.F.] . . . which in any degree contributes to shorten the natural duration of human life" (Vol. I, p. 15). The latter, though the outlines are blurred by the author's delicacy of expression and moral commitments, is complementary. It includes all checks to the birth rate: from "the restraint from marriage which is not followed by irregular gratifications"; through "promiscuous intercourse, unnatural passions" and "violations of the marriage bed"; to "improper arts to conceal the consequences of irregular connections" (Vol. I, p. 16). Elsewhere after "promiscuous concubinage" he brings himself to mention enigmatically "something else as unnatural" (Vol. II, p. 8); i.e. contraception.

But in addition to this method of division he employs a second, cutting right across the first, which is also offered as exclusive and exhaustive, and which is obviously not value-neutral at all. Thus in the *First Essay*, as the sentence immediately following the last passage quoted from this source, he writes: "All these checks may be fairly resolved into misery and vice" (p. 100). And, a little later, "In short it is difficult to conceive any check to population, which does not come under the description of some species of misery or vice" (p. 108). However in the *Second Essay*, as he is at pains to point out in his Preface, he "so far differed in principle from the former, as to suppose the action of another check to population which does not come under the head of either vice or misery; and, in the latter part I have endeavoured to soften some of the harshest conclusions of the first Essay" (Vol. I, pp. vii–viii). The new third category in this trinity is "moral restraint", one of "the preventive checks, the restraint from marriage which is not followed by irregular gratifications" (Vol. I, p. 15). With this vitally important modification the old claim to exhaustiveness is

repeated: "the checks which repress the superior power of population . . . are all resolvable into moral restraint, vice, and misery"
(Vol. I, p. 24).

(f) Finally Malthus makes the point that the values of the various possible checks do not vary entirely independently: "The sum
of all the positive and preventive checks taken together, forms
undoubtedly the immediate cause which represses population . . .
we can certainly draw no safe conclusion from the contemplation
of two or three of these checks taken by themselves, because it so
frequently happens that the excess of one check is balanced by the
defect of some other" (Vol. I, p. 256). Although his general statements about the relations between the various checks considered as
variables are usually, like this one, curiously weak, his particular
arguments again and again depend on the subsistence of far
stronger connections. Thus in the *First Essay* he remarks that Dr.
Price's failure, after supposing that all the checks other than famine
were removed, to draw "the obvious and necessary inference that
an unchecked population would increase beyond comparison, faster
than the earth, by the best directed exertions of man, could produce food for its support", was "as astonishing, as if he had
resisted the conclusion of one of the plainest propositions of Euclid"
(pp. 340–1). Again in the *Second Essay* he quotes with approval
the remark of a Jesuit missionary that "if famine did not, from
time to time, thin the immense number of inhabitants which China
contains, it would be impossible for her to live in peace" (Vol. I, p.
226). And the whole force of his argument for his proposals for
encouraging Moral Restraint lies in the contention that this check
might by these means be substituted, to a greater extent than in
modern Europe it had already been, for those others which he
classed as species of Vice or Misery. "If there were no other
depopulating causes, and if the preventive check did not operate
very strongly, every country would without doubt be subject to
periodical plagues and famines" (Vol. I, p. 530).

* * *

Our examination in the previous section of Malthus' conceptual
framework has, I think, shown: that he was right when he claimed
"I could have intrenched myself in an impregnable fortress . . ."
(*Second Essay*, Vol I, p. vii); but that, if he was taking his actual
guiding ideas to be unassailable just as they were, he was seriously
in error. We are now at last in a position to consider the nature
and function of his theory taken as a whole.

(a) The first thing to remark is the simplicity and familiarity
of the facts and ideas involved. Malthus introduced no new concept and emobdied no factual discovery in his theory. What he did

was to bring together one or two familiar facts of life, make an unfortunately precise and general supposition about a limit on the expansion of food production, and try to deduce the necessary consequences of these facts. All his demographic investigations were generated by these fairly immediate apparent consequences of a few simple ideas and obvious facts, and all his practical recommendations too were conditioned by them. * * *

(b) The second thing to remark is that the master question which stimulates and guides Malthus' population studies is negative: he is asking why and how something does *not* happen. This question is generated by his fundamental law of population, which states the rate at which population increases, *when unchecked.* Malthus' theory here bears a certain resemblance to classical mechanics. For the first law of motion states that: "Every body continues in its state of rest or of uniform motion in a right line *unless it is compelled to change that state by forces impressed upon it*" (*Principia,* Bk. I; italics mine). Since in actual fact most, if not all, bodies are in motion relative to some other bodies and this motion never continues for long in a right line the question arises: Why do bodies *not* continue in a state of rest or of uniform motion in a right line, what forces operate to prevent this, and how? * * *

(c) The third point to remark is that this conceptual framework was originally built as a practical theory, designed as a guide to political and social action (or inaction). Though its fundamental principle generated the speculative question which Malthus by his own work showed to be of great heuristic value, it always retained this essentially practical character. Not only was the evaluative-prescriptive method of classifying checks always used alongside the value-neutral descriptive one (see II (e) and III (e) above): but Malthus also throughout retained the argument of the comparison of the ratios to support simultaneously both the speculatively stimulating conclusion that some checks *are* operating everywhere and the practically crucial contention that there always *must be* checks. * * * Though Malthus made one vitally important addition, the category of moral restraint, and various minor alterations in the *Second Essay* and after, it always remained essentially the conceptual framework of the *First Essay* with which he approached all population questions. It should therefore not surprise us that these ideas are more suited for the rough and ready understanding of broad trends and for guiding the wide lines of general policy than for assisting in detailed demographic analysis. * * *

But for the rough and practically vital understanding of the population explosions now occurring in so many of the under-developed countries Malthus' simple model of an enormous power of increase opposed by various counteracting forces is perhaps both necessary and sufficient. For it can bring out that in these countries the application of modern medical knowledge is weakening the positive check while nothing is occurring to produce a proportionate strengthening of the preventive check.

And if the fallacious argument of the comparison of the ratios is replaced, as it can most easily be * * * by a sound argument for the slightly weaker conclusion that the power of increase is so enormous that it must always be checked in the fairly short run; then Malthusian ideas can be used validly to establish some enormously important general practical conclusions.

Thus if Malthus' facts and arguments, so amended, are correct, and if it is accepted that there can be no right to the physically impossible: then it is surely preposterous to assert or assume that every (married) couple has a right to produce as many children as they wish, regardless of what others may be doing or wanting to do; and that all these children will have a right to support in childhood and as adults to earn a living, to marry and to have a similarly unrestricted right to produce children with similar rights in their turn. Unless you also make the gigantic, utterly unwarranted assumption that the sum of all these separate possible desires will always work out providentially to a practically manageable birth rate. This is a conclusion which Malthus always drew; and its importance can be appreciated by considering how widely and bitterly it was and still is resisted. * * *

JOSEPH J. SPENGLER

Was Malthus Right? (1966) †

I. Outline of Malthus' Conception of the Problem

Recognizing that the "power of increase in plants and animals" was "prodigious" and that man's biotic potential,[1] now at about

† Joseph J. Spengler (b. 1902) is James B. Duke Professor of Economics at Duke University. The present essay was published in the *Southern Economic Journal* and reprinted in *Population Economics* (Durham, N.C., 1972). The author's footnotes have been renumbered; some footnotes have been deleted. Editorial additions appear in brackets.

1. By biotic potential is meant the inherent rate of growth of a population in a logistic model at $t = O$. E.g., see R. Pearl, *Medical Biometry and Statistics* (Philadelphia: Saunders, 1941), p. 461. J. Bourgeois-Pichat's calculations suggest a maximum of about 5 percent. See United Nations, *The Aging of Populations and Its Economic and Social Implications*, Population Studies No. 26 (New York: United Nations, 1956), p. 27. The so-called law of Malthus is sometimes written as if the rate of growth v is constant and the size of a population N at time t is $N(O)e^{vt}$. But if v is inversely related to the size of

5 per cent, was in the neighborhood of 3 per cent, [Malthus] believed this rate needed to be greatly reduced; otherwise mortality would rise until the rate of natural increase was brought down to the level of increase in the food supply, or, better still, the means of existence. Presumably, he wanted to see established a set of institutional commitments which, together with the set of expectations inculcated in the individual would function as a kind of homeostat, prompting the individual to limit his family size sufficiently to bring his standard of life to a suitable level and thereafter at least maintain this level. Action along these lines, he believed, could reduce population elasticity below unity.[2]

* * *

Malthus' emphasis upon the need to establish or strengthen what I called a homeostatic set of arrangements and expectations flowed from: (*a*) his apparent belief that only if fertility could be easily controlled would it be held down in the absence of such arrangements;[3] and (*b*) his hypothesis that produce tended to grow at a decreasing rate—$1/n$ where n denoted the aggregate of produce, and the period to which $1/n$ referred was typically 20–25 years, or the period in which a population could double in the absence of checks. His mode of expression, however, obscured the conduct-determining significance of the indicator of subsistence to which a population adjusted.

We may illustrate the problem by dividing the population P of a crowded closed economy based on land and labor into P_x and P_y, and the labor force L, a fixed percentage of P, into L_x and L_y, where the subscripts x and y signify agricultural and non-agricultural. Let Y_x and Y_y designate the incomes of P_x and P_y, with their sum Y corresponding in value terms to net output O. If $f(x)$ denotes the output of agricultural labor L_x, cultivation will be carried to the point where its marginal product $f'(x)$ coincides with the minimal required "subsistence" income s. The income, in produce, of agricultural labor $= L_x f'(x)$ while the residuum R imputable to land $= L_x (f[(x)/x - f'(x)]$. All of R passes into the hands of P_y which includes landowners, and so does a small fraction of $L_x f'(x)$ which is exchanged for a portion of the output $f(y)$ of the non-

the population, $v = v_0(1 - N/a)$ where v_0 and a are constants, and the solution to the corresponding differential equation $dN/dt = v_0 N(1 - N/a)$ is the "logistic" law of Verhulst and Pearl and Reed. See M. G. Kendall, "Stochastic Processes and Population Growth," *Journal of the Royal Statistical Society*, Series B, XI, 1949, pp. 230–64, esp. pp. 231–32, also 244–45.
2. Malthus, *Essay on the Principle of Population* (London, 1890), pp. 529–31, 540–44.
3. *Essay*, Bk. III, chap. 14. While he pointed to the operation of the preventive check in some countries (e.g., Norway), he commonly associated a cessation of population growth, or a decline in numbers, with a decline in the flow of subsistence (e.g., American Indians, South Sea Islands) rather than with checks immediately operative.

agricultural labor force L_y. Upon completion of the transactions the average incomes of P_x and P_y are Y_x/P_x and Y_y/P_y, with the former approximating s and falling below Y_y/P_y. We thus have an income structure consisting of two sets of incomes, with one set at the subsistence level, by definition, and the other embracing incomes at various levels ranging upward from s, only some of which are high enough to permit population growth in addition to population replacements. If this structure,[4] as just described, is represented by a single value v, this value remains high enough to permit some population growth. If, however, v declines enough, population growth will cease, either because each socioeconomic group just replaces itself, or because the positive growth of some groups is offset by negative growth in others. Malthus did not employ the concept of income structure, though he envisaged a kind of pyramid of incomes, only some of which permitted population growth in then well-settled countries.

* * *

Malthus' stress upon the low elasticity of the food supply probably was based upon general observation rather than upon the rising food costs and rent which must have influenced Ricardo.[5] Of course, had Malthus been fully aware of the general lowness of yields and the very limited improvement achieved, his pessimism would have been fortified.[6]

In Malthus' day a notable change was taking place in the relative importance of the sources upon which Englishmen drew for raw materials. A shift was taking place from organic flow resources to inorganic stock resources, especially from wood to coal and iron and brick. Whence the dependence of industry upon agriculture, so much stressed by Quesnay and Smith, was somewhat relaxed. It was becoming possible to increase some sectors of the economy much more rapidly than ever before, by drawing on long accumulated inorganic reserves instead of on current organic flows of produce and wood in a land-short country with declining forests. The

4. H. Leibenstein uses the term "income structure" to denote a range of incomes, by socioeconomic income groups, which may just suffice for population replacement by each group. See his *A Theory of Economic-Demographic Development* (Princeton: Princeton University Press, 1954), pp. 12–13.

5. In England wheat yield per acre fell from 24 to 22 bushels between 1771 and 1812, with marginal land yielding only 8 bushels, or little more than the average of 9 for France in 1789. See Colin Clark, *The Conditions of Economic Progress*, 2nd ed. (London: Macmillan, 1951), pp. 225–27, and (with M. R. Haswell) *The Economics of Subsistence Agricul-*

ture (London: Macmillan, 1964), pp. 95, 99. The rise in grain prices between the 1790's and 1812 elevated agricultural rents and strengthened the impression that only high prices could evoke an adequate domestic supply of grain. See Kenneth Smith. *The Malthusian Controversy* (London: Routledge & Kegan Paul, 1951), pp. 82–85.

6. "Over a large part of the world today, agricultural productivity is now the same as, or even inferior to, what it was in the leading civilized communities 2,000 years ago." Clark and Haswell, *op. cit.*, p. 78, also pp. 91–92, 105–107, 146–53 on income elasticity of demand for food.

shift from organic to inorganic raw materials, together with the resulting greater concentration of activity, also reduced the relative input of transport, usually heavy in an agricultural economy.[7] If Malthus recognized the partial easing of the agricultural constraint upon industrial expansion and the possible release of landed resources to food production, he ignored it. After all, the elasticity of the food supply had not really been increased, nor had that of population fallen significantly enough. He did not even suggest, as Jevons would less than a half century later, that English industry was living on borrowed time, that a day would come when easily accessible mineral reserves would be exhausted. Malthus' great concern remained the food supply: it stifled other concerns that might have risen within the context of the "population question." * * *

III. Operation of Checks

Much of Malthus' *Essay* dealt with the operation of checks since checks. constituted the response whereby the growth of population was kept in line with the growth of output. * * *

Two misunderstandings have led to criticism of Malthus' reasoning. Checks emerge because the rate of population growth R_p exceeds or threatens to exceed the rate of growth of income R_y. It makes no difference whether R_y is very low and/or falling so long as it is likely to fall short of R_p in some measure. Malthus, as we saw, believed R_y would usually be very low; whence even a low R_p might generate check-exercising behavior which was directed to preserving a level of per capita income rather than a desired rate of increase of income. The rate of growth R_y that was developed in much of Europe and Europe overseas and later in Japan appreciably exceeded R_p, however, and permitted a continuing rise in average income y and hence in the "objective" and the "subjective" standards of life and the spread betwen them.[8] Individuals in the populations of these countries were interested, therefore, not merely in preserving y but in preserving some rate of increase $\Delta y/y$. Accordingly, they resorted to abortion, deferment of marriage, contraceptive practices, celibacy, and occasionally even infanticide to keep R_p sufficiently behind R_y, especially when mortality began to fall and

7. E. A. Wrigley, "The Supply of Raw Materials in the Industrial Revolution," *Economic History Review*, XV, No. 1, 1962, pp. 1–16, esp. 1–4. On transport in agricultural economies, see Clark and Haswell, *op. cit.*, chap. 9; on changes in the composition of the labor force, Phyllis Deane and W. A. Cole, *British Economic Growth 1688–1959* (Cambridge: University Press, 1962), chap. 4.
8. Here the term "objective" refers to actual patterns of consumption or want-satisfaction whereas the term "subjective" refers to the "objective" standard *plus* unsatisfied but actively desired latent wants which border on those satisfied and are or easily could become conduct determining. An increase in the spread between the two standards may produce a change in the composition of the objective standard, reduce fertility, increase the supply of effort, etc.

increase R_p.[9] Malthus' theory of the emergence of voluntary or preventive checks when R_p threatens to outstrip R_y and reduce $(R_y - R_p)R_y$ to a negligible magnitude belongs to the same set of theories as the modern one which stresses prevention of the decline of $(R_y - R_p)/R_y$ below a minimally acceptable positive level. This is the first misunderstanding.

The second misunderstanding is a sequel to the first. Malthus pointed to the possibility of both a decline in incomes in some countries, among them the United States, and an increase in others, especially England.[1] This increase was limited, of course, by limiting factors in a finite universe which limited the realizable upward shifts of returns functions.[2] Of primary concern here, however, is Malthus' failure to develop a social mechanism that would insure a population's continuing to grow less rapidly than income, provided income began for a time to grow more rapidly than population. He was not equipped with such concepts as rising expectations, expanding aspirations, demonstration effects, rising subjective standard of living, etc. Not only were the means of communication and social mobility limited in his day. The marked absence of durable goods from budgets in which outlay upon food, clothing, and housing bulked large also militated against the easy extension of expenditures to complexes of goods whose consumption was likely to entail outlays growing faster than disposable income. Should this category of complexes of goods and services come to bulk sufficiently large in budgets, its further growth would entail diminution in expenditure upon some other components in living budgets.[3] Even today economists and demographers neglect this task with which Malthus was inadequately equipped to deal. * * *

V. *Land Shortage: Achilles Heel*

A high rate of increase in the per capita food supply is essential, in underdeveloped countries, both to the facilitation of economic devel-

9. Davis, "The Theory—," *loc. cit.* [Kingsley Davis, "The Theory of Change and Response in Modern Demographic History," *Population Index*, (October 1963)], pp. 345–66; see also, A. Landry, *La révolution démographique* (Paris: Librairie du Receuil Sirey, 1934), pp. 169–204.

1. *Essay*, pp. 294–95, 360, 461–62.
2. See Ryoshin Minami, "An Analysis of Malthus' Theory," *Journal of Economic Behavior*, April 1961, pp. 60–62.
3. Let y denote an individual's disposable income, N the category of goods and services newly introduced into the individual's living budget, and O the category of old goods, or goods and services consumed prior to the addition of N.

If the income elasticity of demand for $N > 1$, the proportion of y spent upon O must decline, and if expenditure upon N continues to grow, in keeping with this elasticity, expenditure upon some components of O must decline. We thus have a situation in which components of the *subjective* standard of living for which demand had been *latent* are introduced into niches formed in the objective standard by rising income y, but from which they spread (after the manner of some plants when introduced into favorable ecological settings) until the relative and finally the absolute importance of some components of the *objective* standard is reduced. See note 8 above.

opment[4] and to escape from the Malthusian trap in which many such countries are caught. The food supply must annually increase approximately $R_p + iR_y$ where R_p denotes the rate of population growth, R_y signifies the rate of growth of per capita income, and i indicates the income elasticity of demand for food. Since R_p lies between two and 3 per cent, R_y often approximates 2 per cent, and i usually lies between 0.9 and 0.4 (probably between 0.8 and 0.6 in countries with per capita incomes of $50 to $1000), the food supply must increase 3.5 to 5 per cent or more per year in under-developed countries. * * *

How much average yield can be raised is problematical. It is probable that in many areas fertilizer inputs can increase output 100–300 per cent.[5] Within a range the addition of a kilogram of chemical fertilizer plant nutrients tends to be accompanied by an increase of 10 kilograms in the output of grain. In fact, some Japanese rice farmers average about 11,000 pounds of paddy rice per acre of "nearly two-and-one-half times the high national average rice yield of Japan" much as some corn farmers get 150 bushels or more per acre instead of 80 to 85.[6] The response of output to fertilizer increments varies, however, from region to region and from country to country. It is affected by conditions of the soil, cultivation, and so on, tending to be higher in advanced countries than in relatively backward areas.[7] It may be affected by the tendency of the cost of grain production to rise as arable land per capita falls and agricultural intensity rates rise; it will probably be affected by severe limits to the extension of irrigation as well as by the rising costs of an inelastic supply of water.[8] There is, of course, an upper limit to yields per acre,[9] even when a country can produce the required fertilizer, or the foreign

4. B. F. Johnston and J. W. Mellor, "The Role of Agriculture in Economic Development," *American Economic Review*, September 1961, pp. 566–93; T. W. Schultz, *Transforming Traditional Agriculture* (New Haven: Yale University Press, 1964); United Nations (ECAFE), *Economic Survey of Asia and the Far East, 1964* (Bangkok: United Nations, 1965), Part I, esp. pp. 117–36.
5. H. L. Richardson, "What Fertilizers Could Do to Increase World Food Production," *The Advancement of Science*, January 1961, pp. 472–80.
6. Brown, *Increasing World Food Output*, pp. 102–103, and *Man, Land & Food*, pp. 127–28. Colin Clark estimates that in time 20 square meters could be made to supply the annual food requirements of one man, or one acre could, if laboratory conditions were met, feed about 200 men. Clark, in Kendall, ed., *op. cit.* [M. G. Kendall, ed., *Food Sup-*

plies and Population Growth (Edinburgh, 1963)], p. 64. Clark also calls attention to F. Daniels's estimate that the cultivation of algae might yield 50 tons of organic matter, dry weight, per hectare per year. *Conditions of Economic Progress*, 3rd ed., p. 306, note.
7. J. W. Mellor and R. W. Herdt, "Contrasting Response of Rice to Nitrogen," *Journal of Farm Economics*, February 1964, pp. 150–60; Brown, *Increasing World Food Output*, pp. 94–96, and *Man, Land & Food*, pp. 127–28.
8. *Ibid.*, pp. 94–97, 110–11, 127–28; Brown, *Increasing World Food Output*, pp. 90–93.
9. Incremental yields decline as fertilizer input per acre rises. See U.S.D.A., *Yearbook of Agriculture 1957* (Washington, D.C.: U.S. Government Printing Office, 1957), pp. 269–76; C. J. Pratt, "Chemical Fertilizers," *Scientific American*, June, 1965, pp. 70–72.

exchange wherewith to purchase it. If we assume that current yields can shortly be quadrupled, the limit to population will still be reached in about 57 years, should population grow 2.5 per cent per year. If the diet shifts somewhat toward more land-embodying products (e.g., animal products), the limit will be reached even earlier. Whether the upper limit to yields will be reached is doubtful, however, given the many changes besides increased fertilization that must be made in agriculture if yields are to be raised to the maximum levels economically attainable. It should be noted also that non-modern, underdeveloped, land-short, food-short countries are the ones least capable of substituting chemistic Edens for land-based agriculture.[1]

Malthus, it will be recalled, made land or "room" the overriding limitational factor. Whether it is, depends upon the composition of the content of living budgets. If food is the predominant component of the living budget, land will probably turn out to be the limitational factor. If dearth of food operates indirectly to check economic development and transformation, land may prove the limitational factor. If the standard of life rises, however, other components may replace food as the fundamental limitational factor. It is quite likely, however, that limitation of food due to limitation of land will become the limitational factor in parts of Asia, Africa, and Latin America. Elsewhere land in the sense of living space is likely to become the limitational factor. Thus Malthus will have been proven right in stressing the role of limitational factors, above all agricultural land.

1. Jacob Rosen, *The Road to Abundance* (New York: McGraw-Hill, 1953).

Some Contemporary
Anti-Malthusians

A. Y. BOYARSKI

A Contribution to the Problem of the World
Population in the Year 2000 (1965) †

I. *The Significance and Nature of the Problem*

1. In the minds of many, population forecasts are associated with the fundamental questions of population theory. The customary simplified, not to say vulgar, approach to this subject is that if a great increase in population is to be anticipated in the next few decades, then the Malthusians are right; if not, then some of their opponents, in particular the Marxists, are right.

2. In reality, the roots of the absolute incompatibility between these doctrines reach much deeper than the quantitative evaluation of population growth. The crux of the argument lies not in the arithmetical caluclation of rates of population growth tomorrow or the day after, but in determining the causes of the poverty which exists today. The opponents of Malthus maintain that if resources and technology were properly used and goods were properly distributed, the entire population of the world could enjoy an adequate food supply and a sufficiently high general standard of living. The Malthusians, on the other hand, substitute the population problem for the problem of the structure of society and indulge in speculative calculations.

3. In this sense, Marxism does in fact deny the "population problem", although it by no means closes its eyes to the problems connected with population growth. But the relative overpopulation caused in capitalist society not by a shortage of productive forces but by the system of production tends to spread the view that existing ills have a single cause—the population problem. Hence, the hopes and fears connected with the results of demographic forecasts are predicted.

† A. Y. Boyarski is professor and director of the Scientific Research Institute, Central Statistical Office of the USSR, Moscow. The present text is from *World Population Conference, 1965* (United Nations, 1966–67), Volume 2, pp. 5–11.

4. In point of fact, the solution lies in the harmonious development of population and productive forces which can be achieved when the sole purpose served by the productive forces is to ensure the welfare of the population—that is, under conditions of socialism. The socialization of industry is not, of course, enough by itself. To achieve the necessary industrial growth not only labour is required, but also adequate development of the production of the means of production; without that there can be no industrialization or, in the final analysis, improvement in the welfare of people; and a further condition for the latter is that the fruit of the people's labour goes to them and not to a handful of owners. And in this process, if production is to be maintained at the necessary level without lengthening the working day, there must be a corresponding increase in the productivity of labour at the proper level of economic activity of the population.

5. The Malthusians see only one way out: a reduction in population growth. The opponents of Malthus, while not disregarding rates of population growth, believe that all the interdependent aspects of the question must be taken into account; and this means that a solution of the problem can be found through increasing the productivity of labour and ensuring the proper distribution of efforts and resources, on the one hand, between production and other aspects of socially useful activity, and on the other hand, within the sphere of production itself, between the production of the means of production and the production of consumer goods.

* * *

49. We have obtained a world grand total of 4,626 ± 410 million, or, to put it in more suitable form, 4.2 to 5.0 thousand million.

50. Does that mean 5,000 million mouths to feed? Yes, but also 3,000 million workers! And if we equip them with the achievements of modern science and technology and save them and that technology from the senseless waste of war, we shall undoubtedly be able not only to feed all these mouths well, but also, given a proper distribution of wealth, to ensure for all people on earth prosperity and a happy life.

POPE PAUL VI

Humanae Vitae (1968) †

* * *

2. The changes which have taken place are in fact noteworthy and of varied kind. In the first place, there is the rapid demographic development. Fear is shown by many that world population is growing more rapidly than the available resources, with growing distress to many families and developing countries, so that the temptation for authorities to counter this danger with radical measures is great. Moreover, working and lodging conditions, as well as increased exigencies both in the economic field and in that of education, often make the proper education of an elevated number of children difficult today.

* * *

3. This new state of things gives rise to new questions. Granted the conditions of life today, and granted the meaning which conjugal relations have with respect to the harmony between husband and wife and to their mutual fidelity, would not a revision of the ethical norms in force up to now seem to be advisable, especially when it is considered that they cannot be observed without sacrifices, sometimes heroic sacrifices?

* * *

10. * * * conjugal love requires in husband and wife an awareness of their mission of "responsible parenthood," which today is rightly much insisted upon, and which also must be exactly understood. Consequently it is to be considered under different aspects which are legitimate and connected with one another.

In relation to the biological processes, responsible parenthood means the knowledge and respect of their functions; human intellect discovers in the power of giving life biological laws which are part of the human person.[1]

In relation to the tendencies of instinct or passion, responsible parenthood means that necessary dominion which reason and will must exercise over them.

In relation to physical, economic, psychological and social conditions, responsible parenthood is exercised, either by the deliberate

---

† The present text is from the papal encyclical, "Humanae Vitae," dated July 25, 1968. The author's footnotes have been renumbered.

1. Cf. St. Thomas, "Summa Theologia," I–II, Q. 94, art. 2.

and generous decision to raise a numerous family, or by the decision, made for grave motives and with due respect for the moral law, to avoid for the time being, or even for an indeterminate period, a new birth.

* * *

11. These acts, by which husband and wife are united in chaste intimacy and by means of which human life is transmitted, are, as the council recalled, "noble and worthy"[2] and they do not cease to be lawful if, for causes independent of the will of husband and wife, they are foreseen to be infecund, since they always remain ordained toward expressing and consolidating their union. In fact, as experience bears witness, not every conjugal act is followed by a new life. God has wisely disposed natural laws and rhythms of fecundity which, of themselves, cause a separation in the succession of births. Nonetheless the church, calling men back to the observance of the norms of the natural law, as interpreted by her constant doctrine, teaches that each and every marriage act ("quilibet matrimonii usus,") must remain open to the transmission of life.[3]

* * *

14. In conformity with these landmarks in the human and Christian vision of marriage, we must once again declare that the direct interruption of the generative process already begun, and, above all, directly willed and procured abortion, even if for therapeutic reasons, are to be absolutely excluded as licit means of regulating birth.[4]

Equally to be excluded, as the teaching authority of the church has frequently declared, is direct sterilization, whether perpetual or temporary, whether of the man or of the woman.

15. Similarly excluded is every action which, either in anticipation of the conjugal act or in its accomplishment, or in the development of its natural consequences, proposes, whether as an end or as a means, to render procreation impossible.[5]

* * *

23. To rulers, who are those principally responsible for the common good, and who can do so much to safeguard moral customs,

---

2. Cf. Pastoral Const. "Gaudium et Spes," No. 49.

3. Cf. Pius XI, Encyc. "Casti Connubi," in A.A.S. XIV (1930), p. 560; Pius XII, in A.A.S. XLIII (1951), p. 843.

4. Cf. Catechismus Romanus Concilii Tridentini, Part II, Ch. VIII; Pius XI, Encyc. "Casti Connubi," in A.A.S. XXII (1930), pp. 562–64; Pius XII, Discorsi e Radiomessaggi, VI (1944), pp. 191–92; A.A.S. XLIII (1951), pp. 842–43; pp.

857–59; John XXIII, Encyc. "Pacem in Terris," Apr. 11, 1963, in A.A.S. LV (1963), pp. 259–60; "Gaudium et Spes," No. 51.

5. Cf. Catechismus Romanus Concilii tridentini, Part II, Ch. VIII; Pius XII, A.A.S. XLIII (1951), p. 843; A.A.S. L (1958), pp. 734–35; John XXIII, Encyc. "Mater et Magistra," in A.A.S. LIII (1961), p. 447.

we say: Do not allow the morality of your peoples to be degraded; do not permit that by legal means practices contrary to the natural and divine law be introduced into that fundamental cell, the family. Quite other is the way in which public authorities can and must contribute to the solution of the demographic problem: namely, the way of a provident policy for the family, of a wise education of peoples in respect of the moral law and the liberty of citizens.

We are well aware of the serious difficulties experienced by public authorities in this regard, especially in the developing countries. To their legitimate preoccupations we devoted our encyclical letter "Populorum Progressio." But, with our predecessor Pope John XXIII, we repeat: No solution to these difficulties is acceptable "which does violence to man's essential dignity" and is based only "on an utterly materialistic conception of man himself and of his life. The only possible solution to this question is one which envisages the social and economic progress both of individuals and of the whole of human society, and which respects and promotes true human values.[6]

Neither can one, without grave injustice, consider Divine Providence to be responsible for what depends, instead, on a lack of wisdom in government, on an insufficient sense of social justice, on selfish monopolization or again on blameworthy indolence in confronting the efforts and the sacrifices necessary to insure the raising of living standards of a people and of all its sons.[7]

* * *

Given at Rome, from St. Peter's, this twenty-fifth day of July, feast of St. James the Apostle, in the year nineteen hundred and sixty-eight, the sixth of our pontificate.

PAULUS PP. VI.

BARRY COMMONER

The Closing Circle (1971) †

* * *

In the terms described earlier, the Latin Americans wish to pursue, for themselves, the course toward population balance that the advanced nations have followed—increased living standards, reduced mortality, followed by the commonly experienced reduc-

---

6. Cf. Encyc. "Mater et Magistra," in A.A.S. LIII (1961), p. 447.
7. Cf. Encyc. "Populorum Progressio," Nos. 48–55.

† Barry Commoner (b. 1917) is professor of biology at Washington University and Director of the Center for the Biology of Natural Systems. The present text is from *The Closing Circle* (New York, 1971), pp. 243–49, 298–300.

tion in birth rate. For their part, the North Americans are urging on the poorer nations a path toward demographic balance that no society in human history, certainly not their own, has ever followed—deliberate limitation of population to a size compatible with "feasible" resources—at a time when living conditions, as reflected in high death rates and infant mortality, are well below the levels attained by the more advanced nations. The problem of controlling world population growth is clearly a subsidiary part of a larger, political question—the relationships between the rich, technologically advanced nations and the poorer ones that are struggling, against enormous odds, to improve their living conditions. To understand this issue we need to look at the links between the historical development of the two groups of nations.

One of the most important links is established by the two issues that have been under discussion here—the impact of modern technology on the environment in advanced nations, and the effects of poverty and rapid population growth in the developing nations. The wealth of the advanced nations is largely a result of the application of modern science and technology to the exploitation of natural resources. As we have seen, before World War II this was heavily based on the use of natural products. The availability of these materials—such as rubber, fats and oils, and cotton—in undeveloped areas of the world led to their exploitation by the more advanced nations during the colonial period. There is evidence that colonialism had a great deal to do with the development of the rapid rates of population growth that now characterizes so much of the world.

This is the conclusion reached by Nathan Keyfitz of the University of California from an analysis of the effects of colonialism on the present population explosion in the developing nations. He argues that the growth of industrial capitalism in western nations in the period 1800–1950 resulted in the development of a one-billion excess world population, largely in the tropics, as a result of the exploitation of these areas for raw materials (with the resultant need for labor) during the period of colonialism. He argues further that after World War II modern technology replaced tropical raw materials with synthetic ones so that the technologically developed world, "again with no one's intention, rendered functionless in relation to its further self-enrichment almost all the populations of the tropics."

Thus, the Dutch brought into their Indonesian colonies modern techniques that improved living conditions and reduced the mortality rate in the native population. And, according to the anthropoligist Clifford Geertz, who has made a careful demographic study of the colonial period in Indonesia, the Dutch apparently fostered the growth of the Indonesian population in order to increase the labor force that they needed to exploit the colony's natural resources. However, much of the wealth acquired as a result of the increased productivity did not remain in Indonesia. Rather, it was acquired by the Netherlands where it supported the Dutch through their own demographic transition. In effect, the first, or population-stimulating, stage of the demographic transition in Indonesia became coupled to the second, or population-limiting phase of the demographic transition in the Netherlands—a kind of demographic parasitism. Then, in a final irony, with the postwar development of synthetic chemicals, Indonesia's natural rubber trade declined, further depleting the opportunities for the economic advancement that might support their own motivation for population control.

In this way, modern technology becomes a crucial link between the environmental crisis in the advanced nations and the population problem in the developing ones. The postwar trend to replace natural products with synthetic ones has exacerbated ecological stresses in the advanced countries and has hindered the efforts of developing nations to meet the needs of their growing populations. We in the advanced nations like to think that the rest of the world depends on our technological charity. It may soon become clear that help will need to flow the other way. If the world is to return to environmental balance, the advanced countries will need to rely less on ecologically costly synthetics and more on goods produced from natural products—a process which, on both ecological and economic grounds, ought to be concentrated in the developing regions of the world.

Meanwhile, many of the environmental calamaties generated by advanced technology are being exported to the developing nations. At a conference organized by the Washington University Center for the Biology of Natural Systems and the Conservation Foundation observers reported case after case in which new technologies, introduced into developing countries, led to unexpected ecological backlash. The most famous example, the Aswan Dam, was referred to earlier; here, against the power and irrigation which the dam produces, must be balanced the spread of a serious disease, schistosomiasis, by the snails which live in the irrigation ditches. The Kariba Dam, also in Africa, spread a fly-borne disease and disrupted the agriculture of peoples living along the river banks. In Latin America and Asia, introduction of DDT and other synthetic pesticides has often caused new *outbreaks* of insect pests by killing off their natural predators, while the pests themselves become resistant. In Guatemala, some twelve years after the start of a malaria "eradication program" based on intensive use of insecticides, the malarial mosquitoes have become resistant and the incidence of the disease is higher than it was before the campaign. The levels of DDT in the milk of Guatemalan women are by far the highest reported anywhere in the world thus far. Nor should we forget, in this connection, that the United States defoliation campaign has imposed on Vietnam concentrations of various herbicides—of still unknown toxicity to human beings—never achieved anywhere in the world on such a scale. Thus, the developing nations, which so desperately need the benefits of technology, are receiving more than their share of some of its calamities.

Both the environmental and population crises are the largely unintended result of the exploitation of technological, economic, and political power. Their solutions must also be found in this same difficult arena. This task is unprecedented in human history, in its size, complexity, and urgency.

It is natural to seek for easier solutions. Since the basic problems are themselves biological—limitation of population growth and the maintenance of ecological balance—there is a temptation to short-circuit the complex web of economic, social, and political issues and to seek direct biological solutions, particularly for the population crisis. I am persuaded that such reductionist attempts would fail.

Suppose, for example, we were to adopt the solution to the world population problem urged on us by the agriculturists William and Paul Paddock.[1] They propose the application to famine-threatened nations of "triage"—a practice in military medicine that divides the wounded into three groups: those too seriously wounded to be saved, those who can be saved by immediate treatment, and those who can survive without treatment regardless of their suffering. The United States, for example, would decide which nations are too far gone down the road to famine to be saved and which would respond to rescue by American aid. Apart from its abhorrent moral and political features, this scheme is a certain road to biological disaster. Famine breeds disease, and in the modern world, epidemics are rarely confined by national boundaries; the Paddock scheme would condemn the earth to a kind of biological warfare. Nor can we ignore the political consequences. What nation, condemned to death by the very society that has, albeit blindly, brought it to its tragic condition, would willingly refrain from retribution? The Paddock scheme would condemn not merely the "hopeless" nations, but the whole world to political chaos and war. And the first victim of this political degradation might be the United States itself, for to quote the authors of the triage scheme: "The weakness of triage lies in its implementation

1. See below, pp. 230–232 [*Editor*].

by a democratic government like that of the United States." How long would this "weakness" last if the scheme were to be adopted?

* * *

One of the common responses to a recitation of the world's environmental ills is a deep pessimism, which is perhaps the natural aftermath to the shock of recognizing that the vaunted "progress" of modern civilization is only a thin cloak for global catastrophe. I am convinced, however, that once we pass beyond the mere awareness of impending disaster and begin to understand *why* we have come to the present predicament, and where the alternative paths ahead can lead, there is reason to find in the very depths of the environmental crisis itself a source of optimism.

There is, for example, cause for optimism in the very complexity of the issues generated by the environmental crisis; once the links between the separate parts of the problem are perceived, it becomes possible to see new means of solving the whole. Thus, confronted separately, the need of developing nations for new productive enterprises, and the need of industrialized countries to reorganize theirs along ecologically sound lines, may seem hopelessly difficult. However, when the link between the two—the ecological significance of the introduction of synthetic substitutes for natural products—is recognized, ways of solving both can be seen. In the same way, we despair over releasing the grip of the United States on so much of the world's resources until it becomes clear how much of this "affluence" stresses the environment rather than contributes to human welfare. Then the very magnitude of the present United States share of the world's resources is a source of hope—for its reduction through ecological reform can then have a large and favorable impact on the desperate needs of the developing nations.

I find another source of optimism in the very nature of the environmental crisis. It is not the product of man's *biological* capabilities, which could not change in time to save us, but of his *social* actions—which are subject to much more rapid change. Since the environmental crisis is the result of the social mismanagement of the world's resources, then it can be resolved and man can survive in a humane condition when the social organization of man is brought into harmony with the ecosphere.

Here we can learn a basic lesson from nature: that nothing can survive on the planet unless it is a cooperative part of a larger, global whole. Life itself learned that lesson on the primitive earth. For it will be recalled that the earth's first living things, like modern man, consumed their nutritive base as they grew, converting the geochemical store of organic matter into wastes which could no longer serve their needs. Life, as it first appeared on the earth, was embarked on a linear, self-destructive course.

What saved life from extinction was the invention, in the course of evolution, of a new life-form which reconverted the waste of the primitive organisms into fresh, organic matter. The first photosynthetic organisms transformed the rapacious, linear course of life into the earth's first great ecological cycle. By closing the circle, they achieved what no living organism, alone, can accomplish —survival.

Human beings have broken out of the circle of life, driven not by biological need, but by the social organization which they have devised to "conquer" nature: means of gaining wealth that are governed by requirements conflicting with those which govern nature. The end result is the environmental crisis, a crisis of survival. Once more, to survive, we must close the circle. We must learn how to restore to nature the wealth that we borrow from it.

GORAN OHLIN

The New Breed of Malthusians (1974) †

Outside the field of demographers and economists, a whole new breed of Malthusians has arisen, insisting not only as Malthus did on the pressure on the land, but also on resources in general, on the biosphere, on anything else that may be finite in the face of growth. Their claims have been demonstrated by the computerized models of the MIT group in *Limits to Growth*. It is from this group that the most apocalyptic visions of even a few decades of continued population growth tend to emanate. Logically enough, they also suggest the most draconic remedies—such as child rationing, the mass sterilization of populations and controlled extermination.

It has been one characteristic of many of these arguments that they have been presented largely outside of such traditional channels for scientific inquiry as professional publications, and instead have been submitted directly to the general public, without professional scrutiny and assessment. Pamphleteering has, of course, always played an important role in this field, and passions have always run rather high. But at present there seems to be a Gresham's Law in population thought—bad prospects for mankind drive out less bad ones from general circulation. Sometimes one hears the excuse that to get people's attention one has to exaggerate and

† Goran Ohlin is professor of economics at Uppsala University, Sweden. This article appeared in *Family Planning Perspectives*, 6 (1974), 158–59.

shock. I do not accept that, and I do not like to find an increasing part of the general public imbued with a crude Malthusianism and inveighing against the so-called unbridled breeding of the developing countries—an attitude increasingly found also among politicians and national and international civil servants.

Population alarmists tend to assume that population growth will always be excessive unless the "egoistic" desire to have children is checked. Little is to be hoped for from the fertility transition—it is as if it had never occurred or, at any rate, will not occur again. But, in fact, it is already under way in many developing countries and I think I only share a common impression when I find it overwhelmingly probable that it will occur everywhere. Population growth will slow down whether or not governments try to do anything about it. It will, of course, take time—again, whatever is done about it.

Historical evidence of the consequences of population growth is totally inconclusive. The economic/demographic models of recent years, for all their sophistication, do not show very much more than that it is costly to rear children and that per capita income goes down when parents add children to the household.

On the other hand, common sense certainly indicates that growth will continue to subject the institutional structures in poor countries to very heavy strain. Aspirations to provide health, education and welfare services by conventional policies will be more difficult than if populations were growing more slowly; the crises of urbanization will be more acute; the employment problem will be exacerbated—largely because of institutional failure to rearrange the economy rather than to any intrinsic economic impossibility. Mechanical changes in the age distribution will occur—at the present time, in most cases, probably reducing the dependency burden, but also increasing the problem of labor absorption.

These prospects are not very attractive; although by the standards of population pessimists they are wildly optimistic. Is it likely that population growth will bring calamities? Will such modest economic and social improvement as we have seen for some time come to an end? Will there be war, pestilence and famine, crises of global proportions that would not occur if population were growing more slowly or not at all? I am not presumptuous enough to claim such knowledge, but I confess that I find the arguments for those crises highly unconvincing.

While knowledge about the consequences to society as a whole of population growth remains limited and controversial, there is, of course, a grave social problem which is indisputable and well-defined. Parents will have more children than they want or can afford, abortions will continue to be a health hazard, children in large families will be malnourished and their physical and mental development will be retarded.

For some time now the argument has been heard that parents make poor judges of the socially desirable rate of population growth, that simply an effort to eliminate unwanted births will not solve our problems, and that in a not so distant future we will surely have to take more forceful steps against fertility. No matter how hard I try, I do not succeed in seeing things that way. The social consequences of population growth do not seem either so clear-cut or so terrifying to me as to warrant emergency measures. * * *

It is in the developing world that we find most of the experience of modern demographic policy, and it seems to me that, on the whole, it is a very sizable body of experience that has been accumuluated in the last decade. It is true that many countries have not yet gone beyond declarations of policy, and that many of those who have moved toward implementation have so far done it sluggishly. But the range of methods attempted is wide and permits one to form an idea of the building blocks available.

Family planning programs must form the centerpeice. The technical literature trying to evaluate these programs and to isolate their effects is already considerable, and I shall not evoke it here. I shall only note that they have not produced miracles, and that, if I have read the reports correctly, they should not be expected to do so even in the best of circumstances. They make a contribution to fertility decline which, when the time is ripe, may be considerable.

Efforts to change motivation in favor of fertility reduction may, in the future, prove even more important. But at the present time, they are surely in the experimental stage. Propaganda and exhortation alone seem nonstarters, but the potential of population education may prove greater. Incentive systems are being tried in many places, with varied results. Interest is also shown in social policies that reduce dependence on the large family, reduce the profitability of child labor, raise the status of women, etc. And at the end of the spectrum there is the whole complex of rural development, economic change and modernization.

All this adds up to a considerable list where practices that have been tried and tested mingle with ideas that are vague and diffuse but hold out some promise. But many of them cannot and will not be implemented merely or even primarily to influence the course of population.

If these are the kinds of population policies we are likely to have, they are obviously in rather sharp contrast with those demanded by the more vociferous population pessimists. Quite apart from the fact that it does not have a shred of political acceptability in the present world, is there a strong enough case to press for a coercive regime of fertility? It will be apparent from my earlier remarks that I do not think so. * * *

I come to the conclusion that it is wrong, perhaps even slightly dishonest, to suggest that there is a very great deal one can do by means of population policy to influence population. Although there is a strong case indeed for such policies, and especially for efforts to tackle the obvious problem of unwanted births, one is not helping to promote the understanding of these matters by suggesting that population growth is the big problem of mankind which is to be "solved" by population policies.

In my view, it would be useful to indulge less in speculations about population as a policy variable and worry a bit more about population growth as a relatively firm given from which long-term planning has to start and ought to do so immediately. There is no conflict—planners are, in fact, already responsible for much of the awakening to the costs of population growth in developing countries, and exercises seeking to concretize the social and economic situation in a few decades, when population has doubled and urban population may have quintupled, would undoubtedly firm up the determination to help fertility slow down as fast as possible.

OUBOUZAR ALI

The Family and Development (1974) †

* * *

At the 7th meeting, the representative of Algeria introduced a revised draft resolution, contained in E/CONF.60/C.3/L.12/Rev.1, which read as follows:

The Family and Development

The World Population Conference,

Considering that the importance of the family and of the role of women in all societies demands the support of any proposal or solution which aims at improving and affirming the rights of the family and of women,

Considering that birth control cannot in itself solve the problems related to the liberation of women and the equilibrium of the family,

† Oubouzar Ali was the Algerian representative to the World Population Conference in Bucharest, 1974. The present text is from the United Nations Economic and Social Council, *World Population Conference* (E/5585, 2 October 1974), pp. 123–24.

Considering that any policy for improving the status of women and of the family in general can result only from an economic and social development capable of ensuring education and health for all and of raising the income and bettering the living conditions of the most underprivileged,

Considering that development is directly linked to the transformation of international economic relations and to the order governing them, which directly and exclusively benefits the rich countries,

Considering that any Malthusian approach is not only unjust, in that it seriously affects the dignity of the family, but also ineffectual, since the cause of the population problem lies not in the number of individuals, but in the existing inequitable international economic structures, which are aggravated by the continuation of relations of dependence and exploitation of a neo-colonialist character,

1. *Considers* that, in order to create in the countries of the third world a just society in which families can realize their full potentialities, it is necessary to:

(a) *reject* all solutions that ignore these realities and encourage a Malthusian or neo-Malthusian approach which would consolidate the inequalities in the world and retard the progress of the countries of the third world;

(b) *reaffirm* the need to promote at the world level a new economic order which would:

(i) eliminate the still numerous barriers and obstacles to development encountered in trade, financial and monetary relations or the industrialization of the third world;

(ii) ensure the economic independence of those countries and not impede the control, utilization and just exploitation of their natural resources for their development, in particular, by their exercise of full sovereignty over their natural resources;

(iii) put an end to the waste and over-consumption which certain developed countries practise by pillaging and using for commercial purposes the reproducible and non-reproducible resources of the world;

2. *Recommends* that couples and individuals should be allowed full freedom to choose the size of their family, it being incumbent on States to respect such decisions and to facilitate all the assistance necessary for their full implementation;

3. *Advocates* the need to promote measures and policies intended to improve and protect the physical and mental health of women and children.

The Idea of an Optimum Population

WARREN S. THOMPSON

The Optimum Population (1935) †

The concept an optimum population implies a population of the size best fitted to attain some desired state, for example, the greatest welfare, or to achieve some end or purpose which is considered good. * * *

* * * In any society the factors determining maximum production per capita needed to provide the maximum state of well-being are so numerous that in practice it is probably impossible to say just what the economic optimum of population is. To mention a few of the more important factors at work we may call attention to the sex and age composition of a population; to the habits of work that it has developed; to the efficiency with which it uses its tools and machines; to the housing of the people; to their dietary habits; to the climate of the country; to the use made of leisure time; to the amount of leisure time demanded; to the form of the social organization; to the motives dominant in determining the objects for which the people will work; to the distribution of wealth among the different classes in the community; to the religious taboos against the use of certain resources or the employment of time; to the effects of the density and size of population upon the course of invention; to the consumption habits of people and their effects upon the social and economic structure; to the rate of accumulation of capital; to the relative amounts of labor spent upon the production and the distribution of goods; to the amount and the form of the taxes; to the rewards bestowed by the social system upon different kinds of economic and social activity; and to a host of other social and economic factors all of which have an effect upon the productive processes of the community and must be taken account of if one would know with any exactness the economic optimum of population for any area at any time.

† Warren S. Thompson (1887–1973) was director of the Scripps Foundation for Research in Population Problems, Miami University. The present text is from his *Population Problems* (New York, 1935), pp. 422–33.

* * * As a matter of economic theory, we can very plausibly argue that there is an optimum size of population from the standpoint of the operation of any given economic system and any given area of land or the world as a whole. But it is impossible to see a way of so exactly evaluating the different factors that enter into the calculation of the economic optimum that we can ever say with authority that such and such is the optimum population for such and such an area.

2. The Doctrine of Economic Optimum

In spite of this skeptical attitude regarding our ever finding the exact economic optimum population for any land, it may be of interest to discuss rather briefly some of the indications that certain areas have not yet attained or have passed their economic optimum.

* * * [O]ne may ask: Is it likely that England can recover her foreign markets? Do the protective tariffs being everywhere enacted promote increase in foreign trade or otherwise? Are the increasing costs of coal and iron in England due to causes which are temporary in nature? If not, what effects are they likely to have upon the ability of England to compete with other countries for certain types of trade? Are the conditions in England favorable to the rapid increase of industrial efficiency? If not, how are the products of British industry going to meet world competition? Is the entry of the United States into the business of supplying capital to foreign countries going to make the expansion of English industry more difficult? What effect will the development of home industry in the colonies have upon English industry? If one believes * * * that all these changes in world economy, and many more besides, are going to make England's economic position less secure than it has been in the past, then one may look upon her unemployment as a sign of overpopulation without maintaining that the theoretical optimum has been passed. It seems probable, therefore, that unemployment may be useful as indicating that under the conditions actually existing and likely to exist for some time there are too many people in a given territory. The same can be said of underemployment, which is a very serious problem in the populations of China and India. It can be of little comfort to a family that employment yielding a larger real income could be found if certain more favorable conditions were to come to pass, when there is no sound basis for believing that these conditions will materialize. Unemployment or underemployment which is chronic and which appears likely to remain so seems to me then to be proof of overpopulation for all practical purposes.

* * * The very term optimum population implies the best or most desirable population, and there is no essential connection between such a population and the number of people constituting "the most productive ratio between population and natural resources." The use of optimum population implies a value judgment arising from the individual's conception of the "good life" and should not be defined wholly in economic terms. Most of those who speak of the optimum population recognize that this value element exists, but since it is confessedly immeasurable they prefer to rule it out as a factor in population discussion and yet insist that they are considering the optimum population, whereas what they are really talking about is the most desirable population from the standpoint of the per capita consumers' goods available. The term "optimum population" means more to most people than the number of persons who will be able to produce the largest returns from a given amount of natural resources, thus achieving the highest standard of living possible under the circumstances. It has moral and ideal connotations which lead one to think of a population not only free from "carking care" but free from the crushing weight of uncongenial social and economic conditions, free from the compulsion arising from "efficiency" as a system of living, and free from the supervision of the evangelical type of mind which is sure that it has found the true way of life and would force this upon its neighbors. In a word the optimum population is not only the population so related to its resources that it has a high consumption of material goods but one which is also of the proper size to permit of an expansion of personality, the living of the complete life, or the development of those qualities which are peculiarly and distinctly human.

* * *

In so far as a large, real income—a high standard of living—is compatible with the expansion of the human spirit, it is easy to favor it. But if prosperity, like poverty, stultifies the spirit and renders conduct sordid and inhuman, there can be no special virtue in it or in the optimum population which makes such prosperity possible.

But if we reject the economic optimum of population as the optimum, we must likewise reject the political optimum, the ecclesiastical optimum, and all other optima set up by those motivated by interest in some particular institution. All such optima are one-sided and assume that man has fewer capacities for personal development in varied ways than he actually has. I have two quarrels with people who define the good life in terms of a particular human interest. One is almost personal, because they think that they know what is good for man, what is good for each of us, and demand that we submit our wills to their dictation. I rebel at being considered merely part of a producing organism, a fighting organism, or a breeding organism. Such treatment is not consistent with human dignity.

* * *

The truly scientific attitude of mind in the study of any human problem demands that we take into account all the factors in the case, so far as we are able. Therefore we should not talk of the optimum population when we are thinking merely of the number which would be best from some particular standpoint. That the optimum population from this larger human point of view cannot be given a definite quantitative statement leaves it in the same position as the theoretical economic optimum; while as for the political and ecclesiastical optima, they by their very nature can never be attained. A population can never be large enough to meet the demands of the imperialist and the chauvinist or of the churchman who regards ever mounting numbers of worshipers as the end of all life.

GUNNAR MYRDAL

Population: A Problem for Democracy (1940) †

The theory of an optimum population does not belong to the more complicated economic theories. It is, quite simply, as follows: that the highest possible average level of living (greatest national income *per capita*) is attained with a certain size of population, a size which was usually assumed to be considerably smaller than that existing. With any change from this optimum position, whether the movement be upward or downward, there is brought about a lower average level of living. This curve, which reaches its maximum in the optimum population and which denotes the dependence of the average level of living on the size of the population, is, according to the theory, dominated by two counteracting forces. The first force is quite simply the law of diminishing returns: since, *ceteris paribus*, with a smaller population the total amount of land and durable real capital is greater per inhabitant, the marginal productivity of labor and even the average amount of production per worker becomes greater the smaller the population, and *vice versa*. The opposite force is the law of external economics:

† Gunnar Myrdal (b. 1898), Swedish economist. The present text is from Chapter 6 of *Population: A Problem for Democracy* (Cambridge, Mass., 1940).

there are certain advantages dependent on division of labor with a larger population by reason of which the law of diminishing returns cannot prevail down to the smallest population size imaginable. At the position of optimum population the two forces evenly counterbalance one another, resulting in a maximal welfare of the population. Above the optimum position the law of diminishing returns has most effect; under that level the law of external economics dominates.

* * *

I cannot stop to give a thorough criticism of the optimum population theory. For the present purpose it may be enough to hint at some of the points where caution is to be prescribed.

As to the curve itself obtained by this hazardous interpolation—the average level of living as a function of population density—it should be noted that there is actually nothing in its construction which indicates that it could not, for large spaces, have a very level course. It is, likewise, perfectly possible that this curve might have several maximum positions at very different sizes of population and that the difference in height of the average level of living between the maximum positions might be unimportant, particularly in view of the great indeterminateness in theoretical content which the quantity "level of living" shares with all averages and indices. In both cases the conclusion would be that average level of living should be fairly independent of population size for certain values of this last quantity.

It is further clear, and also recognized, that not only the average level of living at any population size but, more primarily, the forms of the productivity functions which are supposed to determine the curve must be thought of as depending upon the available technique. As the amount of applicable technical knowledge is changing and increasing all the time, the assumed curve, and the optimum position, cannot be projected into the future simply on static assumptions. If, then, the curve is supposed to be changing under the influence of future technical change, this makes the theory more valid *in abstracto* in this particular respect, but at the same time increases the difficulties in practical application tremendously.

I shall not go on with this theoretical criticism, even though the points raised are far from inclusive, but conclude with the remark that it has, of course, never been possible anywhere to give for any country a quantitatively expressed answer to the practical question of the actual position of this population optimum. The theory is a speculative figment of the mind without much connection with this world; it does not give any guiding rule for the practical and political judgment of reality. * * *

The Current Demographic and Environmental Situation

KENNETH E. BOULDING

The Economics of the Coming Spaceship Earth (1966) †

The closed earth of the future requires economic principles which are somewhat different from those of the open earth of the past. For the sake of picturesqueness, I am tempted to call the open economy the "cowboy economy," the cowboy being symbolic of the illimitable plains and also associated with reckless, exploitative, romantic, and violent behavior, which is characteristic of open societies. The closed economy of the future might similarly be called the "spaceman" economy, in which the earth has become a single spaceship, without unlimited reservoirs of anything, either for extraction or for pollution, and in which, therefore, man must find his place in a cyclical ecological system which is capable of continuous reproduction of material form even though it cannot escape having inputs of energy. The difference between the two types of economy becomes most apparent in the attitude towards consumption. In the cowboy economy, consumption is regarded as a good thing and production likewise; and the success of the economy is measured by the amount of the throughput from the "factors of production," a part of which, at any rate, is extracted from the reservoirs of raw materials and noneconomic objects, and another part of which is output into the reservoirs of pollution. If there are infinite reservoirs from which material can be obtained and into which effluvia can be deposited, then the throughput is at least a plausible measure of the success of the economy. The gross national product is a rough measure of this total throughput. It should be possible, however, to distinguish that part of the GNP which is derived from exhaustible and that which is derived from reproducible resources, as well as that part of consumption which represents effluvia and that which represents input into the produc-

† Kenneth E. Boulding (b. 1910) is professor of economics at the University of Boulder and director of the Program on General Social and Economic Dynamics of the Institute of Behavioral Sciences.

The present text is from Henry Jarett, ed., *Environmental Quality in a Growing Economy* (Baltimore, 1966), pp. 115–19.

tive system again. Nobody, as far as I know, has ever attempted to break down the GNP in this way, although it would be an interesting and extremely important exercise, which is unfortunately beyond the scope of this paper.

By contrast, in the spaceman economy, throughput is by no means a desideratum, and is indeed to be regarded as something to be minimized rather than maximized. The essential measure of the success of the economy is not production and consumption at all, but the nature, extent, quality, and complexity of the total capital stock, including in this the state of the human bodies and minds included in the system. In the spaceman economy, what we are primarily concerned with is stock maintenance, and any technological change which results in the maintenance of a given total stock with a lessened throughput (that is, less production and consumption) is clearly a gain. This idea that both production and consumption are bad things rather than good things is very strange to economists, who have been obsessed with the income-flow concepts to the exclusion, almost, of capital-stock concepts.

* * *

It may be said, of course, why worry about all this when the spaceman economy is still a good way off (at least beyond the lifetimes of any now living), so let us eat, drink, spend, extract and pollute, and be as merry as we can, and let posterity worry about the spaceship earth. It is always a little hard to find a convincing answer to the man who says, "What has posterity ever done for me?" and the conservationist has always had to fall back on rather vague ethical principles postulating identity of the individual with some human community or society which extends not only back into the past but forward into the future. Unless the individual identifies with some community of this kind, conservation is obviously "irrational." Why should we not maximize the welfare of this generation at the cost of posterity? "*Après nous, le déluge*" has been the motto of not insignificant numbers of human societies. The only answer to this, as far as I can see, is to point out that the welfare of the individual depends on the extent to which he can identify himself with others, and that the most satisfactory individual identity is that which identifies not only with a community in space but also with a community extending over time from the past into the future. * * *

* * * There has always been something rather refreshing in the view that we should live like the birds, and perhaps posterity is for the birds in more senses than one; so perhaps we should all call it a day and go out and pollute something cheerfully. As an old taker of thought for the morrow, however, I cannot quite accept this solution; and I would argue, furthermore, that tomorrow is not only very close, but in many respects it is already here. The shadow of the future spaceship, indeed, is already falling over our spendthrift merriment. Oddly enough, it seems to be in pollution rather than in exhaustion that the problem is first becoming salient. Los Angeles has run out of air, Lake Erie has become a cesspool, the oceans are getting full of lead and DDT, and the atmosphere may become man's major problem in another generation, at the rate at which we are filling it up with gunk. * * *

ALAN R. SWEEZY

Population, GNP, and the Environment (1972) †

The average American consumes far more gasoline and electricity, discards more beer cans, Coke bottles, and automobile bodies, and occupies more space than the average Indian, African, or Latin American. The average American today generates more air and water pollution, disposes of more solid waste, and occupies more space than his predecessors did fifty or even twenty years ago. Some people have concluded from this that population growth is not an important cause of environmental problems. The standard of living and the state of technology so predominate, they say, that for all practical purposes one can forget about population growth when dealing with the environmental problems of the future.

Others draw the opposite conclusion. They point out that although today's affluent American may do more damage than today's Indian or yesterday's American, two of today's affluent Americans would do still more damage than one. It's like the old riddle: What makes more noise than a pig stuck under a gate? The answer: two pigs stuck under a gate.

Who is right? Is population important, or isn't it? The answer depends on two things: First, what effect does the size of the population have on the degree of its affluence? If we have twice as many Americans fifty years from now will they be twice as wealthy and do twice as much damage? Second, what is the relative magnitude of the contributions of population growth and of technological progress to environmental deterioration? Does the latter completely dwarf the former?

† Alan R. Sweezy is professor of economics at the California Institute of Technology and co-director of the Population Research Program. The present text is taken from Harrison Brown and Edward Hutchings, Jr., eds., *Are Our Descendants Doomed?* (New York, 1972), pp. 100–13.

In exploring these questions it will be useful to distinguish between two different sets of environmental problems: pollution and congestion. Population growth affects pollution primarily through its influence on the size and composition of the gross national product (GNP). It has a direct effect on congestion.

* * *

If population remained constant but technical progress and capital accumulation[1] continued at the same rate as in the past, the GNP fifty years from now might be three and a half to four times its present size. If in addition the population doubled—which could easily happen—the GNP might be something like one and three-quarters time as large as *that*, or six to seven times its present size. Thus, in a sense both sides are right. Technological progress has been a bigger factor in accounting for past growth of the economy than population growth. But population growth is far from negligible. * * *

Pollution depends on the size of the GNP and what might be called its pollution coefficient, which in turn depends on the composition of demand and the state of technology. Population is important only as it affects either of these variables. In the case of congestion, population has a more direct effect. Rising per capita income generates a demand for more space. But beyond a certain point the consequences of an increase in the demand for space will differ radically, depending on whether the source of the demand is higher incomes or more people. For example, if people are so poor that most cannot get to the beach on weekends, those few who are able to get there can enjoy relative peace and quiet. But as the standard of living rises, more and more people will be able to go to the beach, and the amount of space they will have once they get there depends on how many people are there. A further rise in per capita incomes will, at worst, mean that the desire for additional space will be unfulfilled. An increase in the number of people, on the other hand, will mean an actual decrease in the space available to each person or family. In the first case, the problem arises because per capita real income is growing. The second case causes per capita real income to decline. It is the inverse of Alice's problem at the mad tea party; in the case of space, you can never have more, but you can always have less.

But what has this to do with the situation in the United States? Haven't we lots of space, not only for our present population, but for any increase that is likely to occur in the next fifty to a hun-

---

1. This assumes, as above, that the size of the residual is independent of the growth of the labor force but that the amount of capital per worker is not. If capital per worker remained constant, doubling the labor force would also double the GNP.

dred years?[2] In answering this question we must first ask: Enough space for what? The traditional view is that a society needs enough space for its dwellings, its factories, offices, roads and streets, and enough land to grow its food and fiber on. Perhaps it also needs a few parks, race tracks, and sports stadiums. Beyond that, space is superfluous, and there is no reason population should not go on increasing until it is all occupied.

This narrow view is rapidly changing. We are coming increasingly to admit the validity of other demands for space. These demands, moreover, are for particular kinds of space rather than for space in general: for beach areas in southern California or northern New Jersey, vacation areas in New England or New York State, actual and potential Yosemites and Yellowstones. As people's horizons widen, even more expansive demands are gaining recognition. An increasing number of people think it is important to preserve unspoiled wildlife habitats, natural forests, and wilderness areas. They are reluctant to see encroachment on areas of unusual natural beauty and grandeur.

Several years ago Murray Gell-Mann was asked what he thought of a scheme for bringing water from Alaska to irrigate land in the Southwest. His reply was, "Why ruin two beautiful and distinctive landscapes to make more ordinary farmland when the same thing can be accomplished through birth control?"[3] This must have seemed idiosyncratic in the extreme at the time. I am sure it would seem less so now.

* * *

I conclude that we can stop arguing about whether affluence or population is the source of our environmental problems. Both are important. Moreover, there is going to be plenty to do on both fronts if future living conditions are to be tolerable.

2. See Coale [Ansley Coale. "Should the United States Start a Campaign for Fewer Births?" Presidential address to the Population Association of America, April, 1968. *Population Index*, Vol. 34, No. 4 (October–December 1968), 467–74.] and Eversley [David Eversley. "Is Britain Being Threatened by Over-Population?" *The Listener*, Vol. LXVIII, Nos. 1999 and 2000 (July 20 and 27, 1967), 78–79, 110–11.]. Eversley's views are much more extreme than Coale's since he thinks even Britain could comfortably absorb double or more its present population.

3. In a private communication.

ROBERT L. HEILBRONER

An Inquiry into the Human Prospect (1974) †

* * * In general the demographic situation of virtually all of Southeast Asia, large portions of Latin America, and parts of Africa portends a grim Malthusian outcome. Southeast Asia, for example, is growing at a rate that will double its numbers in less than 30 years; the African continent as a whole every 27 years; Latin America every 24 years. Thus, whereas we can expect that the industrialized areas of the world will have to support roughly 1.4 to 1.7 billion people a century hence, the underdeveloped world, which today totals around 2.5 billion, will have to support something like 40 billion by that date if it continues to double its numbers approximately every quarter century.

* * *

For the next several generations therefore, even if effective population policies are introduced or a spontaneous decline in fertility due to urbanization takes effect, the main restraint on population growth in the underdeveloped areas is apt to be the Malthusian check of famine, disease, and the like. * * *

These Malthusian checks will exert even stronger braking effects as burgeoning populations in the poor nations press ever harder against food supplies that cannot keep abreast of incessant doublings. At the same time, the fact that their population "control" is likely to be achieved in the next generations mainly by premature deaths rather than by the massive adoption of contraception or a rapid spontaneous decline in fertility brings an added "danger" to the demographic outlook. This is the danger that the Malthusian check will be offset by a large increase in food production, which will enable additional hundreds of millions to reach childbearing age.

Here the situation hinges mainly on the prospects for the new "miracle" seeds, especially in rice and wheat, which have promised a doubling and tripling of yields. Fortunately or unfortunately, the future of the Green Revolution is still clouded in uncertainty. The new strains have not yet been adequately tested against susceptibility to disease, and there are suggestions from recent experience

† Robert L. Heilbroner is Norman Thomas Professor of Economics at the New School for Social Research. The present text is from Chapters 2 and 5 of his *An Inquiry into the Human Prospect* (New York, 1974). The author's footnotes have been renumbered.

that they may be subject to blight. Perhaps more important in the long run is that all the new varieties of grains require heavy applications of water and of fertilizer. Water alone may be a serious constraint in many areas of the world; fertilizer is apt to prove a still more limiting one.

"Some perspective on this point is afforded," Paul Ehrlich writes, "by noting that, if India were to apply fertilizer as intensively as the Netherlands, Indian fertilizer needs alone would amount to nearly half the present world output."[1] Judging by the fact that of the 1.6 billion acres of currently cultivated land in the backward areas, less than 7 percent is now planted in the new seeds, a full "modernization" of agriculture would require enormous investments in fertilizer capacity. It is beyond dispute that these investments exceed by a vast margin the capabilities of the underdeveloped nations themselves, and it is possible that they exceed as well those of the developed world. More sobering yet, the introduction of fertilizers on such a scale may surpass the ecological tolerance of the soil to chemical additives.[2]

The race between food and mouths is perhaps the most dramatic and most highly publicized aspect of the population problem, but it is not necessarily the most immediately threatening. For the torrent of human growth imposes intolerable social strains on the economically backward regions, as well as hideous costs on their individual citizens. Among these social strains the most frightening is that of urban disorganization. Rapidly increasing populations in the rural areas of technologically static societies create unemployable surpluses of manpower that stream into the cities in search of work. In the underdeveloped world generally, cities are therefore growing at rates that cause them to double in ten years—in some cases in as little as six years. In many such cities unemployment has already reached levels of 25 percent, and it will inevitably rise as the city populace swells. The cesspool of Calcutta thus becomes more and more the image of urban degradation toward which the dynamics of population growth are pushing the poorest lands.

Only two outcomes are imaginable in this tragedy-laden historic drama. One is the descent of large portions of the underdeveloped world into a condition of steadily worsening social disorder, marked by shorter life expectancies, further stunting of physical and mental capabilities, political apathy intermingled with riots and pillaging when crops fail. Such societies would probably be ruled by dictatorial governments serving the interests of a small economic

1. Paul and Anne Ehrlich, *Population, Resources, Environment* (W. H. Freeman, 1972), p. 119.

2. Barry Commoner, *The Closing Circle* (Knopf, 1971), pp. 84–93, *passim.*

and military upper class and presiding over the rotting countryside with mixed resignation, indifference, and despair. This condition could continue for a considerable period, effectively removing these areas from the concern of the rest of the world and consigning the billions of their inhabitants to a human state comparable to that which we now glimpse in the worst regions of India or Pakistan.

But there is an alternative—and in the long run more probable —course of action that may avoid this dreadful "solution" to the overpopulation problem: the rise of governments capable of halting the descent into hell. It is certainly possible for a government with dedicated leadership, a well-organized and extensive party structure, and an absence of inhibitions with respect to the exercise of power to bring the population flood to a halt.

What is doubtful is that governments with such a degree of organization and penetration into the social structure will stop at birth control. A reorganization of agriculture, both technically and socially, the provision of employment by massive public works, and above all the resurrection of hope in a demoralized and apathetic people are logical next steps for any regime that is able to bring about social changes so fundamental as limitations in family size. The problem is, however, that these steps are likely to require a revolutionary government, not only because they will incur the opposition of those who benefit from the existing organization of society but also because only a revolutionary government is apt to have the determination to ram many needed changes, including birth control itself, down the throats of an uncomprehending and perhaps resistive peasantry.

Thus the eventual rise of "iron" governments, probably of a military-socialist cast, seems part of the prospect that must be faced when we seek to appraise the consequences of the population explosion in the underdeveloped world. Moreover, the emergence of such regimes carries implications of a far-reaching kind. Even the most corrupt governments of the underdeveloped world are aware of the ghastly resemblance of the world's present economic condition to an immense train, in which a few passengers, mainly in the advanced capitalist world, ride in first-class coaches, in conditions of comfort unimaginable to the enormously greater numbers crammed into the cattle cars that make up the bulk of the train's carriages.

To the governments of revolutionary regimes, however, the passengers in the first-class coaches not only ride at their ease but have decorated their compartments and enriched their lives by using the work and appropriating the resources of the masses who ride behind them. Such governments are not likely to view the vast difference between first class and cattle class with the forgiving eyes of their predecessors * * *.

Finally, and with great reluctance, I must advance one last implication of my argument. It is customary to recognize, but to deplore, the authoritarian tendencies within civil society, especially on the part of those who, like myself, are the beneficiaries of the freedoms of minimally authority-ridden rule. Yet, candor compels me to suggest that the passage through the gantlet ahead may be possible only under governments capable of rallying obedience far more effectively than would be possible in a democratic setting. If the issue for mankind is survival, such governments may be unavoidable, even necessary. What our speculative analysis provides is not an apologia for these governments, but a basis for understanding the critical support that they may be able to provide for a people who will need, over and above a solution of their difficulties, a mitigation of their existential anxieties.

Towards Control of Fertility

FRANCIS PLACE

Illustrations and Proofs of the Principle of Population (1822) †

* * * If * * * it were once clearly understood, that it was not disreputable for married persons to avail themselves of such precautionary means as would, without being injurious to health, or destructive of female delicacy, prevent conception, a sufficient check might at once be given to the increase of population beyond the means of subsistence; vice and misery, to a prodigious extent, might be removed from society, and the object of Mr. Malthus, Mr. Godwin, and of every philanthropic person, be promoted, by the increase of comfort, of intelligence, and of moral conduct, in the mass of the population.

The course recommended will, I am fully persuaded, at some period by pursued by the people, even if left to themselves. The intellectual progress they have for several years past been making, the desire for information of all kinds, which is abroad in the world, and particularly in this country, cannot fail to lead them to the discovery of the true causes of their poverty and degradation, not the least of which they will find to be in overstocking the market with labour, by too rapidly producing children, and for which they will not fail to find and to apply remedies.

* * *

Mr. Malthus seems to shrink from discussing the propriety of preventing conception, not so much it may be supposed from the abhorrence which he or any reasonable man can have to the practice, as from the possible fear of encountering the prejudices of others * * *. It is time, however, that those who really understand the cause of a redundant, unhappy, miserable, and considerably vicious population, and the means of preventing the redundancy, should clearly, freely, openly, and fearlessly point out the means. It is "childish" to shrink from proposing or developing any means,

† Francis Place (1771–1854), British reformer. The present text is from pages 165–75 of his *Illustrations and Proofs of* the *Principle of Population* (London, 1822).

however repugnant they may at first appear to be; our only care should be, that we do not in removing one evil introduce another of greater magnitude. * * * Mr. Malthus has, however, set the question of continence in a very clear point of view; he says, "it may be objected, that, by endeavouring to urge the duty of moral restraint" "we may increase the quantity of vice relating to the sex. I should be extremely sorry to say any thing which could either directly or remotely be construed unfavorably to the cause of virtue; but *I certainly cannot think that the vices which relate to the sex are the only vices which are to be considered in a moral question, or that they are even the greatest and most degrading to the human character*. They can rarely or never be committed without producing unhappiness somewhere or other, and, therefore, ought always to be strongly reprobrated. But there are other vices, the effects of which are still more pernicious; and there are other situations which lead more certainly to moral offences than refraining from marriage. *Powerful as may be the temptations to a breach of chastity, I am inclined to think that they are impotent in comparison with the temptations arising from continued distress*. A large class of women and many men, I have no doubt, pass a considerable part of their lives consistently with the laws of chastity; but I believe *there will be found very few who pass through the ordeal of squalid and* HOPELESS *poverty, or even of long-continued embarrassed circumstances, without a great moral degradation of character*."[1]

1. Malthus, *An Essay on Population*, Everyman's Library ed., Vol. II, p. 175 [*Editor*].

C. V. DRYSDALE

Bradlaugh and Neo-Malthusianism (1877; 1933) †

* * * Malthus showed for all time that unrestricted reproduction must bring the majority of humanity down to poverty and misery, however perfect the social system might be; and he therefore enjoined late marriage, although fully conscious of the obstacle of sex-passion. As a clergyman, he could not bring his mind to face the alternative, but the Utilitarians had no such inhibitions, and the first hint of it was given by James Mill in the *Encyclopædia Britannica* in 1818. Francis Place followed with the "*Diabolical Handbill*" in 1823, and Richard Carlile with *Every Woman's Book* in 1826; while Robert Dale Owen (son of Robert Owen) carried

† C. V. Drysdale (1874–1961) was president of the Malthusian League. Charles Bradlaugh (1833–1891), British radical and atheist, was four times elected to Parliament. The present text is from Chapter 5 of *Champion of Liberty: Charles Bradlaugh* (New York, 1972).

the message to the United States, and published his *Moral Physiology* in 1830, leading to the *Fruits of Philosophy*, by Dr. Charles Knowlton, in 1833, which was destined to play such a great part in the future.

* * *

THE KNOWLTON PAMPHLET

The Knowlton pamphlet, *Fruits of Philosophy*, had found its way to England, and had secured a very limited sale, when in that year a bookseller named Cooke of Bristol was prosecuted for selling it. On making submission and consenting to the destruction of the copies, he was released, but Charles Bradlaugh and Mrs. Besant republished it, gave notice to the police that they were doing so and selling it, and were thereupon themselves prosecuted. Mr. Bradlaugh, with his legal skill, was able to get the case tried at the High Court under Lord Chief Justice Cockburn, and the trial, which commenced on June 18, 1877, is one of the most dramatic in history. It is impossible to read the published report of the trial and the attendant circumstances revealed in Mrs. Bradlaugh Bonner's book without marvelling at the fortitude, eloquence, knowledge, and legal skill of the defendants, who conducted their own case. In spite of the intense odium which then attached to the subject, the jury were so impressed with the obvious high motives of the defendants that they gave the following verdict: "We are unanimously of opinion that the book in question is calculated to deprave public morals, but at the same time we entirely exonerate the defendants from any corrupt motive in publishing it." The Lord Chief Justice held this to be a verdict of guilty, but would have discharged the defendants on their own recognisances, had it not come to his knowledge that they were continuing the sale. He therefore sentenced them to fine and imprisonment, but Bradlaugh was able to quash the indictment on appeal.

* * *

It is only fifty-six years since the trial, and the results have been stupendous. Our own birth-rate in England and Wales has fallen from over thirty-six per thousand in 1876 to about fifteen to-day, which means that we now only have about six hundred thousand births a year instead of about one million four hundred and fifty thousand which would have occurred if the former birth-rate had been maintained. Similar reductions have taken place over the whole of Western Europe, North America, and Australasia; and birth-control instruction is now being given, thanks to the missionary work of Mrs. Margaret Sanger, in India, China, and Japan.

The Knowlton Pamphlet Prosecution

MR. BRADLAUGH'S SPEECH IN HIS DEFENCE

I ask you, then, to consider the issues which I have put to you already and which I put to you again—viz., Is over-population the cause of poverty? Is over-population the cause of misery? Is over-population the cause of crime? Is over-population the cause of disease? Is it moral or immoral to check poverty, ignorance, vice, crime, and disease? I can only think you will give one answer, that it is moral to check these evils. You may say: Try to restrain them, like Malthus, by late marriage. Aye, but even to get late marriage you must teach poor men and women to comprehend the need for it * * *. It is said that this pamphlet tries to defend immorality. You must contradict every page of it—ignore every word in it—to warrant that assumption. You may say it is very unfair, for example, that the agricultural labourer should have children to burden the poor's rate. But put yourself in the position of the agricultural labourers. They have not the training and education that you have, and sometimes mere sexual gratification is the only pleasure of their lives. They cannot read Virgil; they cannot read Dante. They cannot listen to Beethoven; they cannot listen to Handel. They cannot go to a musical reunion; and they cannot visit a sculpture gallery. They have no time occasionally to run across the Alps. They have no opportunity of finding recreation in the Pyrenees. They cannot yacht in the North Sea. They cannot fish for salmon at New Brunswick or St. John's. They are limited to their narrow parish bound, and their bound is only the work, the home, the beerhouse, the poorhouse, and the grave. We want to make them more comfortable; and you tell us we are immoral. We want to prevent them bringing into the world little children to suck death, instead of life, at the breasts of their mother; and you tell us we are immoral. * * * I plead here simply for the class to which I belong, and for the right to tell them what may redeem their poverty and alleviate their misery. And I ask you to believe in your heart of hearts, even if you deliver a verdict against us here—I ask you, at least, to try and believe both for myself and the lady[1] who sits beside me (I hope it for myself, and I earnestly wish it for her), that all through we have meant to do right, even if you think that we have done wrong. * * * [U]nless you feel we are the fit associates of those horrible Holywell Street men, who circulate foul literature day by day, and that we are deserving even of being put in the scale with those who circulate obscene

1. Annie Besant, his co-defendant [*Editor*].

prints, your deliverance must be one of not guilty. It is not a question whether you agree with the methods of checking population; it is not a question whether you are Malthusians or anti-Malthusians. I put it to you, and I ask you to consider it carefully, that the question which you have to determine is this: Is the advocacy of all checks to population lawful except such as advocate the destruction of the fœtus after conception, or of the child after birth? Is it possible to preach abstinence and prudence to the poor without instructing them in the various matters of physiology which have been dealt with in this pamphlet? * * * If we are branded with the offence of circulating an obscene book, many of these poor people will still think "No." They think such knowledge would prevent misery in their families, would check hunger in their families, and would hinder disease in their families. Do you know what poverty means in a poor man's house? It means that when you are reproaching a poor and ignorant man with brutality, you forget that he is merely struggling against that hardship of life which drives all chivalry and courtesy out of his existence. Do not blame poor men too much that they are rough and brutal. Think mercifully of a man such as a brickmaker, who, going home after his day's toil, finds six or seven little ones crying for bread, and clinging around his wife for the food which they cannot get. Think you such a scene as that is not sufficient to make both himself and her hungry and angry too? Gentlemen, it is for you, in your deliverance of guilty or not guilty, to say how we are to go from this court—whether, when we leave this place, if you mark us guilty, his lordship may feel it to be his duty to sentence us, and put upon us the brand of a doom such as your verdict may warrant; or whether, by your verdict of not guilty—which I hope for myself and desire for my co-defendant—we may go out of this court absolved from that shame which this indictment has sought to put upon us.

MARGARET SANGER

My Fight for Birth Control (1931) †

Early in the year 1912 I came to a sudden realization that my work as a nurse and my activities in social service were entirely palliative and consequently futile and useless to relieve the misery I saw all about me.

* * *

† Margaret Sanger (1883–1966), American feminist and first president of the International Planned Parenthood Federation. The present text is from pp. 46–57 and 154–76 of *My Fight for Birth Control* (New York, 1931).

Were it possible for me to depict the revolting conditions exist-ing in the homes of some of the women I attended in that one year, one would find it hard to believe. There was at that time, and doubtless is still today, a sub-stratum of men and women whose lives are absolutely untouched by social agencies.

The way they live is almost beyond belief. They hate and fear any prying into their homes or into their lives. They resent being talked to. The women slink in and out of their homes on their way to market like rats from their holes. The men beat their wives sometimes black and blue, but no one interferes. The chil-dren are cuffed, kicked and chased about, but woe to the child who dares to tell tales out of the home! Crime or drink is often the source of this secret aloofness; usually there is something to hide, a skeleton in the closet somewhere. The men are sullen, unskilled workers, picking up odd jobs now and then, unemployed usually, sauntering in and out of the house at all hours of the day and night.

The women keep apart from other women in the neighborhood. Often they are suspected of picking a pocket or "lifting" an article when occasion arises. Pregnancy is an almost chronic condition amongst them. I knew one woman who had given birth to eight children with no professional care whatever. The last one was born in the kitchen, witnessed by a son of ten years who, under his mother's direction, cleaned the bed, wrapped the placenta and soiled articles in paper, and threw them out of the window into the court below.

* * *

I would never go back again to nurse women's ailing bodies while their miseries were as vast as the stars. I was now finished with superficial cures, with doctors and nurses and social workers who were brought face to face with this overwhelming truth of women's needs and yet turned to pass on the other side. They must be made to see these facts. I resolved that women should have knowledge of contraception. They have every right to know about their own bodies. I would strike out—I would scream from the housetops. I would tell the world what was going on in the lives of these poor women. I *would* be heard. No matter what it should cost. *I would be heard.*

I went to bed and slept.

That decision gave me the first undisturbed sleep I had had in over a year. I slept soundly and free from dreams, free from haunting faces.

I announced to my family the following day that I had finished nursing, that I would never go on another case—and I never have.

II

I asked doctors what one could do and was told I'd better keep off that subject or Anthony Comstock would get me.[1] I was told that there were laws against that sort of thing. This was the reply from every medical man and woman I approached.

* * *

We determined to open a birth control clinic at 46 Amboy Street to disseminate information where it was poignantly required by human beings. Our inspiration was the mothers of the poor; our object, to help them.

* * *

Would the people come? Did they come? Nothing, not even the ghost of Anthony Comstock, could have stopped them from coming! All day long and far into the evening, in ever-increasing numbers, they came. A hundred women and a score of men sought our help on the opening day.

* * *

It was on October 16, 1916, that the three of us—Fania Mindell, Ethel Byrne and myself—opened the doors of the first birth control clinic in America. I believed then and do today, that the opening of those doors to the mothers of Brownsville was an event of social significance in the lives of American womanhood.

News of our work spread like wildfire. Within a few days there was not a darkened tenement, hovel or flat but was brightened by the knowledge that motherhood could be voluntary; that children need not be born into the world unless they are wanted and have a place provided for them. For the first time, women talked openly of this terror of unwanted pregnancy which had haunted their lives since time immemorial. The newspapers, in glaring headlines, used the words "birth control," and carried the message that somewhere in Brooklyn there was a place where contraceptive information could be obtained by all overburdened mothers who wanted it.

* * *

One day a woman by the name of Margaret Whitehurst came to us. She said that she was the mother of two children and that she had not money to support more. Her story was a pitiful one—all lies, of course, but the government acts that way. She asked for our literature and preventives, and received both. Then she triumphantly went to the District Attorney's office and secured a war-

1. Anthony Comstock (1844–1915), American anti-vice crusader [*Editor*].

rant for the arrest of my sister, Mrs. Ethel Byrne, our interpreter, Miss Fania Mindell, and myself.

* * *

I refused to close down the clinic, hoping that a court decision would allow us to continue such necessary work. I was to be disappointed. Pressure was brought upon the landlord, and we were dispossessed by the law as a "public nuisance."

* * *

I admitted the charge of giving birth control advice to the poor mothers of Brownsville. The prosecutor had little to prove. I knew I had violated the letter of the law. I was fighting that law. * * *

* * *

Finally, after what seemed to me a tiresomely repetitious discussion of the same theme, the decisive question was put to me:

"All we are concerned about is this statute, and as long as it remains the law will this woman promise here and now unqualifiedly to respect it and obey it? Now, is it yes or no? What is your answer, Mrs. Sanger?"

"I cannot respect that law as it stands today," I answered. Then I was sentenced:

"Margaret Sanger, with the additional evidence submitted by the learned District Attorney after your case reopened last Friday to meet the claim that the proof was insufficient, there is now additional evidence that makes out a strong case that you established and maintained a birth control clinic where you exhibited to various women articles which purported to be for the prevention of conception, and that there you made a determined effort to disseminate birth control information and advice.

"We are not here to applaud nor to condemn your beliefs; but your declarations and public utterances reflect an absolute disregard for law and order. * * *

"People have the right to free speech, but they should not allow it to degenerate into license and defiance of the law. The judgment of the Court is that you be confined to the workhouse for the period of thirty days."

LOUIS DUPRÉ

Testimony at Hearings on the Foreign Aid Bill (1967) †

What * * * is for a Catholic the moral attitude toward public policy on birth control? Must he abstain from any participation in public programs until the last shred of doubt has disappeared within the Catholic Church? In doing so he fails to live up to the responsibility which the Christian has in the world today. A purely passive attitude would be exactly the kind of other-worldly indifference toward essential human values which nonbelievers deplore so often in their Christian neighbors. * * *

Abstaining from obstruction of government-sponsored aid in family planning is not enough. The Catholic has a positive responsibility in the present population crisis. In taking up this responsibility he can hardly expect that every one adopts the official views of his Church on the subject. But this fact need not paralyze him into non-cooperation. It should make him more watchful that the freedom of each recipient be respected in the implementation of family planning programs. In thus cooperating, the Catholic does not take a stand himself on the objective morality of each particular method which is made available by the program. He may maintain his reservations toward any or all of these methods and yet fully cooperate as long as no hidden or overt attempts are made to coerce the individual recipient of aid into accepting any particular method of birth control. This was precisely the point at stake in the letter of the American bishops of December 1966: The principle remains valid today. No person should be discriminated against because of his refusal to practice contraception. Information and technical means should be made available, but the right to determine the size of the family belongs to the family alone. The population crisis has not yet reached the state of emergency in which the body politic is bound to intervene in a compulsory way to protect the common good. But the avoidance of this specter of the future is a strong reason to cooperate now in making the means of family restriction available while this restriction can still be made on a voluntary basis. The longer we wait, the greater the danger of government intervention becomes.

† Louis Dupré is professor of philosophy at Georgetown University; he testified before the Committee on Foreign Affairs, House of Representatives, May 9, 1967.

JOHN ROBBINS

Unmet Needs in Family Planning: A World Survey (1973) †

The first systematic worldwide survey of fertility control needs and practices indicates that as of 1971 seven in 10 of an estimated 500 million women at risk of having an unwanted pregnancy were using no contraceptive method at all. Some 150 million—about 30 percent of those in need—were taking some action to avert pregnancy; but the worldwide figure must be considered in the light of two significant variances within the total:

• In the developed industrialized countries, 60 percent of the couples at risk were using contraception. In the less developed countries other than China, the comparable figure was 12 percent. For China, which contains nearly one-quarter of the world need, it was estimated that 35 percent of couples at risk were using contraception.

• Only about 70 million, or one-seventh, of the women at risk used the most effective medical methods: the pill, IUD or contraceptive sterilization. The other 80 million contraceptors used less effective traditional methods: the condom, diaphragm, spermicides, rhythm, douche and withdrawal. With so many couples unprotected or using less effective methods (or using effective methods sporadically), it is perhaps not surprising that more than 55 million women terminated their pregnancies by induced abortion—legal or illegal—during the year, for a total worldwide of four abortions for every 10 babies delivered. Given current levels of contraception, the survey data suggest that without induced abortion world birthrates would rise from 35 to close to 50 per 1,000.

A total of about $1.5 billion was spent worldwide in 1971 by governments, private agencies and individuals on contraception (including sterilization). A like amount was spent on induced abortions. Most of the money spent on fertility control—some $1.9 billion, or 62 percent of the $3 billion total—came from individuals who paid for their own services and contraceptive supplies, rather than from governments or other sources.

* * *

† John Robbins is chief executive officer of the Planned Parenthood Federation of America, Inc. The present article appeared in *Family Planning Perspectives*, 5 (1973).

There is wide variation throughout the world in the proportion in need who used contraception. Fewer than 30 percent (141 million) of the 500 million women at risk of unwanted pregnancy in 1971 lived in the world's industrially developed countries; but three-fifths of these (85 million) used contraception.

The less developed countries contained more than 70 percent of the need (355 million); but in these countries fewer than one-fifth of couples in need (68 million) used contraception * * * The record of contraceptive practice would be even poorer without China (which contains nearly one-fourth of the world need). In the remaining less developed countries fewer than one in eight of 243 million couples at risk used any method to avert unintended pregnancy.

In West Africa, where 19 million women are at risk, only one percent practiced contraception; in East Africa, eight percent used a method, out of 17 million in need; in the Indian Ocean region, just 11 percent contracepted of 92 million in need; and in Latin America, 19 percent used any method of 34 million at risk. In China, where there are an estimated 112 million women in need of contraception, the proportion estimated as using a method was exceptionally high among less developed countries—35 percent. Only three less developed countries with at-risk populations of more than a million had records as good as or better than China's: Argentina, reporting 74 percent practicing of 3.2 million in need; Cuba, which reported half of its 1.2 million at-risk couples using contraception; and Taiwan, which reported 44 percent practicing of 1.9 million in need.

Eight out of 10 of an estimated 29 million North American (U.S. and Canadian), and about seven in 10 of 41 million West European women in need were reported to be using a contraceptive method. In developed countries where legal abortion rates are especially high, the proportion using contraception was lower: a little more than half of Japanese, a little under half of Eastern European and about 40 percent of Soviet couples in need were reported to be using contraception.

Although fewer than one-fifth of couples in need from less developed countries used any form of contraception, those who did use contraception were likely to use one of the most effective medical methods. Thus, in less developed countries, two-thirds of contracepting couples used the pill or the IUD or had a contraceptive sterilization. In developed countries, only three in 10 contraceptors used these most effective medical methods, with most relying on traditional contraception, reflecting the greater influence in developing countries of organized programs.

* * *

Abortion

Extrapolations from data for 87 countries build to an estimate that throughout the world in 1971 there were more than four legal and illegal abortions induced for every 10 live births. Reported abortion to live birth ratios range from a low of five per 1,000 in West Africa (almost certainly an underestimate) to a high of 2.4 abortions for every live birth in the Soviet Union (probably an overestimate). Several countries (including Saudi Arabia, Libya, Syria and Yemen) reported that no abortions were performed—which seems hardly believable. No data are reported from the People's Republic of China, although abortion is legal and available there for social as well as medical reasons * * *. The data suggest that about 55 million women had induced abortions during 1971, compared to 48 million who used the pill or the IUD, and to 24 million who had contraceptive sterilizations in that year.

It is estimated that about 12 million abortions, more than one-fifth of the 1971 worldwide total, were performed in the Soviet Union. Almost all of these were legal. About nine million abortions were estimated to have been performed in the Indian Ocean region, and at least four million in Latin America; almost all of these were illegal.

* * *

The survey data strongly indicate that a principal bar to the successful spread of the use of family planning in the less developed world is the unwillingness or inability of governments to allocate a significant amount of resources to the extension of service and training programs. Despite the affirmations made by so many governments that population growth poses a danger to their prosperity and stability, fewer than 10 percent of the governments of the 164 less developed countries assigned a high enough priority to family planning in 1971 to put more than $1 million of their own funds into programs. And, as the survey data dramatically show, the total of funds available from the developed countries for use by the less developed countries is an insignificant fraction of the funds being spent in the world on fertility control.

SUPREME COURT OF THE UNITED STATES

Jane Roe et al., Appellants, v. *Henry Wade* (1973) †

We forthwith acknowledge our awareness of the sensitive and emotional nature of the abortion controversy, of the vigorous opposing views, even among physicians, and of the deep and seemingly absolute convictions that the subject inspires. One's philosophy, one's experiences, one's exposure to the raw edges of human existence, one's religious training, one's attitudes toward life and family and their values, and the moral standards one establishes and seeks to observe, are all likely to influence and to color one's thinking and conclusions about abortion.

In addition, population growth, pollution, poverty, and racial overtones tend to complicate and not to simplify the problem.

II

Jane Roe,[1] a single woman who was residing in Callas County, Texas, instituted this federal action in March 1970 against the District Attorney of the county. She sought a declaratory judgment that the Texas criminal abortion statutes were unconstitutional on their face, and an injunction restraining the defendant from enforcing the statutes.

Roe alleged that she was unmarried and pregnant; that she wished to terminate her pregnancy by an abortion "performed by a competent, licensed physician, under safe, clinical conditions"; that she was unable to get a "legal" abortion in Texas because her life did not appear to be threatened by the continuation of her pregnancy; and that she could not afford to travel to another jurisdiction in order to secure a legal abortion under safe conditions. She claimed that the Texas statutes were unconstitutionally vague and that they abridged her right of personal privacy, protected by the First, Fourth, Fifth, Ninth, and Fourteenth Amendments. By an amendment to her complaint Roe purported to sue "on behalf of herself and all other women" similarly situated.

* * *

† Supreme Court of the United States, No. 70–18, January 22, 1973: *Jane Roe et al., Appellants,* v. *Henry Wade.* On Appeal from the United States District Court for the Northern District of Texas.
1. The name is a pseudonym.

VI

It perhaps is not generally appreciated that the restrictive criminal abortion laws in effect in a majority of States today are of relatively recent vintage. Those laws, generally proscribing abortion or its attempt at any time during pregnancy except when necessary to preserve the pregnant woman's life, are not of ancient or even of common law origin. Instead, they derive from statutory changes effected, for the most part, in the latter half of the 19th century.

* * *

VIII

The Constitution does not explicitly mention any right of privacy. In a line of decisions, however, going back perhaps as far as *Union Pacific R. Co.* v. *Botsford*, 141 U. S. 250, 251 (1891), the Court has recognized that a right of personal privacy, or a guarantee of certain areas or zones of privacy, does exist under the Constitution. * * *

* * *

This right of privacy, whether it be founded in the Fourteenth Amendment's concept of personal liberty and restrictions upon state action, as we feel it is, or, as the District Court determined, in the Ninth Amendment's reservation of rights to the people, is broad enough to encompass a woman's decision whether or not to terminate her pregnancy. The detriment that the State would impose upon the pregnant woman by denying this choice altogether is apparent. Specific and direct harm medically diagnosable even in early pregnancy may be involved. Maternity, or additional offspring, may force upon the woman a distressful life and future. Psychological harm may be imminent. Mental and physical health may be taxed by child care. There is also the distress, for all concerned, associated with the unwanted child, and there is the problem of bringing a child into a family already unable, psychologically and otherwise, to care for it. In other cases, as in this one, the additional difficulties and continuing stigma of unwed motherhood may be involved. All these are factors the woman and her responsible physician necessarily will consider in consultation.

* * *

XI

To summarize and to repeat:

1. A state criminal abortion statute of the current Texas type, that excepts from criminality only a *life saving* procedure on

behalf of the mother, without regard to pregnancy stage and without recognition of the other interests involved, is violative of the Due Process Clause of the Fourteenth Amendment.

(a) For the stage prior to approximately the end of the first trimester, the abortion decision and its effectuation must be left to the medical judgment of the pregnant woman's attending physician.

(b) For the stage subsequent to approximately the end of the first trimester, the State, in promoting its interest in the health of the mother, may, if it chooses, regulate the abortion procedure in ways that are reasonably related to maternal health.

(c) For the stage subsequent to viability the State, in promoting its interest in the potentiality of human life, may, if it chooses, regulate, and even proscribe, abortion except where it is necessary, in appropriate medical judgment, for the preservation of the life or health of the mother.

* * *

This holding, we feel, is consistent with the relative weights of the respective interests involved, with the lessons and example of medical and legal history, with the lenity of the common law, and with the demands of the profound problems of the present day. * * *

J. MAYONE STYCOS

Demographic Chic at the UN (1974) †

A resurgence of anti-Malthusian ideology associated with the observance of World Population Year is giving some older hands in the population business a bad case of déjà vu. Two decades ago, when India was the only developing country dabbling with family planning programs, and international assistance in population was just a gleam in some visionaries' eyes, Malthus was almost a dirty word. At the United Nations, the Soviet bloc vociferously insisted that population problems could not occur in a well-organized (read socialist) state and that the whole population issue was a blue herring invented by capitalists to divert attention from the true causes of poverty. The Catholic nations, citing the magisterium of the Church that contraception was unnatural and therefore sinful, maintained that improved technology and greater Christian charity

† J. Mayone Stycos is professor of sociology and director of the International Population Program, Cornell University. The present article appeared in *Family Planning Perspectives*, 6 (1974), 160–64. Editorial additions appear in brackets.

in the distribution of the world's goods would take care of the growing numbers at life's table.

* * * By the late 1960s many governments had introduced
their own programs and, following the collapse of opposition from
the Catholic and socialist nations, the United Nations was granting
funds and technical assistance. So respectable had the topic become
that the United Nations could schedule the massive World Population Conference for governments and the Population Tribune for
nongovernmental organizations, both of which were held in Bucharest in August [1974].

* * * [At Bucharest] I realized that every old ghost of the anti-
Malthusian past had resurfaced, clothed in the new slick trappings
of demographic chic. * * *

Consider the most innocuous-seeming slogan in the [UN "Action
Pack"] kit, one which has the distinction of being reproduced
twelve times on self-stick glue, "Love the World's People." It
would take a foolhardy bigot to contest this sentiment in any
general way; but when we note the context of this message—
given by the accompanying phrase "World Population Year"—it is
about as appropriate as an unqualified "Love Motherhood" sticker
at a Planned Parenthood convention. * * * At worst, the slogan
conjures up images of increasing a race (the human one) already
populous enough; at best, it 'cools out' concerns for world population growth. How can there be too many of something as lovable
as "the world's people"?

The second most important slogan (two stickers, one poster and
one order form) proclaims, "Take Care of the People and the
Population Will Take Care of Itself." This is complemented by a
third poster captioned "Population Is Only a Problem If the World's
Wealth Cannot Support the World's People." * * * What we are
hearing is the echo of an old argument between Malthus and
Marx. Marx insisted that only faulty social organization can cause
poverty and only good social organization can cure it. Any other
therapy, such as population planning, he considered a diversion-
ary ruse of the capitalists. This line, although recently muted, has
long been espoused by spokesmen of socialist nations. Is there
anything new in the present arguments?

What is new is that many nonsocialist intellectuals in the Third
World are beginning to espouse such arguments, fueled partly by
allegations that "family planning has failed," and partly by concerns that other aspects of developmental assistance may suffer
if population is given too much emphasis. * * *

India is the favorite example of the "failure" of family planning. Pradervand refers to India's losing "twenty precious years" in
"trying to persuade illiterate women to adopt the rhythm method

by bribing them with coloured beads. . . ." We leave to the Indians the task of responding to this condescending caricature of the Indian family planning program. It is certainly true that national birthrates in India have not fallen to the levels originally projected by enthusiastic family planners. But success stories on *any* front are hard to come by in India, for reasons which should be obvious; and modest progress should not be labeled as "dismal failure." Twenty years ago what scholar or administrator would have believed that in the early 1970s as many as 14 percent of Indian women of reproductive age would currently be contracepting, that over four million IUDs would have been inserted, and over 11 million sterilizations performed? Is it just to regard this as "dismal failure?"

India's program is exceptionally mature; but most programs are in their infancy. So eager are the critics to pass sentence on family planning that they hardly wait for the programs to be initiated before they declare them a failure. As of 1973, about 60 countries were giving official support of family planning activities, but 35 of these have been giving support for no more than five years, and only eight programs have reached their tenth birthday.

* * *

There is a long way to go before family planning programs become really effective. More resources, better management and better research are all needed. We must learn how better to adapt technology to different cultures, how to integrate family planning programs into other developmental programs without obliterating family planning, and, most of all, we must learn how to learn more from our experience. We need to learn from the Chinese experience, from the Indian experience and from the U.S. experience, too. In this quest for more useful knowledge about the control of population growth, nothing will be served by insisting that population problems will go away if only the problem of poverty is solved. Population problems will be with us for a long time. They must be faced squarely and they must be dealt with directly.

UNITED NATIONS
WORLD POPULATION CONFERENCE

Resolutions and Recommendations (1974) †

The World Population Conference, having due regard for human aspirations for a better quality of life and for rapid socio-economic development, and taking into consideration the interrelationship between population situations and socio-economic development, decides on the following World Population Plan of Action as a policy instrument within the broader context of the internationally adopted strategies for national and international progress.

* * *

C. *Recommendations for Action*

1. POPULATION GOALS AND POLICIES

(a) *Population growth*

16. According to the United Nations medium population projections, little change is expected to occur in average rates of population growth either in the developed or in the developing regions by 1985. According to the United Nations low variant projections, it is estimated that as a result of social and economic development and population policies as reported by countries in the Second United Nations Inquiry on Population and Development, population growth rates in the developing countries as a whole may decline from the present level of 2.4 per cent per annum to about 2 per cent by 1985; and below 0.7 per cent per annum in the developed countries. In this case the world-wide rate of population growth would decline from 2 per cent to about 1.7 per cent.

17. Countries which consider that their present or expected rates of population growth hamper their goals of promoting human welfare are invited, if they have not yet done so, to consider adopting population policies, within the framework of socio-economic development, which are consistent with basic human rights and national goals and values.

18. Countries which aim at achieving moderate or low population growth should try to achieve it through a low level of birth and death rates. Countries wishing to increase their rate of population

† From the United Nations Economic and Social Council, *World Population* *Conference* (E/5585, 2 October 1974), pp. 4–14.

growth should, when mortality is high, concentrate efforts on the reduction of mortality, and where appropriate, encourage an increase in fertility and encourage immigration.

19. Recognizing that *per capita* use of world resources is much higher in the developed than in the developing countries, the developed countries are urged to adopt appropriate policies in population, consumption and investment, bearing in mind the need for fundamental improvement in international equity.

* * *

29. Consistent with the Proclamation of the International Conference on Human Rights, the Declaration of Social Progress and Development, the relevant targets of the Second United Nations Development Decade and the other international instruments on the subject, it is recommended that all countries:

(a) Respect and ensure, regardless of their over-all demographic goals, the right of persons to determine, in a free, informed and responsible manner, the number and spacing of their children;

(b) Encourage appropriate education concerning responsible parenthood and make available to persons who so desire advice and means of achieving it;

(c) Ensure that family planning, medical and related social services aim not only at the prevention of unwanted pregnancies but also at elimination of involuntary sterility and subfecundity in order that all couples may be permitted to achieve their desired number of children, and that child adoption be facilitated;

(d) Seek to ensure the continued possibility of variations in family size when a low fertility level has been established or is a policy objective;

(e) Make use, wherever needed and appropriate, of adequately trained professional and auxiliary health personnel, rural extension, home economics and social workers, and non-governmental channels, to help provide family planning services and to advise users of contraceptives;

(f) Increase their health manpower and health facilities to an effective level, redistribute functions among the different levels of professionals and auxiliaries in order to overcome the shortage of qualified personnel and establish an effective system of supervision in their health and family planning services;

(g) Ensure that information about, and education in, family planning and other matters which affect fertility are based on valid and proven scientific knowledge, and include a full account of any risk that may be involved in the use or non-use of contraceptives.

* * *

31. It is recommended that countries wishing to affect fertility levels give priority to implementing development programmes and educational and health strategies which, while contributing to economic growth and higher standards of living, have a decisive impact upon demographic trends, including fertility. International co-operation is called for to give priority to assisting such national efforts in order that these programmes and strategies be carried into effect.

32. While recognizing the diversity of social, cultural, political and economic conditions among countries and regions, it is nevertheless agreed that the following development goals generally have an effect on the socio-economic context of reproductive decisions that tends to moderate fertility levels:

(a) The reduction of infant and child mortality, particularly by means of improved nutrition, sanitation, maternal and child health care, and maternal education;

(b) The full integration of women into the development process, particularly by means of their greater participation in educational, social, economic and political opportunities, and especially by means of the removal of obstacles to their employment in the non-agricultural sector wherever possible. In this context, national laws and policies, as well as relevant international recommendations, should be reviewed in order to eliminate discrimination in, and remove obstacles to, the education, training, employment and career advancement opportunities for women;

(c) The promotion of social justice, social mobility, and social development particularly by means of a wide participation of the population in development and a more equitable distribution of income, land, social services and amenities;

(d) The promotion of wide educational opportunities for the young of both sexes, and the extension of public forms of pre-school education for the rising generation;

(e) The elimination of child labour and child abuse and the establishment of social security and old age benefits;

(f) The establishment of an appropriate lower limit for age at marriage.

* * *

36. The projections in paragraph 16 of future declines in rates of population growth, and those in paragraph 22 concerning increased expectation of life, are consistent with declines in the birth rate of the developing countries as a whole from the present level of 38 per thousand to 30 per thousand by 1985; in these projections, birth rates in the developed countries remain in the region of 15

per thousand. To achieve by 1985 these levels of fertility would require substantial national efforts, by those countries concerned, in the field of socio-economic development and population policies, supported, upon request, by adequate international assistance. Such efforts would also be required to achieve the increase in expectation of life.

37. In the light of the principles of this Plan of Action, countries which consider their birth rates detrimental to their national purposes are invited to consider setting quantitative goals and implementing policies that may lead to the attainment of such goals by 1985. Nothing herein should interfere with the sovereignty of any Government to adopt or not to adopt such quantitative goals.

* * *

Some "Neo-Malthusian" Proposals

WILLIAM and PAUL PADDOCK

Proposal for the Use of American Food: "Triage" (1967) †

* * * Only four countries produce enough wheat to play a major role in the Time of Famines, countries I term "The Granary."

(*e*) However, three of these countries, Canada, Australia and Argentina, have in the past given only small amounts of food as charity to the hungry nations, and it is unlikely they will do more in the future. They will sell their stocks on the international market to anyone with cash in hand. Whatever these three countries may give to the needy will be only a token gesture.

(*f*) This leaves the United States as the sole hope of the hungry nations.

(*g*) Yet the United States, even if it fully cultivates all its land, even if it opens every spigot of charity, will not have enough wheat and other foodstuffs to keep alive all the starving.

THEREFORE, the United States must decide to which countries it will send food, to which countries it will not.

The Thesis of "Triage"

"Triage" is a term used in military medicine. It is defined as the assigning of priority of treatment to the wounded brought to a battlefield hospital in a time of mass casualties and limited medical facilities. The wounded are divided on the basis of three classifications:

† The present text is from *Famine 1975!* (Boston, 1967), pp. 206–29. See comments on this proposal by Barry Commoner (p. 188) and the editor (p. xxii). In the preface to *Famine 1975!*, the Paddock brothers describe themselves in this way: "The one is an agronomist and plant pathologist, who has headed a tropical research station and also a school of agriculture in Central America and is now a Washington-based consultant in tropical agricultural development. The other is a retired Foreign Service Officer of the State Department, with nearly all of his experience in the developing countries of Asia and Africa, including Russia and Communist China." The authors' footnotes have been deleted.

(1) Those so seriously wounded they cannot survive regardless of the treatment given them; call these the "can't-be-saved."

(2) Those who can survive without treatment regardless of the pain they may be suffering; call these the "walking wounded."

(3) Those who can be saved by immediate medical care.

The practice of triage is put into effect when the flow of wounded fills the tents of the battlefield hospitals and when it becomes impossible for the available medical staff to give even rudimentary care to all. Furthermore, the number allowed to be sorted into the third group for immediate treatment must be limited by the number of doctors available. The marginal cases must then also be selected out into the other two groups.

It is a terrible chore for the doctors to classify the helpless wounded in this fashion, but it is the only way to save the maximum number of lives. To spend time with the less seriously wounded or with the dying would mean that many of those who might have lived will die. It would be a misuse of the available medical help.

* * *

Triage Applied to the Time of Famines

President Johnson has proposed "that the United States lead the world in a war against hunger." On the battlefields of this forthcoming war the practice of triage will be vital because choices must be made as to which wounded countries will receive our food.

The leadership in Washington comprises the medical staff. The stricken ones in need of medical attention (American food aid) are the hungry nations. To provide maximum effective treatment the medical staff must divide them into the three classifications of triage:

(1) Nations in which the population growth trend has already passed the agricultural potential. This combined with inadequate leadership and other divisive factors make catastrophic disasters inevitable. These nations form the "can't-be-saved" group. To send food to them is to throw sand in the ocean.

(2) Nations which have the necessary agricultural resources and/or foreign exchange for the purchase of food from abroad and which therefore will be able to cope with their population growth. They will be only moderately affected by the shortage of food. They are the "walking wounded" and do not require *food* aid in order to survive.

(3) Nations in which the imbalance between food and population is great but the *degree* of the imbalance is manageable.

Rather, it is manageable in the sense that it can give enough time to allow the local officials to initiate effective birth control practices and to carry forward agricultural research and other forms of development. These countries will have a chance to come through their crises provided careful medical treatment is given, that is, receipt of enough American food and also of other types of assistance.

* * *

Washington may dally and shuffle and procrastinate, but the Moment of Truth will come the morning when the President must make a choice whether to save India or to save Latin America, when he must sign a piece of paper to send available food to one of two neighboring countries but not to the other, though both are equally friendly to the United States, both equally worthy of help.

Let us hope that before this Moment of Truth arrives there has been wide discussion of this problem in the press, in church councils, in Congress and in the departments of the government.

* * *

Finally, everyone—the Bolivians, the Indians, the Gambians, the Zambians, the Trinidadians and, most of all, the Americans—must realize that when a 10,000-ton freighter loaded to the scuppers with Food for Peace wheat sails out of New York or Baltimore or Seattle or Buffalo or Houston a specific component of American wealth is shipped out, wealth in the form of 200 tons of nitrogen, 41 tons of phosphorus and 50 tons of potassium. Multiply these figures by the approximately 14,600 freighter loads shipped out from 1954 to July 1965 and one sees that the portion of our soil's fertility thus lost forever is a significant part of our national resources, resources which we are denying to our children and grandchildren.

* * *

When we pour out this wealth we ought to get something in return for it. Let us make certain that what we get from our future shipments is a "better" world for our children. They are the ones who will suffer if we fail to obtain a fair return on this forfeiture of national resources.

Triage would seem to be the most clean-cut method of meeting the crisis. Waste not the food on the "can't-be-saved" and the "walking wounded." Send it to those nations which, having it, can buttress their own resources, their own efforts, and win the fight through to survival.

KINGSLEY DAVIS

Population Policy:
Will Current Programs Succeed? (1967) †

The need for societal regulation of individual behavior is readily recognized in other spheres—those of explosives, dangerous drugs, public property, natural resources. But in the sphere of reproduction, complete individual initiative is generally favored even by those liberal intellectuals who, in other spheres, most favor economic and social planning. Social reformers who would not hesitate to force all owners of rental property to rent to anyone who can pay, or to force all workers in an industry to join a union, balk at any suggestion that couples be permitted to have only a certain number of offspring.

* * *

If excessive population growth is to be prevented, the obvious requirement is somehow to impose restraints on the family. * * * As a means of encouraging the limitation of reproduction within marriage, as well as postponement of marriage, a greater rewarding of nonfamilial than of familial roles would probably help. A simple way of accomplishing this would be to allow economic advantages to accrue to the single as opposed to the married individual, and to the small as opposed to the large family. For instance, the government could pay people to permit themselves to be sterilized;[1] all costs of abortion could be paid by the government; a substantial fee could be charged for a marriage license; a "child-tax" could be levied;[2] and there could be a requirement that illegitimate pregnancies be aborted. Less sensationally, governments could simply reverse some existing policies that encourage childbearing. They could, for example, cease taxing single persons more than married ones; stop giving parents special tax exemptions; abandon income-tax policy that discriminates against couples when the wife works; reduce paid maternity leaves; reduce family allowances;[3] stop awarding public housing on the basis of family

† Kingsley Davis (b. 1908) is Ford Professor of Sociology and Comparative Studies, University of California at Berkeley. The present article appeared in *Science*, 158 (10 November 1967), 730–39. The author's footnotes have been renumbered.

1. S. Enke, *Rev. Economics Statistics* 42, 175 (1960); *Econ. Develop. Cult. Change* 8, 339 (1960); *ibid.*, 10, 427 (1962); A. O. Krueger and L. A. Sjaastad, *ibid.*, p. 423.
2. T. J. Samuel, *J. Family Welfare India* 13, 12 (1966).
3. Sixty-two countries, including 27 in Europe, give cash payments to people for having children [U.S. Social Security Administration, *Social Security Programs Throughout the World, 1967* (Government Printing Office, Washington, D.C., 1967), pp. xxvii–xxviii].

size; stop granting fellowships and other educational aids (including special allowances for wives and children) to married students; cease outlawing abortions and sterilizations; and relax rules that allow use of harmless contraceptives only with medical permission. Some of these policy reversals would be beneficial in other than demographic respects and some would be harmful unless special precautions were taken. The aim would be to reduce the number, not the quality, of the next generation.

A closely related method of deemphasizing the family would be modification of the complementarity of the roles of men and women. Men are now able to participate in the wider world yet enjoy the satisfaction of having several children because the housework and childcare fall mainly on their wives. Women are impelled to seek this role by their idealized view of marriage and motherhood and by either the scarcity of alternative roles or the difficulty of combining them with family roles. To change this situation women could be required to work outside the home, or compelled by circumstances to do so. If, at the same time, women were paid as well as men and given equal educational and occupational opportunities, and if social life were organized around the place of work rather than around the home or neighborhood, many women would develop interests that would compete with family interests. Approximately this policy is now followed in several Communist countries, and even the less developed of these currently have extremely low birth rates.[4]

GARRETT HARDIN

The Tragedy of the Commons (1968) †

We can make little progress in working toward optimum population size until we explicitly exorcise the spirit of Adam Smith in the field of practical demography. In economic affairs, *The Wealth of Nations* (1776) popularized the "invisible hand," the idea that an individual who "intends only his own gain," is, as it were, "led by an invisible hand to promote . . . the public interest."[1] Adam Smith did not assert that this was invariably true, and per-

4. Average gross reproduction rates in the early 1960's were as follows: Hungary, 0.91; Bulgaria, 1.09; Romania, 1.15; Yugoslavia, 1.32.

† Garrett Hardin (b. 1915) is professor of biology and human ecology, University of California, Santa Barbara. The present text is from Appendix B of *Exploring New Ethics for Survival: The Voyage of the Spaceship "Beagle"* (New York, 1972). The author's footnotes have been renumbered.

1. A. Smith, *The Wealth of Nations* (Modern Library, New York, 1937), p. 423.

haps neither did any of his followers. But he contributed to a dominant tendency of thought that has ever since interfered with positive action based on rational analysis, namely, the tendency to assume that decisions reached individually will, in fact, be the best decisions for an entire society. If this assumption is correct it justifies the continuance of our present policy of *laissez-faire* in reproduction. If it is correct we can assume that men will control their individual fecundity so as to produce the optimum population. If the assumption is not correct, we need to re-examine our individual freedoms to see which ones are defensible.

Tragedy of Freedom in a Commons

The rebuttal to the invisible hand in population control is to be found in a scenario first sketched in a little-known pamphlet in 1833 by a mathematical amateur named William Forster Lloyd (1794–1852).[2] We may well call it "the tragedy of the commons," using the word "tragedy" as the philosopher Whitehead used it:[3] "The essence of dramatic tragedy is not unhappiness. It resides in the solemnity of the remorseless working of things." He then goes on to say, "This inevitableness of destiny can only be illustrated in terms of human life by incidents which in fact involve unhappiness. For it is only by them that the futility of escape can be made evident in the drama."

The tragedy of the commons develops in this way. Picture a pasture open to all. It is to be expected that each herdsman will try to keep as many cattle as possible on the commons. Such an arrangement may work reasonably satisfactorily for centuries because tribal wars, poaching, and disease keep the numbers of both man and beast well below the carrying capacity of the land. Finally, however, comes the day of reckoning, that is, the day when the long-desired goal of social stability becomes a reality. At this point, the inherent logic of the commons remorselessly generates tragedy.

As a rational being, each herdsman seeks to maximize his gain. Explicitly or implicitly, more or less consciously, he asks, "What is the utility to *me* of adding one more animal to my herd?" This utility has one negative and one positive component.

1) The positive component is a function of the increment of one animal. Since the herdsman receives all the proceeds from the sale of the additional animal, the positive utility is nearly +1.

(2) The negative component is a function of the additional over-

2. W. F. Lloyd, *Two Lectures on the Checks to Population* (Oxford Univ. Press, Oxford, England, 1833), reprinted (in part) in *Population, Evolution, and Birth Control*, G. Hardin, Ed. (Freeman, San Francisco, 1964), p. 37.
3. A. N. Whitehead, *Science and the Modern World* (Mentor, New York, 1948), p. 17.

grazing created by one more animal. Since, however, the effects of overgrazing are shared by all the herdsmen, the negative utility for any particular decision-making herdsman is only a fraction of −1.

Adding together the component partial utilities, the rational herdsman concludes that the only sensible course for him to pursue is to add another animal to his herd. And another. . . . But this is the conclusion reached by each and every rational herdsman sharing a commons. Therein is the tragedy. Each man is locked into a system that compels him to increase his herd without limit—in a world that is limited. Ruin is the destination toward which all men rush, each pursuing his own best interest in a society that believes in the freedom of the commons. Freedom in a commons brings ruin to all.

* * *

Pollution

In a reverse way, the tragedy of the commons reappears in problems of pollution. Here it is not a question of taking something out of the commons, but of putting something in—sewage, or chemical, radioactive, and heat wastes into water; noxious and dangerous fumes into the air; and distracting and unpleasant advertising signs into the line of sight. The calculations of utility are much the same as before. The rational man finds that his share of the cost of the wastes he discharges into the commons is less than the cost of purifying his wastes before releasing them. Since this is true for everyone, we are locked into a system of "fouling our own nest," so long as we behave only as independent, rational, free-enterprisers.

The tragedy of the commons as a food basket is averted by private property, or something formally like it. But the air and waters surrounding us cannot readily be fenced, and so the tragedy of the commons as a cesspool must be prevented by different means, by coercive laws or taxing devices that make it cheaper for the polluter to treat his pollutants than to discharge them untreated. * * *

The pollution problem is a consequence of population. It did not much matter how a lonely American frontiersman disposed of his waste. "Flowing water purifies itself every ten miles," my grandfather used to say, and the myth was near enough to the truth when he was a boy, for there were not too many people. But as population became denser, the natural chemical and biological recycling processes became overloaded, calling for a redefinition of property rights.

* * *

Freedom to Breed Is Intolerable

The tragedy of the commons is involved in population problems in another way. In a world governed solely by the principle of "dog eat dog"—if indeed there ever was such a world—how many children a family had would not be a matter of public concern. Parents who bred too exuberantly would leave fewer descendants, not more, because they would be unable to care adequately for their children. David Lack and others have found that such a negative feedback demonstrably controls the fecundity of birds.[4] But men are not birds, and have not acted like them for millenniums, at least.

If each human family were dependent only on its own resources; *if* the children of improvident parents starved to death; *if*, thus, overbreeding brought its own "punishment" to the germ line—*then* there would be no public interest in controlling the breeding of families. But our society is confronted with another aspect of the tragedy of the commons.

In a welfare state, how shall we deal with the family, the religion, the race, or the class (or indeed any distinguishable and cohesive group) that adopts overbreeding as a policy to secure its own aggrandizement?[5] To couple the concept of freedom to breed with the belief that everyone born has an equal right to the commons is to lock the world into a tragic course of action.

* * *

Mutual Coercion Mutually Agreed Upon

The social arrangements that produce responsibility are arrangements that create coercion, of some sort. Consider bank-robbing. The man who takes money from a bank acts as if the bank were a commons. How do we prevent such action? Certainly not by trying to control his behavior solely by a verbal appeal to his sense of responsibility. Rather than rely on propaganda we * * * insist that a bank is not a commons; we seek the definite social arrangements that will keep it from becoming a commons. That we thereby infringe on the freedom of would-be robbers we neither deny nor regret.

The morality of bank-robbing is particularly easy to understand because we accept complete prohibition of this activity. We are willing to say "Thou shalt not rob banks," without providing for

4. D. Lack, *The Natural Regulation of Animal Numbers* (Clarendon Press, Oxford, 1954).

5. G. Hardin, *Perspec. Biol. Med.* 6, 366 (1963).

exceptions. But temperance also can be created by coercion. Taxing is a good coercive device. To keep downtown shoppers temperate in their use of parking space we introduce parking meters for short periods, and traffic fines for longer ones. We need not actually forbid a citizen to park as long as he wants to; we need merely make it increasingly expensive for him to do so. Not prohibition, but carefully biased options are what we offer him. A Madison Avenue man might call this persuasion; I prefer the greater candor of the word coercion.

Coercion is a dirty word to most liberals now, but it need not forever be so. As with the four-letter words, its dirtiness can be cleansed away by exposure to the light, by saying it over and over without apology or embarrassment. To many, the word coercion implies arbitrary decisions of distant and irresponsible bureaucrats; but this is not a necessary part of its meaning. The only kind of coercion I recommend is mutual coercion, mutually agreed upon by the majority of the people affected.

To say that we mutually agreed to coercion is not to say that we are required to enjoy it, or even to pretend we enjoy it. Who enjoys taxes? We all grumble about them. But we accept compulsory taxes because we recognize that voluntary taxes would favor the conscienceless. We institute and (grumblingly) support taxes and other coercive devices to escape the horror of the commons.

* * *

Recognition of Necessity

Perhaps the simplest summary of this analysis of man's population problems is this: the commons, if justifiable at all, is justifiable only under conditions of low-population density. As the human population has increased, the commons has had to be abandoned in one aspect after another.

First we abandoned the commons in food gathering, enclosing farm land and restricting pastures and hunting and fishing areas. These restrictions are still not complete throughout the world.

Somewhat later we saw that the commons as a place for waste disposal would also have to be abandoned. Restrictions on the disposal of domestic sewage are widely accepted in the Western world; we are still struggling to close the commons to pollution by automobiles, factories, insecticide sprayers, fertilizing operations, and atomic energy installations.

* * *

Every new enclosure of the commons involves the infringement of somebody's personal liberty. Infringements made in the distant past are accepted because no contemporary complains of a loss. It is the newly proposed infringements that we vigorously oppose; cries of "rights" and "freedom" fill the air. But what does "freedom" mean? When men mutually agreed to pass laws against robbing, mankind became more free, not less so. Individuals locked into the logic of the commons are free only to bring on universal ruin; once they see the necessity of mutual coercion, they become free to pursue other goals. I believe it was Hegel who said, "Freedom is the recognition of necessity."

The most important aspect of necessity that we must now recognize, is the necessity of abandoning the commons in breeding. No technical solution can rescue us from the misery of overpopulation. Freedom to breed will bring ruin to all. At the moment, to avoid hard decisions many of us are tempted to propagandize for conscience and responsible parenthood. The temptation must be resisted, because an appeal to independently acting consciences selects for the disappearance of all conscience in the long run, and an increase in anxiety in the short.

The only way we can preserve and nurture other and more precious freedoms is by relinquishing the freedom to breed, and that very soon. "Freedom is the recognition of necessity"—and it is the role of education to reveal to all the necessity of abandoning the freedom to breed. Only so, can we put an end to this aspect of the tragedy of the commons.

PAUL R. and ANNE H. EHRLICH

Population Resources Environment (1972) †

Summary

To recapitulate, we would summarize the present world situation as follows:

1. Considering present technology and patterns of behavior our planet is grossly overpopulated now.

2. The large absolute number of people and the rate of population growth are major hindrances to solving human problems.

3. The limits of human capability to produce food by conventional means have very nearly been reached. Problems of supply

† Paul R. Ehrlich (b. 1932) is professor of biology at Stanford University. Anne H. Ehrlich (b. 1933) is research assistant in biology, Stanford University. The present text is from the final chapter of *Population Resources Environment: Issues in Human Ecology* (San Francisco, W. H. Freeman and Company, 1972). Copyright © 1970. Editorial additions appear in brackets.

and distribution already have resulted in roughly half of humanity being undernourished or malnourished. Some 10–20 million people are starving to death annually.

4. Attempts to increase food production further will tend to accelerate the deterioration of our environment, which in turn will eventually *reduce* the capacity of the Earth to produce food. It is not clear whether environmental decay has now gone so far as to be essentially irreversible; it is possible that the capacity of the planet to support human life has been permanently impaired. Such technological "successes," as automobiles, pesticides, and inorganic nitrogen fertilizers are major contributors to environmental deterioration.

5. There is reason to believe that population growth increases the probability of a lethal worldwide plague and of a thermonuclear war. Either could provide a catastrophic "death rate solution" to the population problem; each is potentially capable of destroying civilization and even of driving *Homo sapiens* to extinction.

6. There is no technological panacea for the complex of problems comprising the population-food-environment crisis, although technology, properly applied in such areas as pollution abatement, communications, and fertility control can provide massive assistance. The basic solutions involve dramatic and rapid changes in human *attitudes*, especially those relating to reproductive behavior, economic growth, technology, the environment, and conflict resolution.

Recommendations: A Positive Program

Although our conclusions must seem rather pessimistic, we wish to emphasize our belief that the problems can be solved. Whether they *will* be solved is another question. A general course of action that we feel will have some chance of ameliorating the results of the current crisis is outlined below. Many of the suggestions will seem "unrealistic," and indeed that is how we view them. But the system has been allowed to run downhill for so long that only idealistic and very far-reaching programs offer any hope of salvation.

1. Population control is absolutely essential if the problems now facing mankind are to be solved. *It is not, however, a panacea.* If population growth were halted immediately, virtually all other human problems—poverty, racial tensions, urban blight, environmental decay, warfare—would remain. The situation is best summarized in the statement, "whatever your cause, it's a lost cause without population control."

2. Political pressure must be applied immediately to induce the United States government to assume its responsibility to halt

the growth of the American population. Once growth is halted, the government should undertake to regulate the birth rate so that the population is reduced to an optimum size and maintained there. It is essential that a grassroots political movement be generated to convince our legislators and the executive branch of the government that they must act rapidly. The program should be based on what politicians understand best—votes. Presidents, Congressmen, Senators, and other elected officials who do not deal effectively with the crisis must be defeated at the polls and more intelligent and responsible candidates elected.

3. A massive campaign must be launched to restore a quality environment in North America and to *de-develop the United States*. De-development means bringing our economic system (especially patterns of consumption) into line with the realities of ecology and the world resource situation. Resources and energy must be diverted from frivolous and wasteful uses in over-developed countries to filling the genuine needs of the under-developed. This campaign would be largely political, especially with regard to our overexploitation of world resources, but the campaign should be strongly supplemented by legal and boycott action against polluters and others whose activities damage the environment. The need for de-development presents our economists with a major challenge. They must design a low-consumption economy of stability, and an economy in which there is a much more equitable distribution of wealth than in the present one. Redistribution of wealth both within and among nations is absolutely essential. Marxists claim that capitalism is intrinsically expansionist and wasteful, and that it automatically produces a monied ruling class. Can our economists prove them wrong?

4. Once the United States has clearly started on the path of cleaning up its own mess it can then turn its attention to the problems of the de-development of the other DCs [developed countries], population control, and ecologically feasible semi-development of the UDCs [underdeveloped countries]. It must use every peaceful means at its disposal to bring the Soviet Union and other DCs into the effort, in line with the general proposals of Lord Snow and Academician Sakharov. Such action can be combined with attempts to achieve a general detente with the Soviets and the Chinese. Citizens, through the ballot, letter writing, and continued peaceful protest, must make clear to American leaders that they wish to move toward disarmament in spite of its possible risks. They must demand detailed appraisal of the risks of continuing the "balance of terror" versus the risk that the other side might "cheat" in a controlled disarmament situation. Americans should inform themselves of what is known about the causes and the psychology of conflict and about deterrence theory, and attempt to elect officials who are similarly

informed. They must, above all, learn to behave in ways that will convince the poor of the Third World that the days of exploitation will end and that genuine aid is on its way.

5. It is unfortunate that at the time of the greatest crisis the United States and the world have ever faced, many Americans, especially the young, have given up hope that the government can be modernized and changed in direction through the functioning of the elective process. Their despair may have some foundation, but a partial attempt to institute a "new politics" very nearly succeeded in 1968. In addition many members of Congress and other government leaders, both Democrats and Republicans, are very much aware of the problems outlined in this book and are determined to do something about them. Others are joining their ranks as the dangers before us daily become more apparent. These people need public support in order to be effective. The world cannot, in its present critical state, be saved by merely tearing down old institutions, even if rational plans existed for constructing better ones from the ruins. We simply do not have the time. Either we will succeed by bending old institutions or we will succumb to disaster. Considering the potential rewards and consequences we see no choice but to make an effort to modernize the system. It may be necessary to organize a new political party with an ecological outlook and national and international orientation to provide an alternative to the present parties with their local and parochial interests. The environmental issue may well provide the basis for this.

6. Perhaps the major necessary ingredient that has been missing from a solution to the problems of both the United States and the rest of the world is a goal, a vision of the kind of Spaceship Earth that ought to be and the kind of crew that should man her. Society has always had its visionaries who talked of love, beauty, peace, and plenty. But somehow the "practical" men have always been there to praise the smog as a sign of progress, to preach "just" wars, and to restrict love while giving hate free rein. It must be one of the greatest ironies of the history of the human species that the only salvation for the practical men now lies in what they think of as the dreams of idealists. The question now is: can the "realists" be persuaded to face reality in time?

LESTER R. BROWN

In the Human Interest (1974) †

As of the mid-1970s, it has become apparent that the soaring demand for food, spurred by both population growth and rising affluence, has begun to outrun the productive capacity of the world's farmers and fishermen. The result is declining food reserves, skyrocketing food prices, and increasingly intense international competition for exportable food supplies.

* * *

Since the invention of agriculture roughly 12,000 years ago, the earth's food-producing capacity has increased several hundredfold. Yet hunger has remained the lot of a large segment of humanity. Now food price inflation is helping to undermine the prosperity and economic stability of the well-fed countries as well. At issue today is whether or not man can break the dismal cycle in which increased food production has been largely absorbed by an ever growing population.

* * *

New Constraints on Protein Supplies

At a time when rising affluence is manifesting itself in the form of rapidly growing demand for high-quality protein, we suddenly find ourselves in difficulty in our efforts to rapidly expand the supplies of three major protein sources—beef, soybeans, and fish.

There are two major constraints on beef production. Agricultural scientists have not been able to devise any commercially satisfactory means of getting more than one calf per cow per year; for every animal that goes into the beef production process, one adult animal must be fed and otherwise maintained for a full year. There does not appear to be any prospect of an imminent breakthrough on this front. The other constraint on beef production is good grassland. The grazing capacity of much of the world's pastureland is now almost fully utilized. This is true, for example, in much of the U.S. Great Plains area, in large areas of sub-Saharan Africa, and in parts of Australia. There are opportunities for using improved grasses and for improved range management, but these are limited and slow to be realized.

† Lester R. Brown (b. 1934) is senior fellow of the Overseas Research Council and president of the Worldwatch Institute. The present text is from Chapters 4, 11, and 13 of *In the Human Interest* (New York, 1974).

Another potentially serious constraint on efforts to expand supplies of high-quality protein is the inability of scientists to achieve a breakthrough in per acre yields of soybeans. Soybeans are consumed directly as food by more than a billion people throughout densely populated East Asia, and they are an important high-quality protein ingredient in livestock and poultry feeds throughout the world.* * *

In the United States, which now produces two-thirds of the world's soybean crop and supplies more than four-fifths of all soybeans entering the world market, soybean yields per acre have increased by just over 1 percent per year since 1950; corn yields, on the other hand, have increased by nearly 4 percent per year. One reason soybean yields have not climbed very rapidly is that the soybean, a legume with a built-in nitrogen supply, is not very responsive to nitrogen fertilizer.

In these circumstances, more soybeans are produced essentially by planting more land to soybeans. Almost 85 percent of the dramatic fourfold increase in the U.S. soybean crop since 1950 has come from expanding the area devoted to it. As long as there was ample idle cropland available, this did not pose a problem, but with this cropland reserve rapidly disappearing and with one in every six acres of U.S. cropland already planted to soybeans by 1973, serious supply problems could emerge.

Deep Trouble in Ocean Fisheries

The oceans are one of mankind's major sources of protein. From 1950 to 1970, the world fish catch expanded rapidly, going from 21 million to 70 million tons. This phenomenal growth in the catch of nearly 5 percent [annually], which far exceeded the annual rate of world population growth, greatly increased the average supply of marine protein per person.

But since 1970, the catch has declined for three consecutive years, falling by an estimated 8 million tons * * *. With population continuing to grow, the per capita availability of fish declined 16 percent during this three-year span, triggering dramatic price rises. As stocks of many key commercial species are depleted, the amount of time and capital expended to bring in the shrinking catch continues to rise every year.

Many marine biologists now feel that the global catch of table-grade fish is at or near the maximum sustainable level. A large number of the thirty or so leading species of commercial-grade fish currently may be overfished; that is, stocks will not sustain even the current catch.

* * *

In sum, despite the substantial opportunities for expanding the world's food output, it now seems likely that the supply of food, particularly protein, will lag behind the growth in demand for some time to come, resulting in significantly higher prices during the decade ahead than those of the 1960s. We are witnessing the transformation of the world protein market from a buyer's to a seller's market, much as the world energy market has been transformed over the past few years.

Scarce Resources: Land, Water, and Energy

As the world demand for food climbs, constraints on efforts to expand food production become increasingly apparent. The means of expanding food supplies from conventional agriculture fall into two categories: either increasing the amount of land under cultivation, or raising yields on existing cropland through intensified use of water, energy, and fertilizers. In either direction, we face scarcity problems.

From the beginning of agriculture until about 1950, expanding the cultivated area was the major means of increasing the world's food supply. Since mid-century, however, raising output on existing cultivated area has accounted for most of the increase. Intensification of cultivation has progressed steadily since 1950; during the early 1970s it has accounted for an estimated four-fifths of the annual growth in world food output, far overshadowing expansion of the cultivated area.

The traditional approach to increasing production—extending the area under cultivation—has only limited scope for the future. Indeed, some parts of the world face a net reduction in agricultural land because of the growth in competing uses, such as recreation, transportation, and industrial and residential development. Few countries have well-defined land use policies that protect agricultural land from other uses. In the United States, vast areas of farmland have been diverted indiscriminately to other purposes in recent years, with little thought to the possible long-term consequences.

Some more densely populated countries, such as Japan and several Western European countries, have been experiencing a reduction in the land used for crop production for several decades. Other parts of the world, including particularly the Indian subcontinent, the Middle East, North and sub-Saharan Africa, the Caribbean, Central America, and the Andean countries, are losing disturbingly large acreages of cropland each year because of severe soil erosion.

* * *

The intensification of agricultural production on existing cultivated area in most developing countries will involve a severalfold
increase in energy requirements. Energy is required for more
thorough seedbed preparation, weeding, irrigation pumps, application of fertilizer and pesticides, and for harvesting the heavier
crop. With world energy prices rising rapidly, the costs of intensify-
ing food production will rise commensurately. In countries already
engaged in high-energy agriculture, such as the United States,
Japan, and those in Western Europe, high energy prices may
reduce future food production prospects below what they would
otherwise be.

The future availability of fertilizer will be directly affected by the
scarcity of energy. Manufacture of nitrogen fertilizer, the most
widely used chemical fertilizer, commonly utilizes natural gas or
naphtha as a raw material, and the manufacturing process itself
consumes large amounts of energy. Fertilizer is already in short
supply, largely because of a lag in the construction of new production facilities, but the high cost of energy inputs will also ensure
higher fertilizer prices. Yet fertilizer requirements over the remaining years of this century will soar to phenomenal levels.

Even more ominous than the price rises are the absolute shortages of fertilizers which appeared in 1973. By early 1974, there
were signs that many nations—including some very populous ones,
such as Indonesia, India, and the Philippines—would be unable to
obtain the needed amounts of fertilizer *regardless of price*. Japan,
a principal supplier of nitrogenous fertilizers in Asia, was forced to
cut production and exports substantially as a result of the energy
crisis. Simultaneously, the United States, due to the combination of
increased fertilizer demand accompanying the return of idle land to
production and energy shortages, reduced its fertilizer exports. In
early 1974, it appeared virtually certain that reduced fertilizer supplies would cause a drop in food production in the 1974–75 crop
year in several key developing countries even with favorable
weather conditions. * * *

The Green Revolution: Opportunity Lost?

Efforts to modernize agriculture in the poor countries in the
1950s and early 1960s were well-intentioned but frequently frus-
trated. When farmers in these countries attempted to use varieties
of corn developed for Iowa, they often failed to produce any corn
at all. Japanese rice varieties introduced into India were not suited
to either local cultural practices or consumer tastes. Intensive application of fertilizer to local cereal varieties often resulted in a
limited, and occasionally even negative, yield response.

It was against this backdrop of frustration that a Rockefeller Foundation team under the leadership of Nobel Prize winner Dr. Norman Borlaug developed the high-yield dwarf wheats in Mexico in the 1950s. Three unique characteristics of these wheats endeared them to farmers in many countries—their fertilizer responsiveness, lack of photoperiod (day length) sensitivity, and early maturity.

When farmers applied more than 40 pounds of nitrogen fertilizer per acre to traditional varieties having tall, thin straw, the wheat often lodged or fell over, causing severe crop losses. By contrast, nitrogen applications to the short, stiff-strawed dwarf varieties of Mexican wheat allowed the efficient application of up to 120 pounds of nutrient per acre. Given the necessary fertilizer and water and the appropriate management, farmers found they could easily double the yields they had been getting from indigenous varieties.

Beyond this, the reduced sensitivity of dwarf varieties to day length permitted them to be moved around the world over a wide range of latitudes, stretching from Mexico, which lies partly in the tropics, to Turkey in the temperate zone. Because the biological clocks of the new wheats were much less sensitive than those of the traditional ones, planting dates were much more flexible. Another advantageous characteristic of the new wheats was their early maturity. They were ready for harvest within 120 days after planting; the traditional varieties took 150 days or more. This trait, combined with the reduced sensitivity to day length, created broad new opportunities for multiple cropping (the harvesting of more than one crop per year on the same land) wherever water supplies were sufficient.

Within a few years after the spectacular breakthrough with wheat in Mexico, the Ford Foundation joined the Rockefeller Foundation to establish the International Rice Research Institute (IRRI) in the Philippines. Its purpose was to attempt to breed a fertilizer-responsive, early-maturing rice capable of wide adaptation—in effect, a counterpart of the high-yield wheats. With the wheat experience to draw upon, agricultural scientists at IRRI struck pay dirt quickly. Within a few years, they released the first of the high-yield dwarf rices, a variety known as IR-8.

The great advantage of the new seeds was that they permitted developing countries to utilize quickly agricultural research that had taken decades to complete in the United States, Japan, and elsewhere. In those areas of the developing countries where there were requisite supplies of water and fertilizer, and appropriate price incentives were offered, the spread of the high-yield varieties of wheat and rice was rapid. Farmers assumed to be bound by tradition were quick to adopt the new seeds when it was obviously profitable for them to do so.

* * * Among the principal Asian countries to benefit from using the new seeds are India, Pakistan, Turkey, the Philippines, and, more recently, Malaysia, Indonesia, and Sri Lanka.

During the late 1960s, the Philippines was able to achieve self-sufficiency in rice, ending a half century of dependence on imports. Unfortunately, this situation was not sustained because of a variety of factors, including civil unrest, the susceptibility of the new rices to disease, and the failure of the government to continue the essential support of the rice program.

Pakistan greatly increased its wheat production, emerging as a net exporter of grain in recent years. In India, where advances in the new varieties were concentrated largely in wheat, progress has been encouraging. During the seven-year span from 1965 to 1972, India expanded its wheat production from 11 million tons to 27 million tons, an increase in a major crop unmatched by any other country in history.

* * *

This is not to suggest that the Green Revolution has, by any stretch of the imagination, solved the world's food problems, either on a short- or long-term basis. The 1972 drought clearly demonstrated that Indian agriculture is still at the mercy of the weather. A second monsoon failure would seriously disrupt the pattern of progress that has characterized Indian agriculture over the past five years. The fertilizer shortage emerging in 1974, impairing the effectiveness of the high-yield cereals, will probably contribute to rapid growth in the need for Indian food imports, though the potential magnitude was not yet clear by early 1974.

It has been fashionable in many circles to criticize the Green Revolution, but it can be properly assessed only when we ask what things would have been like in its absence. The alternative scenario is a grim one and helps put its accomplishments in appropriate perspective. Increases in cereal production made possible by the new seeds did arrest the deteriorating trend in per capita food production of the early 1960s in the developing countries. The massive famine anticipated by many has been thus far avoided. Although relatively little progress has been made in raising the per capita production of cereals among the poor countries as a whole, it brought spectacular localized successes in raising cereal output. In sum, the Green Revolution does not represent a solution to the food problem; rather, it has been a means of buying time, perhaps an additional fifteen years, during which some way might be found to apply the brakes to population growth.

Almost a decade has now passed since the launching of the Green Revolution, but success stories in national family planning programs in the poor nations are too few. Among the population giants of Asia, China appears to be substantially reducing its birth rate and India is very gradually bringing its birth rate down, but reductions to date in Indonesia, Pakistan, and Bangladesh are minimal. The futility of relying solely on the new agricultural technologies to "solve" the population problem is evident in Mexico, the country where the Green Revolution began. Fifteen years of dramatic advances in wheat production made Mexico a net exporter of cereals in the late 1960s, but a population growth rate that ranks among the highest in the world has again converted Mexico into an importer of food.

* * *

Population Growth: Independent or Dependent?

Given the numerous ecological and social stresses and resource scarcities emerging during the early 1970s, we must ask whether it is any longer realistic to consider population growth as a largely independent variable—whether it is realistic for demographers to project future population growth without assessing the prospect for supporting the projected populations at levels of consumption *they* find acceptable. In order to do this meaningfully, extensive inputs from several other related disciplines are required. As additional information is taken into account, the discrepancy between the projected growth in population and that which would be tolerable, or even possible, appears to be widening.

Population growth per se is not the only additional claimant on resources. The aspiration of mankind for higher consumption levels appears to be universal. We do not know what the relative roles of these two forces will be in the final quarter of this century. But we do know that the more resources required to meet the additional requirements of population growth, the less there will be for raising per capita consumption levels.

Existing demographic projections, like the economic ones, have assumed a more or less business-as-usual condition for the future periods covered by the projections. But as we analyze current ecological and social stresses and resource scarcities, even a doubling of world population without any further improvement in per capita consumption becomes a rather frightful prospect in light of the social stresses and potential political conflict that would be likely to accompany it. Similarly, a doubling of per capita consumption levels worldwide, which would still leave the world at only a fraction of North American levels, would put a great strain on the earth's resources—even assuming no further growth in population. A 50 percent increase in world population, combined with a 50 percent rise in individual affluence worldwide, would bring a 125 *percent* increase in world consumption of goods and services. Even this modest growth in population, assuming it is matched by growth in per capita consumption, as was the case during the third quarter of this century, will not only further aggravate existing ecological stresses and resource scarcities, but generate many more as well.

The time has come to broaden the information and analytical base from which population projections are made. The growing scarcities of many vital resources and, more important, the reaction to these scarcities at the individual, national, and global levels, must be fully taken into account in considering future population prospects. Inputs from agronomists, ecologists, human toxicologists, meteorologists, and resource specialists must be included in future population projections, if they are to have any validity, any relationship to the real world.

As the consequences of continuing population growth become more clearly and widely understood, it seems likely that we will be forced to treat future population growth as a dependent rather than an independent variable. As it becomes more difficult and costly to achieve the inevitable balance between supply and demand by expanding the supply, it will become necessary to adjust the demand. It is in this context that efforts to stabilize population growth everywhere, and to simplify life styles among the world's more affluent, begin to loom large.

Any consideration of alternative demographic trends is in reality a consideration of alternative futures for the human race. Virtually all the important problems facing mankind will be aggravated, and their solutions made more difficult, by population growth. * * *

Creating a Workable World Order

The need to stabilize population sooner rather than later must not be viewed in isolation, but as part of a broader effort to create a workable world order. Such an effort must not only strive to slow population growth as rapidly as possible, but it must also seek to arrest the pursuit of superaffluence. An indefinite increase in either the number of people in the world or in the amount of goods and services consumed by each individual would eventually put unbearable stress on the earth's ecosystem and resources. If the developed countries continue the pursuit of superaffluence as they have so successfully over the past quarter century, then the world will be threatened as surely as if its population had multiplied several times.

Creating a workable world order means creating new supranational institutions to cope with emerging global problems. * * *

Creating a workable world order requires that national leaders perceive the changing relative threats to the well-being of their people. The real threats to man's future may have their origins much less in the relationship of man to man, and much more in the relationship of man to nature. If uncontrolled human fertility poses a greater threat to our future well-being than any other single factor, as many informed analysts now believe, then national governments must rethink the question of national security and the allocation of budgetary and human resources. At present, expenditures on the direct control of fertility worldwide total perhaps $3 billion per year. This compares with global military expenditures far in excess of $200 billion per year, exceeding the income of the poorest half of mankind. The question is whether leaders at the national level can perceive the changing nature of the threat to national security and well-being soon enough to achieve a more rational ordering of priorities before major global problems become unmanageable.

* * *

There is need for a major increase in the general flow of resources from rich countries to poor, both to help the latter achieve higher growth rates and to give them the capacity better to meet the basic needs of the poor. Though it is now clear that economic growth alone will not solve the problems in the low-income countries, neither will these problems be readily solved without higher growth rates. Quite simply, higher rates of growth make it easier for a determined government to carry out necessary reforms without major violence or extreme authoritarianism. Higher rates of growth require more machinery, raw materials, and technical know-how, all of which require foreign exchange. Thus it is no accident that most of the economic development and family planning "successes" have taken place in countries that have broad access to foreign aid, trade, and investment.

Many less developed countries can acquire some additional foreign exchange by adopting more outward-looking economic policies; however, the international economic environment frequently is no more congenial to their development than is the national environment in many countries to the poor majority of their people. Policies of developed countries and the structure of international institutions frequently discriminate, often inadvertently, against the poor countries in both trade and finance. Yet there must be major changes in the ways rich countries relate to poor countries if there is to be anything like the needed increase in the transfer of resources in the 1970s. Additional sources of foreign exchange must come from trade, investment, aid, and from such new global sources as the raw materials of the sea bed and the foreign exchange made available by the International Monetary Fund through its Special Drawing Rights.

Combined with appropriate national and international policies in the trade, monetary, and aid areas, the systematic simplification of life styles in the more affluent countries would free resources which could then be used to help the less developed countries solve their basic economic and social problems. A 10 percent reduction in beef consumption by Americans would free several million tons of grain for use in hungry countries. A reduction in the size of automobiles within the United States from large to medium or small automobiles would greatly reduce pressure on world energy supplies, making it considerably easier for the food-scarce less developed countries to obtain the enormous supplies of energy needed to expand their food output. This would be a small price to pay for the slowing of population growth and the creation of a more workable world order.

If we fail to understand and meet this challenge, we face the ominous prospect that the poorest countries will be hopelessly trapped at low levels of development because of the high prices of the energy fuels, foodstuffs, and fertilizers they must import. Under these circumstances, survival would become the overriding objective, forcing the abandonment of any hope for social and economic improvement. The scenario then unfolding in Asia, Africa, and Latin America would involve spreading food scarcity, continuously rising prices, and growing political instability. Governments would change hands with increasing frequency. Malnutrition would spread and rising death rates would begin to rise to reestablish the inevitable equilibrium between population and resources.

The encouraging thing about efforts to satisfy social needs and slow population growth is that they can reinforce each other positively. Progress made on one front enhances the prospects for progress on the other. Unfortunately, it is equally true that these two trends can reinforce each other negatively. Rapid population growth makes it more difficult to satisfy basic social needs, and this in turn hinders efforts to slow population growth. The need today is to tilt the scales in favor of the positive reinforcements.

COMMITTEE ON AGRICULTURE, HOUSE OF REPRESENTATIVES

Malthus and America (1974) †

II. The Reason for This Report

This report is the result of hearings called by Congressman E de la Garza, Chairman of the Department Operations Subcommittee, on July 23, 24, and 25, 1974. These public sessions examined the world food supply, demand, and population equation, world food reserves relative to the stocks on hand and the general policy question. The hearings were held in response to the leadership of House Speaker Carl Albert and House Minority Leader John Rhodes who earlier this year sent each Member of the House a letter and a memorandum entitled "Declaration of Food and Population."

In their letter, these two distinguished leaders called attention to the fact that "not only will the extent of death by famine and disease in developing countries over the next few years depend primarily on the actions taken by their own governments, but it will also depend to a large extent on the leadership and assistance of the United States and other industrialized countries in alleviating the crises caused by rapid population increases and tragic food shortages."

* * *

XIII. Summary

Building quietly and ominously these days is a voice that will rock the world in our lifetime, and that voice articulates the world food and people equation. . . . and it is to our blessed land of abundance from across the threshold of scarcity that this voice cries.

Will Americans discover too late that Thomas Malthus is a 200-year-old alarmist whose time has finally arrived?

The Subcommittee concludes that unless present trends in population growth and food production are significantly altered, a food crisis that will have the potential to affect everyone from every walk of life will hit with more impact than the energy crisis of 1973–74.

---

†From *Malthus and America, A Report about Food and People* by the Subcommittee on Department Operations of the Committee on Agriculture, House of Representatives, October, 1974.

Unfortunately most of the citizens of this and every country of the world are yet unaware of the phenomenal problem that looms on the horizon, and if the hearings held by the Subcommittee and this followup report can serve to make people at least aware of what the statistics show we are headed for, our goal will have been achieved. Americans, who heretofore have been rather complacent about this subject, inasmuch as abundant food supplies have been available at low prices in years past and since the growth rate of our population has slowed considerably, cannot afford to sit idly by thinking that this problem does not affect us. Did you ever stop to think, for example, what the effects on our national security would be if, say, the governments of three or four major countries collapsed due to a shortage of food, resulting in riots in the streets and an overthrow of the government? Can we live in peace in a whole world neighborhood of sick and hungry people?

The United States of America, comprising approximately 5 to 6 percent of the world's population, consumes more than 40 percent of the world's resources. The demand for food, like the demand for oil, metals, minerals, and other resources, is obviously going to skyrocket, and that rocket is going to be fueled by fires of inflation and joblessness.

Can we boil the complex issues down to a very elementary proposition, namely tradeoffs and sacrifices? How do we manage the demands? What formula do we use to determine who gets how much of what we have? We have to decide to what extent the interest of certain groups, among others, taxpayers, consumers, farmers, domestic industry, foreign customers, and the humanitarian interest, are served and/or sacrificed. Let us further examine this statement. Our country has, throughout its history, operated our political and social systems within the perimeters of abundance and has seldom had to cope with the politics of scarcity. But last summer, Americans were forced to cope with scarcities and found it none too pleasant. Price controls were applied to beef. Export controls were set on soybeans. Import restrictions on nearly all commodities were lifted. Humanitarian food shipments under Title II of Public Law 480, our Food for Peace program, were suspended.

These central contemporary questions arise: Should we limit the amount of commodities we export from this country at the expense of our balance of trade and humanitarian interests so we can have "cheap food" here at home; or should we sell all of the commodities we can on the world market to bolster our balance of trade and strengthen the dollar and our economy at the expense of American consumers who will have to pay higher prices for food and hungry people around the world who don't have money to pay for food and will starve as a result; or should we give away large quantities of food to feed hungry people and save lives around the world at the expense of the American taxpayer who would be called upon to finance such a venture and the American consumer who would have to pay higher food prices as a result; or should we establish large governmentally or internationally held and controlled grain reserves which quite possibly could be used against the best interests of the American farmer who in turn would probably reduce production due to a lack of incentive to produce, at the expense of the American consumer who again would have to pay higher food prices and the American taxpayer who would be called upon to finance the largest portion of any such undertaking?

The aforementioned alternatives briefly outline the question of whose interests are to be served or sacrificed before any conclusive policy can be forthcoming. However, the Subcommittee is certain that the U.S. Government can no longer afford to take a piecemeal approach to food policy as we have done in past years. The problem with the piecemeal approach is that it never allows for all of the pieces to really be put together and thus have never solved the puzzle. What is needed is an integrated social policy approach in the formulation, debate, and implementation of the policy position to be taken by the United States. An integrated social policy approach sees the issue of food in terms of its relationship to the other elements of socio-economic-political development in a highly interdependent world. Income distribution, health care systems, literacy programs, land reform in the agricultural sector, employment policies in the industrial sector, encouragement of savings among the poor, and the possibility of political participation by all sectors—these are some of the elements which give people a stake in society and thus motivates them to do something for the sake of society and for themselves, namely to have smaller families. Additionally, issues such as world prices (inflation), trade, preferential tariffs, international money structures, et cetera, should be taken into consideration. In other words, the issue is much broader than just a question of food supply and demand or population, and all factors which might conceivably enter into the picture as previously stated should be discussed.

In conclusion, the Subcommittee feels that at least a part of its obligation is to create a greater understanding and awareness of the fact that a potentially devastating crisis is on the horizon, and it is drastically affecting us already. Therefore, the Subcommittee plans to follow up these hearings with additional hearings, including meeting with our delegations to the United Nations Population and the World Food Conferences.

Will America allow a food shortage to surprise us such as we allowed the energy crisis to do this year, and only then react *after* we find people standing in line from 7 a.m. to 9 a.m. on Tuesday and Thursday mornings waiting to get into their local grocery store to buy a limited quantity of food? The Department Operations Subcommittee sincerely hopes not.

The answers aren't easy, but the price of inaction will be cruel.

Think about it, Congress.

Think about it, America.

Index

Index • 259